Understanding family meanings

A reflective text

Details of Open University modules can be obtained from the Student Registration and Enquiry Service, The Open University, PO Box 197, Milton Keynes MK7 6BJ, United Kingdom (tel +44 (0)845 300 60 90, email general-enquiries@open.ac.uk).

www.open.ac.uk

Understanding family meanings related audio discussions

Audio discussions with leading authorities in the field are available online to enhance the content and key concepts of *Understanding family meanings*.

The Open University's Megan Doolittle joins four leading academics (Professors Ros Edwards, David Morgan, Lynn Jamieson, and Carol Smart) from the field of sociology to tackle the issues of what 'family' really means.

They look at how families communicate and behave, and they talk about family personal life and what is meant by the term 'intimacy'. Finally, they discuss the future of family studies.

These files, and related transcripts, can be obtained at: http://itunes.apple.com/us/itunes-u/theories-concepts-in-family/ id380231496

Understanding family meanings

A reflective text

Jane Ribbens McCarthy, Megan Doolittle and Shelly Day Sclater

First published in 2008 by The Open University

This edition first published in 2012 by

The Policy Press, University of Bristol, Fourth Floor, Beacon House, Queen's Road, Bristol
BS8 1QU, UK

www.policypress.co.uk

in association with

The Open University, Walton Hall, Milton Keynes, MK7 6AA, United Kingdom

www.open.ac.uk

British Library Cataloguing in Publication Data
A catalogue record for this book is available from the British Library.

Library of Congress Cataloging-in-Publication Data
A catalog record for this book has been requested.

ISBN 978 1 44730 112 7 paperback
ISBN 978 1 44730 113 4 hardcover

Cover design by Qube Design Associates, Bristol.
Front cover: image kindly supplied by istock.com
Printed and bound in Great Britain by Henry Ling, Dorchester.
The Policy Press uses environmentally responsible print partners.

Contents

Chapter 1
Why family meanings?

Jane Ribbens McCarthy

Contents

1   Introducing 'family meanings'

Wendy: *What's important about being in a family?*

Juliet: *I've got mixed feelings in a way, cause I sometimes feel they are over-rated … You don't have to be suffocated in a two parents and a couple of kids situation. To me that is not the be all and end all.*

…

Fred: *… it's the natural flow of family life isn't it. You know that you get old enough to get married, you find someone, you get married, you have children, it's just the natural thing to do and I feel yeah that's important about a family. It's having that self-respect and having that family around you. You've got your own people then haven't you. They're your little gang if you like. You've all, you've all got one thing in common, that you're all together. You've basically come from the same place haven't you and that's a good start isn't it. You're always going to be reasonably of like minds.*

(Langford et al, 2001, pp. 16–7)

Ideas of family Chapter 1?can raise strong emotions in all of us, and the great majority of people, when asked in research interviews, describe their idea of 'family', like Fred, in very positive, perhaps idealised, terms. Dissenting voices, like Juliet's, which question whether or not family is the most useful framework for understanding personal relationships, are not often heard in such studies.

In this book you will encounter many different voices and views of 'family', and sometimes you will also be invited to reflect on your own views and assumptions. So, we welcome you to the fascinating study of family meanings. By putting 'meanings' at centre stage, and using this as a framework to examine families and relationships, this book will give you an opportunity to explore the shifting and subtle ways in which people themselves, researchers, policy-makers and professionals make sense of the idea of 'family'. In the process, you will also consider how issues of power, inequalities, and values are integral to any understanding of family meanings. As you will see, ideas of family can be imbued with some of our deepest personal desires and fears, as well as being a major focus for wider social anxieties and concerns. Families are thus crucial to any understanding of social lives, both for us as individuals and for social processes more widely. While families are sometimes described as if they somehow stand 'outside' of society, from another point of view, families and relationships may be seen as the very core of social life, binding individuals into the fabric of society.

1.1   Core questions

The *idea* of 'family' is thus very powerful, at least in the contemporary cultures of Europe and the New World. At the same time, family lives have been under constant scrutiny from all sides – from family members themselves, politicians, professionals, and media pundits. And this scrutiny does not seem to be abating, as people and governments struggle to deal with anxieties about the complexities and uncertainties of changing and diverse communities in a globalising world. How does this debate and anxiety impact upon, but also reflect, people's everyday experiences? How does it relate to professional and policy developments? And how can the academic study of family lives progress within the context of such ongoing and widespread debates?

In this book we will approach these questions by taking a step back from these anxious debates, to focus on family meanings as the key feature for academic study. Thus we will *not* be seeking to observe family as a structure about which we can develop objective knowledge from a position of total detachment. Rather, our concern will be to explore the ways in which 'family', as an *idea*, forms a key construct through which people develop meanings in a whole variety of social settings. Further, we will demonstrate how 'meanings' come to have practical consequences, contesting and complicating our everyday assumptions around family lives. In this regard, some 'family' meanings may develop into systematic and enduring sets of meanings, while other meanings may be more changeable and idiosyncratic. Meanings may become more systematised because they are embedded in institutions and legal systems which also give these meanings some power in society, or meanings may be systematised in the sense that they are regularly exchanged and drawn upon between networks of people over time, and thus become widely used and established. But at other times, 'family' may represent more fluid and contingent meanings as individuals develop their own understandings of their everyday lives and interactions in varied contexts. But, in either case, 'family' can serve as a symbol around which many features of personal and social lives intertwine and coalesce. This book, then, centralises the question, what *is* 'family' – what do we mean by it?

1.2 Exploring values and assumptions

As you progress through this book, we would like you to consider how values and moral assumptions are deeply embedded in family meanings. A central argument of the book is that 'family' is a notion which is suffused with values, desires and fears. This results in 'family' being a powerful ideal to which we may all react strongly, with regard to both our own lives and the lives of others. It is therefore very rare for people to discuss families without making judgements. Sometimes such evaluations are embedded in the assumptions which underpin the language being used – for example, as in the medicalised language of what is healthy or unhealthy, functional or dysfunctional. Furthermore, family lives may be one of the most difficult areas for academic study, as they are literally so 'close to home' and 'familiar' that it's hard for us to step outside of ourselves to see what is happening, or even to realise what assumptions we are bringing to our observations. Indeed, such 'stepping outside' may be an impossible endeavour to achieve in any absolute sense.

Nevertheless, as you read, we ask you to attempt to set aside presumptions of what is right or wrong, and focus instead on listening to the ways in which people express and live out family meanings in their own lives and in their interactions with others in varied contexts. As you progress through these chapters you should carefully and continually reflect on your own assumptions and values. Rather than trying to work out what is good or bad about family lives, then, in this book you will explore how people themselves, as well as researchers and professionals, make sense of the circumstances and contexts in which they find themselves, and work out their lives through variable meanings of family.

While this approach is rooted in a strong academic social science tradition (discussed further in Chapter 2) that stresses the importance of understanding the meanings by which people frame their lives, this is not a common way to approach discussion of families outside of academic contexts. Instead, we generally encounter debates and discussions in the media, and in our own everyday conversations, that launch into what is going wrong or right about families, and how we think people *should* conduct their relationships.

Figure 1.1
Family life is often portrayed as going wrong

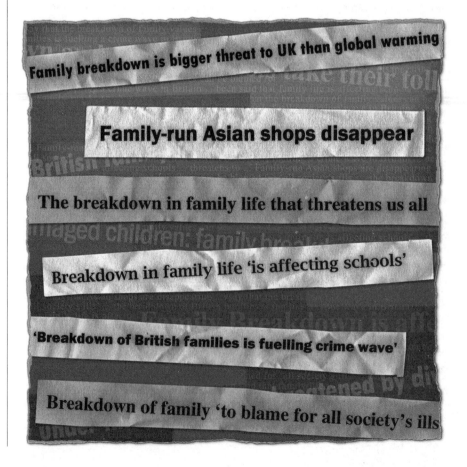

Family breakdown is bigger threat to UK than global warming

Family-run Asian shops disappear

The breakdown in family life that threatens us all

Breakdown in family life 'is affecting schools'

'Breakdown of British families is fuelling crime wave'

Breakdown of family 'to blame for all society's ills'

You may find yourself, then, reacting to what you read here with such judgements – perhaps towards your own life, as well as the lives of others. It may be that you find yourself thinking about how your life compares, and how you might judge yourself and feel judged by others. You may at times feel that we, as the writers of this book, have ourselves implicitly – if unintentionally – conveyed such judgements, or you may become aware of the values through which you yourself view other people's families. We invite you to watch out for such moments in your reading, and to note them and ponder upon them as part of your learning process. Sometimes these judgements may be obvious to you, and sometimes they may be more subtle – apparent, perhaps, through a sense of unease or disapproval rather than through any explicit and conscious evaluative thought-process. But, most subtly of all, it can occur through taken-for-granted assumptions of what is 'normal', and what 'makes sense' to us, or, alternatively, what seems incomprehensible or even 'exotic' to our general way of thinking about families.

Another key way in which moral judgements may occur implicitly is through the language of what is 'natural'. As you saw with the opening quote from Fred, families are often discussed as being 'natural' – an inevitable part of the flow of 'normal' life. Yet, at the same time, there may often be moral disapproval of those who don't live up to this image of the 'natural' and 'normal' family. But, from a social science perspective, what may appear in social life to be 'natural', and a matter of 'commonsense', needs to be opened up for scrutiny, since these terms are often used to describe what are actually matters of culture and history. Thus our assumptions about families and relationships may be taken as quite unremarkable, and taken-for-granted, but to an outsider they might appear strange and reprehensible. As social scientists, then, we seek to *make the familiar strange* in order to see what is happening more clearly.

1.3   Structures of power and inequalities

At the same time, such judgements and responses are not just personal matters: they are also embedded in all sorts of wider and interpersonal processes of power and inequality. These processes shape social policies, professional interventions, and representations in the media, as well as underpinning everyday social interactions in family lives and relationships. If we focus on family meanings, we may not always put issues of power, material inequalities, and moral evaluations at the centre of our analysis. But they will be important to meanings of family and the ways in which we think about our lives. Such issues as gender, class, ethnicity, or sexuality form features of wider social structure, in the sense that they form major and regular social patterns that can be seen to occur in people's lives, reflecting and revealing significant dimensions of power and the distribution of resources. Structural issues can then fundamentally shape the contexts in which people live, and it is by reference to these contexts that people work out how to make sense of their families and relationships. An attention to meanings may, then, not centralise issues of power and inequality as such, but it is important to understand the significance of meanings-in-contexts. As mentioned earlier, meanings don't just appear from nowhere, but can be seen to represent the ways in which people try to make sense of their lives, and understand their situations, in relation to the contexts and circumstances in which they find themselves. People experience such contexts in all sorts of ways – in terms of direct interactions with others, physical and material phenomena, media representations, and legal and institutional structures which set the parameters of much of life in developed societies. Most of this will be taken completely for granted as people get on with their daily lives, but, as they do so, they will be developing and drawing on meanings that help them to make sense of their lives as these occur in the particular contexts they experience. We will return to this theme in later chapters, particularly in Part 3.

Families also carry a widespread expectation of privacy and freedom from 'outside' interference, perhaps making a 'world of their own'. Nevertheless, families are equally a major focus for both professional interventions and policy developments as there is so much at stake if things are thought to be 'going wrong' in family lives – both for vulnerable individuals and for society at large. But relying on common-sense assumptions, or unexamined ideas about the 'naturalness' and fundamental desirability of 'the traditional family', limits our ability to understand what is happening. Academic study is necessary to bring into focus the fluid and dynamic nature of contemporary families and to consider how we can study and 'know' them.

In this introductory chapter, then, we will begin our exploration by raising this question: what is 'family'? Starting from, but then moving beyond, various attempts to pin down the concept and define it, you will be invited to consider the question afresh through the eyes of Borg, an extraterrestrial, androgynous cyborg (whom you will meet later in the chapter). Borg sets out on the apparently straightforward quest to locate families, but ends up with the view that we have to listen in order to see. And in many ways, this is the view that frames this book.

2   Can we, and should we, define what we mean by 'family'?

2.1   Attempting definitions

A common foundation for any academic discussion – as you may be well aware – is to start by defining the key terms. Not only may this help towards clear thinking and communication, it can also itself constitute a very significant theoretical task, since concepts make up the basic framework for developing knowledge about any subject.

Activity 1.1

Without any further reading, you may like to spend a couple of minutes writing down how you might define 'family' if you were embarking on an academic essay about family lives. What key elements do you think should be included in any definition?

Comment

You may have found this to be quite a straightforward task, or you may have found it really difficult. Either way, as you read on, you can compare your own definition with the following discussion of the academic debates. Social scientists have also varied as to how far they regard the task of defining 'family' as relatively straightforward or fraught with difficulties. Indeed, students sometimes joke about how much social scientists seem to love endlessly discussing key terms and their meanings, and defining 'family' could certainly serve as an example!

Some writers thus offer definitions of 'family' with apparent confidence, as if the term is unproblematic:

> A group of people, related by kinship or similar close ties, in which the adults assume responsibility for the care and upbringing of their natural or adopted children.
>
> (Jary and Jary, 1995)

Others pay more attention to diversity and variation, but even so, may presume some shared underlying features, so that the definition of 'family' becomes variations on a theme. Common elements include:

■ co-residency and domesticity

■ blood, legal or (hetero)sexual ties

■ the care of children.

You may have observed, however, that these themes – taken together – evoke strong resonances with the notion of the nuclear family: i.e. the model of 'the family' that encompasses two married parents living together with their shared biological children. Nevertheless, some sociological definitions also take care to point out that this is indeed a *model* which is taken to represent an (idealised) institution. In this sense, then, it is something that needs to be understood separately from people's lived experiences of family, which may or may not correspond to this model. It is also a model with limited historical and cultural relevance.

As these debates have developed, then, efforts have been made to:

■ identify the institutionalised model of 'family' separately from the lived experience of family

■ incorporate diversity and variations

■ acknowledge the gap between ideals and (sometimes harsh) realities.

Some writers have gone further still, putting the uncertainty about the meaning of family at the centre of any attempt at definition:

> *family* Most commonly, a social group defined in some combination by parentage, kinship (including marriage), and co-residence. Historically, the family has been taken to be the basic unit of social organization, but the latter half of the twentieth century has seen a widespread breakdown of consensus about the meaning of the term. Once presumed to be a universal feature of human societies (subject to certain variations), both structural definitions of the family based on the kin relations that compose it and ... definitions based on the functions that it performs (e.g., reproduction) have failed to meet the challenge of the observed variety of forms of collective, small-group life in human societies.
>
> (Calhoun, 2002)

These are very important insights which go beyond the days when the family was seen as a solid, natural and unremarkable object of study or policy-making, as in the UK Beveridge Report, for example. This report, which formed the foundation of the Welfare State after 1945 and the Second World War, was based on the assumption of the nuclear white heterosexual family. More recent policy debates, and guidelines used by professionals such as social workers, struggle between wanting to deploy the rhetoric of 'the family' as if this is unproblematic, whilst also recognising diversity of family forms and cultures in order to be able to 'speak' to the population at large. (This is something you will look at in greater detail in Chapter 8.) So what is seen as new about diversity and change in contemporary family lives in European and New World countries may in fact be a recognition of the variable and diverse *meanings* that we give to this term. By acknowledging diversity, it is easier to think about and acknowledge the variations and ambiguities in family meanings and in families themselves. Nevertheless, this recognition of the varied meanings of 'family' does not happen consistently. Furthermore, particular meanings may also confer moral judgements and evaluations about what are the 'best' or most 'normal' families. The meanings attached to family have thus become more open to argument, not only in everyday and policy contexts, but also in academic discussions.

2.2 Responding to the problems

Consequently, some academics have increasingly voiced concerns about whether it is possible to define family satisfactorily at all – or, indeed, whether it serves any useful purpose even to try. The extract you will look at in the following activity is taken from an Introduction to a four-volume collection of readings on *Family: Critical Concepts in Sociology*. In this Introduction, the author seeks to find a way of defining family that will work across the four volumes of readings on aspects of family lives across the world.

Activity 1.2

As you read the following extract, consider these key questions:

1 Why do definitions matter, and what do they need to achieve?

2 What different approaches does David Morgan identify in response to the difficulties of defining 'family'?

Reading 1.1   David Morgan, 'Defining "family"'

Definitions are always important in all areas of social enquiry and not just in terms of the more immediate concerns and projects of the scholars themselves. In the case of family, these issues come to be of particular importance, partly because the terms used overlap with several everyday usages and partly because, in certain parts of the world, these words – family, marriage, parents etc. – have come to take on an ideological or political significance. A critical examination of family and family practices must be aware of some common themes and concerns across different cultures (if only to make some kind of cross-cultural comparison possible) while remaining sensitive to the culturally embedded character of these key concerns. Put another way there must be an awareness of the different ways in which family terms are deployed not only between cultures but also within a single society. Thus demographers, constructors of family policy and informal carers (to indicate just three sets of interested social actors) have different concerns and different practices. A critical sociology of family must be ever alive to these different usages.

We may examine these usages in a variety of ways. One common usage is as a noun where one talks about 'the' family. The dangers of this approach have been well-rehearsed ...; it gives the family a fixed, reified, quality which runs the danger of losing sight of the wider context and of obscuring more fluid or more everyday understandings. Nevertheless, it might be argued that this usage does have some value in comparative research ... and to talk about ' the family' can itself be of some critical use when it opens up a gap between 'my' family, the immediate and taken-for-granted family world which I inhabit, and some sense of 'the family in general'.

However, it could be argued that there has been a shift within the sociological literature to using the word as an adjective, as something that gives a particular quality or character to some other, overlapping, sets of practices. Thus, in this present collection, we have references to 'family policy' ... or 'politics' ..., 'family caregiving' ..., 'family time' ... and 'family power' ... My own discussion of 'family practices' attempts to explore what is entailed when scholars attempt to use the word 'family' in this way (Morgan, 1996). This character is partly provided by the range of practices signified by the use of the term 'family' (roughly, those practices to do with marriage or partnering and with parenting and generations) but also by the particular emotional significance that seems to accompany this usage of the word 'family'. Thus, 'family time' is not just part of the broader patterns of time use within social settings but is frequently invested with further emotional or, indeed, moral significance.

Another usage, which is entering into the literature (at least by implication) is to treat the word as a verb or in terms of some verb-like usages. In the English language 'to family' still seems awkward, as does the associated idea of 'doing family'. Nevertheless, the usage has considerable potential in reminding the reader of a more active and variable understanding of the word 'family'. Thus step-parents may have to 'do family' more explicitly and more vigorously than some other parents partly because of some assumed suspicion that step-parents are not 'proper' families ... To talk in a more active sense of 'doing family' is to point to the interchanges between families and significant others, whether these be other families or households, professionals of various kinds or representatives of state agencies. ... [This means] we are talking about the active presentation of family in everyday life.

Reading source

Morgan, 2003, pp. 1–2

Comment

In this discussion, Morgan makes a number of key points:

1   Family definitions matter, not just for academic reasons, but because there are several overlapping usages at stake, constituting a serious risk of confusion and misunderstandings around the term. Moreover, these various usages invoke political and ideological issues. Thus, the ways in which definitions of family matter may depend to quite a large extent on the purposes we have in mind when we use the word. At the same time, there are a number of different interests and agendas at stake in discussions around family, depending on who is involved in the discussion. Some of these different agendas may be associated with ideological, political, emotional and moral dimensions, which may be attached to, and evoked by, 'family'.

2   In discussing these various conundrums, Morgan suggests two possible ways forward, both of which involve moving away from 'the family' (or even 'families') as an object or structure. The first possibility is to use 'family' as a descriptive word – an adjective – to refer to features we take to be present in another object or facet of social life. The second possibility is to use it as an action word – a verb – in which case it informs us of the social practices that involve 'doing family' as a presentation to others. Note also that Morgan himself doesn't see it as too

problematic to know how to identify 'family', whether as an adjective or a verb, which he defines in terms of partnering, parenting and generations.

2.3   What's so difficult?

Morgan's discussion helps us to think about how we can develop research, policies and interventions around 'family' when the key term is so problematic. But we also need to explore further just what *is* so difficult about this endeavour. There are also some clues to this in Morgan's discussion, in which he points out that:

- there is a close linkage between everyday and academic language of family

- there is a whole variety of agendas and interests at stake

- the word 'family' involves a great range of emotional and moral investments that work at individual, psychological, and social levels

- there are also political and practical issues at stake.

Despite such discussions, it is common to find references to 'the family' as a definite object in both academic and policy debates. On the other hand, many academic writers now consciously avoid using this term, referring instead to 'families' in the plural, or 'family lives' (using 'family' as an adjective). Jon Bernardes (1993, 2003[1985]), however, argues that it is not enough to recognise diversity and change around contemporary family lives in Europe and New World countries, or to talk about 'families' in the plural. He suggests that the conceptual problem of 'family' goes much deeper than this, to the point that academics should avoid defining 'family' at all. Instead, he suggests the focus of study should shift to explore '*how, why and when actors define particular aspects of their lives as "family life"*' (Bernardes, 1987, p. 882). By attempting to pin down the meaning of 'family', academics risk contributing to a situation where particular understandings and versions of 'family' become more powerful than others. This may result in people thinking about their own or others' lives in ways that are really unhelpful and which create evaluations and judgements; this undermines the ability to 'hear' and 'see' how people's family lives make sense on their own terms.

Bernardes further argues that the persistent tendency to revert to discussions of 'the family' as if 'it' exists, are not simply due to the intellectual deficiencies of social scientists. Rather, there are many questions that social scientists wish to ask about social life that seem to *require* the concept of 'the family' as an object that exists and can be studied. Questions such as: How does the family function for society? Does the family change in response to industrialisation? Is the family converging towards a common form around the world? Similarly, social policy-makers and professional practitioners may also feel the need for a clear model of what family is, in order to develop legislation, general procedures, and guidelines in relation to people's family lives and relationships. (This is something you will explore further in Chapter 8.) And yet, as the quote from Bernardes suggests, such models may be pernicious.

So far we have seen, then, that 'family' is so difficult to define that academic writers have sought various ways to shift the language that we use to study families and relationships, with some writers suggesting that it is not even useful to try to pin down the concept, and any attempt may indeed be harmful.

In line with such debates, this book seeks to go beyond the important insights of family change and diversity, to consider much more fundamentally what we mean by 'family' at all. How far, and in what circumstances, is it a useful concept, for either social science or for professional practice? What are the different facets of using this concept, and in what ways can we use it effectively in research and in practice? Can it be modified or adapted to make it work better, or do we need other concepts altogether? In what ways can it help to illuminate social lives, yet marginalise others, and whose interests are served in these processes?

2.4 The slippery language of 'family'

Most fundamentally, however, we need to understand how language is used, and what 'work' it does as we interact with others in our everyday lives. As the sociologist and philosopher Alfred Schutz (1954) argued, it is important to pay careful attention to the relationship between sociological and everyday concepts, since everyday concepts express the meanings by which social interactions are framed. So how do people themselves understand, encounter, interpret and evoke the very slippery concept of 'family' in their everyday lives? As mentioned above, social theorists, policy-makers and professionals may raise questions that seem to require them to discuss 'the family' as a definite object or structure, but in everyday life the word may work effectively for people precisely *because* it can't be pinned down.

The slipperiness of 'family' may occur in many different directions, ranging from quite concrete issues of who 'belongs', or who should be invited to a 'family' event such as a wedding, to more emotional and value-laden issues of how we feel about (our) families and how we evaluate them. The historian John Gillis (1997) distinguishes between 'the families we live with', and 'the families we live by', with the former referring to our daily experience of family life, and the latter referring to idealised images of what we think family life ought to be like. Bernardes (1993, 2003[1985]) also suggests that people can hold several different meanings of 'family' at once, which are mutually contradictory, but can coexist in ways that are very useful in holding together some of the tensions in their relationships and daily activities. Bernardes thus argues that, despite such ambiguities, most people in their everyday lives need to carry an assumption that there is something general or common about how family occurs. Furthermore, he suggests, sociologists have been similarly seduced into confusing such an assumed generality with the concrete existence of something that can be called 'the family'.

The position taken here is to suggest that everyday actors, as a matter of course, hold at least two distinct concepts of 'the Family'. These will be called the 'specific', that is personal or individual and the 'general' that is a concept used in relation to society at large ...

... individuals feel no discomfort about describing their own family life as 'unusual' and yet believing that they are seen by other people as having a 'usual family life', and finally asserting that most families 'conform to a pattern or type'.

...

Individuals are able to, indeed must, simultaneously accommodate both 'general' and 'specific' concepts of 'the Family'. Individuals are able to, first, assume that there is a single uniform type of 'the Family'; second, believe that their own family life is divergent from this model, and third, remain unaware that all families may diverge from a single dominant type.

(Bernardes, 2003[1985], pp. 87–96)

3 So what is 'family'?

However, if the concept is so tremendously complex, how then can we study family?

Activity 1.3

I would now like you to read the following piece from Jaber Gubrium and James Holstein (1990), where you are introduced to Borg, the extraterrestrial cyborg. This extract is central to the themes of this book, so read it thoughtfully and in detail.

As you read, you may like to write some notes in answer to the following questions:

1   What did Professor Caswell hope to demonstrate to his students by introducing Borg?

2   What did Professor Caswell hope to demonstrate in the analogy of the table and the family? On what grounds did Borg object to this analogy?

3   What advice did Professor Caswell give Borg in her search for 'family'?

4   What were some of the difficulties that Borg encountered in identifying 'family'?

Figure 1.2

Humpty Dumpty and Alice

"IF HE SMILED MUCH MORE THE ENDS OF HIS MOUTH MIGHT MEET BEHIND," SHE THOUGHT

Reading 1.2   Jaber Gubrium and James Holstein, 'What is family?'

'When I use a word,' Humpty Dumpty said in rather a scornful tone, 'it means just what I choose it to mean – neither more nor less.'

'The question is,' said Alice, 'whether you can make words mean so many different things.'

'The question is,' said Humpty Dumpty, 'which is to be master – that's all.'

(Lewis Carroll, *Alice Through the Looking Glass*)

Professor Caswell, a renowned scholar of the family, quoted from Lewis Carroll whenever he had the opportunity to make a point about human nature. As he once concluded, 'Alas, friends, big brass, and pedestrians, words are what we make of them.' Nevertheless, Caswell expected more from the language of serious scholarship. Family studies was a science, and he believed that science harboured clear thinking and precise meanings.

... [O]ne day ... Caswell turned to a favored classroom technique for prodding students out of their taken-for-granted view of things. 'I shall assume the perspective of an extraterrestrial visitor,' he told his students, 'and you will see how your familiar world must look to a stranger.' Caswell instructed them to imagine him as an androgynous cyborg – a cybernetically operated organism named 'Borg.'

...

Attempting to show his class how to sort through the variety of ties that have been called family, Caswell asked the students to put themselves in Borg's place. 'Pretend that you don't know what words mean at all, that you don't know to what or how words should be applied. Now let's try to figure out what the family really is.' Caswell wanted to show the students how the word 'family,' while highly variable in its historical and cultural meanings, nonetheless could be used to designate a concrete form of life, one he had studied for the greater part of his scholarly career.

Caswell started by talking about tables rather than households or homes. Using the classroom table next to him, he noted that, like the table, the family had parts and at the same time was a whole. ...

... Caswell indicated how tables come in as many sizes and shapes as the family. 'Some are big, some small, some do certain things – just as some tables hold dishes and others hold saws, different families do altogether different things.' He cautioned that, nonetheless, they are all families, Caswell described structure and function as something common to all, even while he carefully denoted family's human variations. ...

Now Borg – that curmudgeon in Caswell's mind – emerged to speak in her own voice. Like Humpty Dumpty, she asked in a scornful tone, 'But, Professor Caswell, I see the table, the students see the table, but I don't recall having seen the family, any family. ...' Borg added that, in her casual wanderings on Earth, she hadn't actually seen a family, only people.

Caswell picked up the assigned family textbook. Like most such textbooks, it included colorful pictures of diverse families and households, showing a variety of cultural and historical origins. Caswell opened the book to the appropriate pages and told Borg that the pictures would be her guide to a mission: to locate family in its many forms.

Before Borg left, she repeated that all she could see in the pictures were people and houses, just as she could see people in the classroom and people out in the street. Borg wondered how she would be able to distinguish just any collection of people from the collection that constituted a family; in particular, she wondered whether housing could help distinguish what these humans called 'family.' She asked Caswell how she could differentiate a collection that looked just like the people in one of the textbook pictures from what, on an earlier trip around Earth, she had heard called a 'gang.' Caswell responded that she had found the key; namely, that Borg had to combine looking with listening. He explained that she needed to discover how collections of people referred to themselves before she could locate families.

As Borg set out, she understood that this mission was going to be more difficult than finding more tables after seeing a table. What if people disagreed? What if they claimed to be family in one place and disclaimed it in another? Tables didn't talk to, or about, themselves. ...

Several weeks later Professor Caswell announced to the class that Borg had returned from her search. He asked her what she had found. To begin with, Borg had found many collections of people whom other people referred to as families, but whose alleged members did not. She found that when she revisited the members of the gang she had mentioned earlier and paid close attention to what they said about themselves, she heard the members not only refer to themselves as family, but also call each other brothers and claim filial responsibility for their actions. Yet this 'family' wasn't a household. She added, 'And what about Laura, a teenage girl who shrieked that she didn't have a sister when her twin spilled grape juice on Laura's brand new cashmere sweater?'

...

Borg wondered how ... experts could possibly study the family if there was so little consensus about what it was. How did they create a scientific literature on the family if they didn't define it in a common way? Could these experts have been looking at the same thing? Who did know what the family was and what it was like? ...

Borg took delight in the confusion that seemed to rule the experts' search for the family. She teased Caswell that they were no better at it than she was. She enjoyed recounting the ways humans connected words and things; in general, it seemed to have no universal rhyme or reason. Yet everyone seemed to understand one another. She'd been keeping track of what people said when she asked about families, and it was clear that she had actually heard much more about the thing she was searching for – family – than legal status or biological kinship implied. What seemed most evident, she noted, was that people seemed to use family in ways that legal or biological definitions could not capture. She wondered aloud, 'Could it be that what family is to people is how family is used by them?' Borg was beginning to sound like Humpty Dumpty.

Caswell was both surprised and annoyed by the question. Was Borg implying that family was nothing more than a human construct and that people applied family imagery and familial categories like brother, sister, and cousin to all sorts of human relations, in and out of homes? ... Was Borg saying that family was not so much a thing, but a way of interpreting interpersonal ties?

Caswell calmed himself and asked hastily, 'Well, then, my sceptical alien sidekick, if that's all the family is – just words – then it's not much of anything! What are we to do? Study words?' ...

Borg explained that no one she had talked with, or whom she had heard talk with others, acted as if family were just a word. She added, in a curious turn of phrase, that all the words she heard about family were words about 'it' or some form of 'it,' something concretely part of experience. The people she heard were making statements about something either real, not real enough, or too real to them, and were not just uttering words. 'It' seemed to link words to concrete aspects of life.

...

Borg pointed out that ... [i]n order to 'see' what people were referring to, one had to listen to the way they used words and described their social relations, paying particular attention to the factors that affected their descriptions. Looking straight at Caswell, Borg blurted out, 'You have to listen in order to see, Caswell!'

... [Caswell] hadn't intended the listening business to become so central to locating the familial; he had meant it only as a handy guide. Yet, now intrigued by Borg's reasoning, Caswell was bent on learning more about Borg's thoughts on seeing and hearing. He turned toward her and asked warmly, 'Well, then, my friend, what is family?'

Reading source

Gubrium and Holstein, 1990, pp. 1–6

Comment

1   By introducing Borg to his students, Caswell hoped to help them make the familiar strange, but he was still expecting to be able to work out a precise guideline which defined 'family' for academic study.

2   In likening the family to the table, Professor Caswell was drawing attention to the ways in which families seem to be composed of various parts that together create a whole. There can be varieties of sorts of families, but, nevertheless, they may share certain 'functions' (a word which we encountered in Calhoun's

Figure 1.3
Do we need to listen in order to know how to see?

definition of family earlier). Borg's objection, however, centred on the impossibility of identifying family when you see it, even in pictures. Knowing that families are diverse doesn't actually solve the problem of knowing when one is, or is not, looking at a 'family' grouping.

3   Professor Caswell advised Borg that maybe we have to listen in order to be able to know how to look, in order to know how people refer to families and identify families in their lives. By listening as well as looking it may then be possible to identify the meanings of 'family'.

4   But attending to meanings did not provide any easy answers for Borg to know how to identify families, as meanings have to be interpreted. This is what Borg found out when she then set out on a major exploration to discover how people use and develop the language of family, along with its associated meanings in their lives. All of these might vary in very subtle ways, as interpretations vary among speakers and listeners, according to their purposes, and the local and broader cultural contexts. This is the sort of exploration that constitutes the heart of this book.

4   What's next?

In this chapter I have introduced you to some of the key concerns and themes of the book as a whole. We have considered how social scientists have struggled with the term 'family', to the point where the difficulty in designating clear guidelines for the term itself takes centre stage, and becomes transformed into the central question for consideration rather than an obstacle to scientific understanding. Our primary focus thus becomes an exploration of how family meanings change and shift in response to the contexts and situations at hand, including the ways in which such meanings are imbued with emotion and moral evaluations. Nevertheless, some family meanings are more institutionally embedded than others, and all are contextualised by structures of power and inequality. The implications of these issues, and the exploration of family meanings, also need to be considered in the context of policies and professional practices. But, as you read, we have recommended that you try to set aside your own evaluations and judgements in order to be able to listen to others' family meanings as they seek to make sense of their lives and relationships in a variety of contexts. We hope therefore that you will read thoughtfully, and listen openly and reflectively to the evidence and ideas we present about family meanings.

This book is divided into three parts. In Part 1 you will explore the meanings of family by focusing on qualitative and quantitative research evidence (mainly from the UK); while in Part 2 you will turn towards a more theoretical discussion of the terms and frameworks we might use to understand people's family lives and relationships. In Part 3, you will focus more directly on understanding family meanings in variable contexts, including historical and global variations and diversities, and family meanings in the contexts of social policies and professional practices. Although you will focus on three different areas, the distinction between research and theory, meanings and contexts, is more of a useful device than a clear-cut division, since all research is underpinned by concepts and theories, all theoretical frameworks are developed in relation to research evidence, and contexts are always mediated through meanings even as the contexts also shape those meanings.

In the first two chapters of Part 1 (Chapters 2 and 3), you will begin to consider what we mean by the term 'family meanings', and whether family meanings matter. Drawing on qualitative UK research, these chapters focus on the everyday family meanings of people living in various localities. Chapter 4 will take you into different territory, as you will consider the meanings of family that are involved when researchers draw on studies using surveys and census data. Surveys require that families and households are grouped and counted by reference to certain categories, so you will be asked to consider the underlying social and historical processes, and how these help to construct particular meanings of family. You will also be asked to examine some data to see what sorts of things we can learn about families through these avenues.

These three chapters complete Part 1 of this book. Part 2 (Chapters 5 and 6) then turns to a more theoretical discussion of the underlying conceptual frameworks available. In Chapter 5 you will encounter the notions of family discourses and family practices. Both of these offer frameworks for studying families that seek to move beyond the straightforward view of family as a fixed entity, by using 'family' as an adjective, and by focusing on the ways in which family meanings occur through talk and concrete practices. Chapter 6 shifts the theoretical framework again, to ask what happens if we decentre the concept of 'family', as such, and instead explore relationships through the concepts of intimacies and personal lives.

So, in Parts 1 and 2 of the book you will encounter debates and research which are based largely on contemporary developed societies, especially the UK. In Part 3 (Chapters 7 and 8) you will focus in more detail on the question of context. In Chapter 7 you will look beyond contemporary UK contexts to consider the diversity of family meanings in earlier historical periods, and across the globe. This highlights the need for researchers to set aside their own assumptions and taken-for-granted preconceptions in order to understand diversity and difference, whether this involves looking at societies around the world, or variations of family meanings that are closer at hand. A key issue here, then, is how we identify commonalities and differences in order to make such comparisons, and move beyond the specifics of particular relationships to make generalisations within and across contexts of time and space.

Particularities and generalities are also key issues for Chapter 8, where you will consider the family meanings at stake in the contexts of social policies and professional practices in contemporary UK society. Such meanings may be embedded in all sorts of policy assumptions and practical interventions, including significant judgements and evaluations about what is proper or improper about how people live out their family meanings. Finally, in Chapter 9, you will return to the issue of values and moral assumptions as we review the book as a whole.

As you work through the rest of this book, I hope that – like Caswell and Borg – you will become engaged with, fascinated and perhaps challenged by, the exploration and study of family meanings, as we try to understand 'what is family?'

References

Bernardes, J. (1987) '"Doing things with words": Sociology and "Family Policy" debates', *Sociological Review,* vol. 35, no. 4, pp. 679–702.

Bernardes, J. (1993) 'Responsibilities in studying postmodern families', *Journal of Family Therapy*, vol. 14, no. 1, pp. 35–49.

Bernardes, J. (2003[1985]) 'Do we really know what "the family" is?' in Cheal, D. (ed.) *Family: Critical Concepts in Sociology*, London, Routledge, vol. I, pp. 83–102.

Calhoun, C. (ed.) (2002) *Dictionary of the Social Sciences* [online], Oxford University Press, http://www.oxfordreference.com/views/ENTRY.html?subview=Main&entry=t104.e601 (Accessed 18 February 2008).

Gillis, J. (1997) *A World of Their Own Making: the History of Myth and Ritual in Family Life*, Oxford, Oxford Paperbacks.

Gubrium, J. and Holstein, J. (1990) *What is Family?*, London, Mayfield.

Jary, D., and Jary, J. (1995) *Collins Dictionary of Sociology* (2nd edn), Glasgow, Harper Collins.

Langford, W., Lewis, C., Solomon, Y. and Warin, J. (2001) *Family Understandings: Closeness, Authority and Independence in Families with Teenagers*, London, Family Policy Studies Centre/ Joseph Rowntree Foundation.

Morgan, D.H.J. (2003) 'Introduction' in Cheal, D. (ed.) *Family: Critical Concepts in Sociology*, London, Routledge.

Schutz, A. (1954) 'Concept and theory formation in the social sciences', *Journal of Philosophy*, vol. 51, pp. 257–73.

Part 1
Research

Introduction to Part 1

Jane Ribbens McCarthy

In this part of the book we focus on research issues in relation to family meanings. In Part 2 we will focus more on theories and concepts, and in Part 3 on the contexts of family meanings.

Specifically, in the first two chapters of this Part 1 (Chapters 2 and 3), you will explore research in which people have been asked to talk about their everyday lives, largely on their own terms. These interviews have then been analysed to consider how people make sense of 'family'. In Chapter 4 you will consider research that has been undertaken from the perspective of policy-makers and social scientists who want the sorts of large-scale data that guide policies and paint general overviews of family lives.

The research that we present in Part 1 is all based on empirical studies. This means that the researchers set out to study the world through talking to people or observing their lives. Through this process they are able to provide empirical data, i.e. sets of information, that represent the observations and interviews that the researchers have undertaken. The data is then analysed to produce research findings; these findings are subsequently treated as information which provide us with knowledge about the world. For our purposes here, empirical research is significant because it provides us with knowledge and understanding of families and family meanings that goes beyond everyday individual experiences and 'common sense'. But research is itself a complex social process, so knowledge is always shaped by the decisions, constraints and practicalities of the particular project which produced it.

In considering research that may help us to explore family meanings, there are thus two elements to our discussion.

1   We consider existing data and what this can tell us about families and family meanings in the contemporary UK context.

2   We also look at some of the underlying issues of how such research is undertaken, and the questions this raises, including how research itself draws upon, and helps to construct, particular meanings of family.

Research is not just important in providing academics and policy-makers with information about contemporary family lives, however. In developing research evidence and accounts, studies not only *reflect* and *interpret* lived experiences, they also help to *shape* them. This was sharply illustrated for me when my son was a teenager in secondary school, and one day brought home a copy of a newspaper article concerning changing gender roles, which he had to read in preparation for a lesson. The article itself drew upon social science research undertaken by people that

I happened to know. So I could see in a very concrete way how academic work was filtered through a variety of social and institutional processes to end up informing my son's thinking and shaping his cultural understandings of gender. These processes included (amongst others): publication of the original work; its incorporation into a journalist's writing; its inclusion in a newspaper publication; and its adoption by the teacher in my son's school within the terms of the curriculum they were studying. As a consequence, the class discussion impacted on my son's views of gender. But the ways in which young people think about gender roles was itself part of the subject of the research, so the process came full circle.

You saw in Chapter 1 how some writers (e.g. Bernardes, 1993) argue forcefully for the need for researchers to be more self-conscious about such issues. This is because the findings of research, along with their underlying assumptions and meanings, get reflected back into people's own understandings and meanings, as well as policy and professional practice, sometimes with negative effects. This process has been described as the 'reflexivity of social science', and it is a two-way process, since social scientists cannot stand outside their subject matter. So researchers studying family meanings also have relationships and families of their own, and their own taken-for-granted assumptions and perspectives on families, that may inevitably affect the way the research is conducted. Indeed, perhaps you are wondering about the family lives and relationships of the authors of this book! Furthermore, not only do social scientists draw upon cultural meanings when conducting research, but their writings

Social science may shape social life, as well as reflect it

in turn may help to shape cultural meanings. (We explore issues of culture more fully in Part 3.)

The three chapters in this part of the book focus on two types of research: qualitative research (Chapters 2 and 3), and quantitative research (Chapter 4). At its most basic level, the distinction between qualitative and quantitative research concerns data which is expressed as numbers, and data which is not. But, while this is a common divide that is made around variable types of research, it does need to be approached critically. There are thus a number of other related issues that are often associated with, but may also cross-cut, this divide. Furthermore, any one piece of research may itself draw on more than one approach.

Nevertheless, the distinction between the two types of research often provides a useful basis for categorising different sorts of research evidence, and as such, we have found it helpful in organising the research evidence for Part 1. The following questions may help to illuminate the kinds of features that relate to the two different types of research you will encounter in the following chapters:

- How many people (or units of study) have been included in the research? Compared with quantitative research, qualitative studies tend to be more limited in terms of numbers and scale, but more intensive in the depth and detail involved.

- Do the researchers set out with definite ideas and questions they want to answer (associated with quantitative research), or is the research more open-ended and exploratory (associated with qualitative research)?

- Do the researchers set out to measure 'variables' i.e. precise empirical components for demarcating and measuring different aspects of social lives (indicating quantitative research) or do they seek to study social lives 'in the round', as one set of integrated relationships (qualitative research)?

- Is the research analysed in terms of statistical patterns that are found amongst these variables (quantitative research), or is it analysed through the interpretation of the meanings of participants' actions and words (qualitative research)?

You will find these dimensions discussed at various points in the chapters that follow.

In this book, we take a view of all knowledge as something that is socially produced and socially situated, rather than something that reflects a pre-given 'reality', which we seek to 'know' through detached objectivity. In other words, research doesn't just gather up 'facts' that are already present in the world, waiting to be garnered – as Borg found when she set out at to fulfil Professor Caswell's request to study 'families' (discussed in Chapter 1). But this does not mean that empirical evidence is 'created' out of nowhere – indeed, we suggest that research can only be useful if it provides a convincing account of people's lived experiences of social and material worlds. What it does mean, however, is that it is crucial to pay close attention to the ways in which research is undertaken, and knowledge is 'produced' – not least in terms of the language which frames and underpins it. Within this, the concepts or terms that are used are crucial in providing the framework which structures how we look and listen. (We discuss concepts further in Part 2.)

In the qualitative projects that you will encounter in Chapters 2 and 3, the research seeks to stay 'close' to people's own understandings, based on interviews that used a variety of open-ended techniques. Such techniques aim to provide interviewees with opportunities to express in their own words what is important to them about their lives, through such methods as life-history interviews, or open-ended questions. However, it is important to remember that the researchers' own understandings and assumptions are always present too, even if only implicitly. In the more structured, quantitative studies discussed in Chapter 4, there are issues of how these large-scale categories (largely dependent on the notion of 'household') have been developed and specified. Furthermore, for our purposes here, there is the question of how far these categories can reveal family meanings, while also in themselves helping to shape such meanings.

So, we will start our focus on research in Chapter 2, when we explore the question of whether or not family meanings do indeed 'matter'.

Chapter 2

Family meanings in contemporary contexts

Jane Ribbens McCarthy

Contents

1   Introduction

In this chapter and in Chapter 3, you will explore family meanings in different settings by focusing on evidence from contemporary qualitative research conducted in contemporary European and New World societies. This evidence will introduce you to some overarching themes of 'family meanings'. In Chapter 3, you will go on to explore these themes in greater detail, teasing apart any cross-cutting threads. Before we start our focus on research evidence, though, I'd like to begin at a more general level of discussion.

So, in this chapter we will first set the scene by discussing the various ways in which family meanings might be said to 'matter' in contemporary contexts. We will then focus more directly on what is meant by 'meanings' in academic discussion. In the subsequent sections of the chapter we will focus on evidence from qualitative research, introducing you to some broad themes of contemporary family meanings which arise from research interviews. We will then explore these themes in more detail through a discussion of research conducted in South Wales in various localities. In the process, we begin to consider some research issues including how to:

■   interpret and represent the varying and subtle nuances – or 'layers' – of family meanings in any one person's research interview

■   discuss differences and diversities, alongside generalities

■   reflect on the research process and analysis.

2   Do family meanings matter?

We spent time in Chapter 1 considering the difficulties of pinning down family definitions and meanings. We open this chapter by asking whether it is indeed important to explore and unravel these complexities. Do the varieties of family meanings – or the meaning of 'family' itself – matter, or do they just provide a minor intellectual diversion? You may like to pause here for a moment to consider how you would answer this question for yourself. Do you think they matter, and if so, in what ways?

We consider this question by reference to three main areas – people in their individual lives and relationships; social policies and professional practices; and family studies as an academic area.

2.1   Family meanings matter to people in their individual lives and relationships

Survey research in the UK, reported by Jacqui Scott (1997), shows the extent to which families matter when people are asked about the key events in their lives over the previous year. While there were some differences by gender and age, the overall pattern was clear: events concerning family lives were considered to be the most significant. And, in the intricacies of personal lives and relationships, family meanings can be complex and powerful.

Writing from a US perspective, Barbara Cox Walkover (1992) conducted interviews with young American couples who were having difficulties with conceiving a child, which they cast in terms of 'wanting to start a family'. Walkover was struck by the starkly polarised images and emotions that arose in these interviews; indeed, she refers to 'the family' as 'an overwrought object of desire', as her interviewees struggled to reconcile their hopes of a perfect future family life with their fears of becoming imperfect parents who might resent their loss of freedom and individuality. What Walkover is at pains to acknowledge, however, is that this situation is rooted in much wider – but unrecognised – contradictions in this particular culture about what a family *ought* to be. These young couples were trying to deal with wider dilemmas through their own individual hopes and failings. Cultural meanings are thus translated into personal meanings, generating much tension for the individuals concerned.

While the tensions that Walkover discusses are particularly stark in the context of young couples trying to conceive a child, they can also be seen in interviews I conducted with mothers in the late 1980s (Ribbens, 1994). The interviewees were white mothers living in middle-income households in the South East of England, all with an eldest child aged seven. In my discussion of these interviews (part of which is reproduced below), I consider the extent of the efforts made by mothers to create their 'families'. However, this work is largely discussed as unremarkable by the mothers themselves, as families are understood to be 'natural'.

Becoming 'a family'

For households in circumstances similar to those of my own study, it is largely the mother's task to create 'the family'. There are two very important processes in this:

1   internal cohesion, welding the individual members together into a meaningful unit, and

2   external demarcation, drawing clear boundaries and separating the family clearly from other social units.

...

If 'the family' is indeed impossible to identify at a concrete level (as Gubrium and Holstein argue), in what ways is its unity signified and symbolised and made to appear concrete? A number of powerful symbols appeared in the women's accounts, including the home, spending time together (whether meals, playing board games, or family outings) and pictorial representations such as photographic collections. Yet in all these cases, it is the presence of children that is crucial to 'family' symbolism.

When the first child is born to a married couple, this is expected to produce a different sort of social unit – the baby is not seen as a simple addition to a 'household', but an essential ingredient in the creation of 'a family'. The household is thus expected to be more than a collection of individuals who have to learn to live together. There is the additional central expectation that they constitute a social unit that can be demarcated from those around, and that is made special by the presence of children. So when the baby arrives, the woman is in the position of being confronted with this new being, for whom she is responsible as an individual, but at the same time, the arrival of this baby is expected (by her and by others) to lead to the establishment of a new social unit, which is 'the family' ... Furthermore, providing this 'family' may be construed as the essence of loving children:

> *Jane:*   *Could you say in what ways you think perhaps you make a good job of being a mother yourself?*
>
> *Susan:*   *... Giving them loving I think is the main thing.*
>
> *Jane:*   *And loving involves all the things you mentioned?*
>
> *Susan:*   *Yeah, giving them a good family life, I think.*
>
> (Ribbens, 1994, pp. 58–9)

Research interviews, such as the ones we've considered above, show us that family meanings have a powerful impact on people in their individual lives, particularly when those meanings involve a cultural or personal ideal of what it means to be 'a family'. Thus, family meanings matter to individuals and impact on their lives in the following ways:

- People who hope to constitute a 'normal family' try to live up to virtually impossible associated expectations in their own lives (as with the studies discussed above, and with those you'll explore in Chapter 3).

- People who don't feel that they can hope to (or don't want to) 'fit' the image of a 'normal family' may feel marginalised and excluded.

- Alternatively, people may try to redefine the term to claim its emotional and moral significance for new patterns of living – in effect, to diversify the meanings of family.

Family meanings also matter when people interact with one another – whether with family members, researchers or professionals – as there may be much scope for misunderstanding. This is an issue we'll explore later on in the chapter.

2.2 Family meanings matter in social policies and professional practices

In the studies by Walkover and Ribbens, above, we can see individuals caught between a generalised cultural ideal and the messiness and ambivalences of everyday lives. This tension between the generality of 'family' as an idealised model, and the fluidity of individual lives in everyday contexts, is also a key difficulty for the development of social policies, and for the procedures and administrative structures of professional practices. This takes us back to Bernardes' question (1987) which we discussed in Chapter 1: how is it possible to develop social policy and professional practice without having some sort of model or structure in mind of what family actually is? And yet, any generalisation or model of family – even if there is an attempt to incorporate diversity – will have the effect of creating potentially harmful stereotypes and generalisations. Attention to family meanings may help us to see how such harmful effects occur, which may be a crucial step towards avoiding the pitfalls of stereotyping, stigmatising, and misunderstanding people's family lives and relationships.

In the following activity, I would like you to look at a couple of definitions of family. These give an example of how law and welfare bureaucracies may attempt to accommodate fluid and diverse meanings of family, on the one hand, and set out categorical rules about them, on the other. Example A concerns written guidelines provided for services dealing with emergency humanitarian crises that require them to liaise with 'family members'. Example B concerns guidance given to local-authority social workers about who counts as a 'relative' in terms of private fostering arrangements (which are made, or are intended to be in place, for twenty-eight days or more).

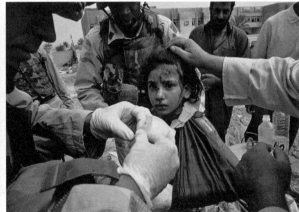

Figure 2.1

Responding to needs in emergency situations

Activity 2.1

As you read the following two examples:

1   Compare and contrast the wording used in each one to describe 'family'.

2   See if you can identify issues that might arise about how to apply the guidelines in practice.

3   Consider what might account for the differences between them.

Example A

In the context of these guidelines [for humanitarian assistance centres] the term *family* includes: partners, parents, siblings, children, guardians, carers, friends, and others who might have a direct, close relationship with the missing, injured or deceased person. The identification of what makes up an individual's family is extremely important in the context of these guidelines. It is important to recognise the potentially wide variations of the 'family', which can be influenced by culture, lifestyle and by preference. Care should be taken to establish the wishes of the family at all times with sensitivity and understanding exercised around families with diverse lifestyles. Some people interpret 'family' to just mean their close relatives. As a result, care should taken in using the term 'family' – 'family and friends' is a useful phrase.

(Humanitarian Assistance in Emergencies: Non-Statutory Guidance on Establishing Humanitarian Assistance Centres, UK Department of Culture, Media and Sport and the Association of Chief Police Officers, p. 13)

Example B

Private fostering: ... [A private foster carer is] anyone who ... is neither a LA [Local Authority] foster carer, nor a relative within the meaning of s.105 CA [Children Act 1989] i.e. not a grandparent, sibling, aunt or uncle (half or full blood or by affinity) or step-parent (including civil partners).

(quoted in Bridget Lindley, 2007, UK Family Rights Group handout)

Comment

1   What is notable about Example A is its flexibility in the face of what could be very variable individual situations caught up in a general crisis, with a recommendation to use the phrase 'family and friends'. Nevertheless, there is still an underlying assumption that there is something that the professionals can try to identify as 'the family'. Example B, by contrast, seeks to draw up a tight definition that will be very clear about who does or does not 'count' as a relative, which it does by reference to who is not included in legal definitions used in the Children Act. This also includes references to half-blood relatives.

2   While the phrase 'direct, close relationship' (in Example A) provides quite an open point of reference, what is not included here is any guidance about how to prioritise different individuals in terms of who to contact, who needs information, or whose wishes or needs should take precedence if there is a dispute among these 'family and friends' about what needs to be done for the deceased, missing or injured person. Whose wishes or views should be given greatest weight? There is much scope left to the professional, then, to work out family meanings on the ground. And, while Example B seeks to be more directive, there is still scope for ambiguity about who to count in or out of the definition, e.g. would it include an auntie 'by affinity' who has no biological connection with the child but has a relationship based on cultural ideas of 'fictive kin'?

3   In relation to the situation of humanitarian crisis discussed in Example A, there are no immediate bureaucratic issues at stake, and the guidelines seek to allow room for fluidity and openness about who counts as 'family and friends'. In Example B, however, it is important for bureaucracy to demarcate family members from non-family, in order to draw a firm line between private fostering and public foster-care arrangements, since different funding and supervision arrangements apply to each of these. Additionally, then, there is also a time element to the definition of private foster care, such that the arrangement needs to either be, or be intended to be, for 28 days or more. (Lindley, 2008, personal communication)

These examples point to key dilemmas about how family meanings may come to be defined and redefined through different social processes around policy and professional practices. On the one hand, clear-cut definitions may be limiting and unhelpful and difficult to work with in practice. But, on the other hand, fluid and open-ended definitions require professionals to be make contingent decisions in particular cases. This points to the need for professionals to be aware of their own assumptions, and to have the ability to cope with the variety of family meanings that may occur between different family members themselves. (These are issues which we'll return to in Chapter 8.)

2.3   Family meanings matter in family studies

Researchers and students of family studies need to pay attention to family meanings because it is not possible to stand outside of such meanings. Thus, it is important to be able to reflect upon the ways in which these meanings shape and impinge upon research, and, in the process, come to be reconstructed and reproduced. Such reflection is relevant whether we are considering the interpretations of people's lives undertaken within qualitative research (Chapters 2 and 3) or the categories of households and relationships underpinning statistical surveys and censuses (Chapter 4).

Research cannot stand outside of social life as it is always founded upon particular conceptual ideas, and different theoretical frameworks may bring variable understandings and ideas of how to identify and interpret family meanings. As we started to consider in Chapter 1, academics who study families and relationships have struggled to know how to deal with these conceptual difficulties, especially when the language of 'family' is so emotionally and morally loaded. Consequently, research and academic writings may themselves contribute their own moral and evaluative charge, whether or not this is the authors' intention. This may result in people feeling excluded if they don't conform to the dominant models that emerge from research that goes on to shape wider policies and representations concerning families. In grappling with these dilemmas, academics have tried to find ways of modifying the language of 'family', or moving beyond it. (This is something you will explore in Chapters 5 and 6.)

Additionally, family meanings matter to family studies, and to social sciences in general, because they shape the lives and actions of individuals, and, at the same time, they are a core feature in their own right of the social worlds we want to understand. I explain this issue further in the following section, where we will consider what is meant by 'meanings' in academic discussion.

Summary

So far, then, we have seen that family meanings matter for individuals, for social policy and professional practices, and for family studies – both for the ways in which family studies are undertaken, and for the ways in which such academic work impinges upon wider understandings and social processes. Each area of family meanings may thus also shape each of the other areas.

3   What do social scientists mean by 'meanings'?

3.1   Meanings in social lives

An attention to meaning is stressed in a number of academic and applied fields of study, cutting across academic disciplines. Meanings are often also a key aspect of professional interventions, including therapeutic approaches that seek to modify and improve people's experiences. Thus there are branches of psychology, sociology, history and anthropology that reflect strong intellectual traditions – sometimes described as 'hermeneutic' approaches – that emphasise the importance of seeing people primarily as meaning-makers. Those taking a hermeneutic approach argue that we cannot understand social lives without paying attention to meanings. If we take this point of view, we cannot study social life by the same methods we would use to study the natural world, since the meanings which people use to make sense of their situations will always shape what they do. The social world cannot be studied as a neutral object, like the planets or an earthquake can be observed and measured, because human actions are influenced and determined by the meanings which people bring to those actions. At the same time, these meanings are rooted in the social and material contexts in which people live, even as they are recreated anew by people within the circumstances of their lives. These processes of shaping and reflecting existing meanings are structured by social power, determining which meanings will become more dominant than others. Indeed, one of the key strengths of attending to meanings is that they can capture this sense of the *duality* and *dynamism* of meanings, which are simultaneously constructed and effective at *both* cultural and individual levels of social lives – as we discussed in Chapter 1. Meanings thus do not represent something fixed or inherent in the objects of study, nor are they purely individual creations; instead they constitute the interface between culture and individuals. (We return to the notion of 'culture' in Part 3).

So why are meanings significant for social lives? First, because they have consequences for human actions – since humans do not simply respond in any automatic way to external events, but shape their actions by reference to the meanings that frame their understandings of the world. In this regard, even researchers who use quite structured, quantitative methods in the search for statistical patterns in human behaviour, may also stress the need to understand the meanings that people give to situations in order to understand how they respond to them (Rutter, 2000). Second, meanings are significant for social lives because they emerge from ongoing and everyday social interactions, while they are also laid down and formalised through institutions (such as law, and welfare), in ways that help to shape social realities in the first place. The meanings by which we understand what it is to be 'a child' in the UK, for example, are fundamental to the ways in which we relate to younger people, and are also enshrined in child labour laws, the educational system, and so on.

3.2 Evaluating meanings?

There are, however, some important differences of emphasis in the ways in which meanings are discussed in different fields, particularly in terms of the difficult question of whether or not we want to judge some meanings as desirable or undesirable. This is a particularly important issue in relation to family meanings, since, as we discussed in Chapter 1, 'family' is a term that carries many moral and ideological values that are often only implied rather than explicitly argued for. Can we, and should we, as social scientists, also expect to evaluate some family meanings as more worthwhile and desirable than others, while other meanings might be regarded as reprehensible?

To take a particular emotive example, there might be a set of family meanings around the idea that children need protection in their families in order to enjoy the freedom and (sexual) innocence of a special period of life that we understand as 'childhood'. But another set of family meanings might suggest that children need the freedom to explore their own sexuality, including with other children or adults if they so desire. How do you find yourself reacting to these different sets of meanings? These are difficult ideas to consider without evaluating them and responding to them emotionally: indeed, the very terms in which they are couched – 'innocence', 'freedom' – may themselves evoke strong reactions. Yet understandings of appropriate physical contact with children, and of what childhood means, may be very variable. Some anthropologists have sought to establish meanings of child sexual abuse that can be universally applied, despite cultural diversity across the world. Such universalised meanings may be seen as crucial in underpinning the work of international child-welfare organisations, but how do we decide which meanings are desirable, and which aren't? We will return to such questions of values and cultural relativity in Chapter 9.

In many social science disciplines the goal is not to evaluate meanings in this way: they are not to be seen as right or wrong in themselves, desirable or undesirable. Instead of offering opinions about which meanings are right or best, social scientists may seek to explore them in all their varieties and nuances as a key, intrinsic, part of the way in which social lives and interactions occur. Thus, for hermeneutic branches of sociology, psychology and anthropology, understanding and analysing these meanings is the central task for study.

3.3 Two meanings of 'meaning'

To complicate matters further, there are two main ways in which 'meaning' may be used. First, meaning can be used in terms of 'making sense', as in, '*I don't understand what you mean*'. Second, meaning can be used in terms of 'purpose', as in, '*I didn't mean to cause such a problem*', and it is easy for this sense of meaning as 'purpose' to be seen as something desirable and positive. This can be exemplified by the situation where it is taken as a sign of mental well-being to be able to articulate a set of meanings around a particular experience in life, especially if it was a difficult or traumatic experience, as in, '*Can I find any meaning in my partner's death?*' Thus the language of 'meaning' itself implicitly conveys moral evaluations unless we take care to consider what we mean by 'meaning'.

Hermeneutic social scientists, however, emphasise the goal of interpreting family meanings, in terms of how people *make sense* of their family lives and relationships, rather than in terms of whether or not people find their lives 'meaningful' or *purpose*ful. Social scientists are themselves social beings who cannot stand outside the moral terrain in which family meanings are located. Their endeavour (which we share in this book) is to make this moral groundwork visible, seeking to consider what the contexts are which shape this terrain, rather than plunging in to make evaluative judgements. Furthermore, this search to interpret and understand others' family meanings may be multifaceted. It may lead to questions about whether meanings are always necessarily expressed through language, and whether they are always consciously known to people. So meanings might be found, not only in language, but also in embodied actions, in symbols and in objects themselves.

3.4 Meanings in context

This approach, then, suggests that people don't create their family meanings from nowhere. Instead they draw creatively and actively on the meanings available to them in their social and material contexts. As we discussed in Chapter 1, we can see that meanings are interchanged in social lives and become more or less systematised over time. But we need to be careful not to see such culturally systematised meanings as right or wrong, good or bad. Rather, we need to understand that they are the result of certain social processes, which may be seen in the ways that individual and collective lives unfold over time. Furthermore, these lives occur in particular social, material and historical contexts, which are shaped by relationships of power. As people go about their varied daily activities, then, they may draw upon the meanings that are available to them in the contexts and cultures in which they live. At times individuals may invoke and modify such meanings, in quite fluid and pragmatic ways, to help them to make sense of their lives and circumstances. But at other times, meanings may be more forcefully or emphatically imposed on individuals, according to the views and interests of powerful social groups. They may also become part of the ways in which people judge their own lives or feel judged by others. Meanings may thus be the outcome of struggles as well as creativity, involving processes of oppression, resistance and contestation.

In this book, then, our concern is to explore and interpret individualised and culturally systematised meanings, which may be expressed verbally or symbolically, or in everyday practices – as we explore more fully in Chapters 5 and 6. We will also seek to understand how these meanings help people to make sense of their lives in the circumstances and contexts in which they find themselves, which is the particular focus of Chapter 7. But when we are studying contexts close to our own lives, subtle variations in the meanings of family can also be very difficult to identify, because meanings tend to be very much embedded in conscious and unconscious thought processes, as well as in wider cultures. In this book, we aim to work towards a framework that enables us to think beyond particular and cultural meanings of 'family' – whether we are interested individuals, professionals or policy-makers, or researchers and academics. In the remainder of this chapter, we start this endeavour by seeking to make the familiar strange, to help us uncover what is normally quite taken-for-granted about family meanings within social contexts located in European and New World societies. As discussed in Chapter 1, then, we will follow Borg's journey to identify families by listening in order to know how to see.

Summary

So far in this chapter, we have discussed whether family meanings do indeed 'matter' in contemporary UK contexts. We considered the ways in which meanings of family matter:

- to individuals
- within policies and interventions
- to family studies as an academic field.

We then examined the significance of meanings to social scientists, who regard meanings as 'sense-making'. This refers to a fundamental human and social process which enables individuals to work out how to survive and live satisfactorily in their particular social and physical worlds, shaped by material conditions and processes of power and inequalities. Meanings as 'sense-making' are studied by social scientists in ways that seek to get close to people's own understandings without using value judgements.

4   Everyday family meanings

As you saw in Chapter 1, any attempt to answer the question 'what is family?', requires much more than the production of a coherent and workable definition of 'family'. Maybe 'family' defies definition, and this is a useful thing because we must learn to listen in order to know how to look and to pay attention to varieties of family meanings – and, thus, to the meaning of 'family' itself. So how does this word 'work' in social life, both in individual lives and understandings, and in wider social processes? This is something we will consider in the rest of this chapter.

Activity 2.2

I invite you now to undertake an extended reflective activity, by spending some time, perhaps twenty minutes or so, thinking about your own 'family' and the 'families' of others that you know.

1   Who would you consider to be your 'family' in your life right now, and how would this alter if you look back in time to your younger years?

How do you feel your 'family' compares to others that you know?

Try to think about these issues in various ways: in terms of actual people, places and times, as well as perhaps considering what sorts of emotions may be associated with these issues. Then make some notes on your thoughts and responses to these questions for your personal use and insight.

2   Having done this, consider what difference it would make if you were to share some of your responses to this activity with others (e.g. other students, colleagues

or friends). Which aspects would you be prepared to share with others, and which ones would you want to keep more 'private', and why?

Once you've thought about this, I'd like you to consider your answer in the light of the following questions:

What do such self-imposed boundaries – of openness or privacy – suggest about the ways in which we talk and interact around our family lives?

What does your answer tell you about the areas where you might feel exposed and open to the judgements, or perhaps misunderstandings, of others?

In what ways does this alert us to the need to both respect, and listen out for, other people's self-imposed silences? And what issues does this suggest for researching others' family lives?

Comment

1   People vary a great deal in what they mean by 'family', whom they would include and how they feel about these issues (as you will explore in more detail in Chapter 3). As you read through the discussion below, you may like to compare this with your own responses to the activity above.

2   Considering whether, and what, you would be prepared to share with others about your family life perhaps highlights the need to be sensitive to these issues of openness and privacy in other people's family lives. We thus need to listen to others with respect and care, listening to what is *not* said as well as to what *is*. We also need to be aware that people may have underlying concerns that they are being evaluated and judged. Therefore, reflecting on our own assumptions and family meanings, and trying to respect others' views, is no easy task. In light of this difficulty, there may be an additional question that needs to be asked here: Do you commonly consider 'family' to be an important and relevant part of your life, or has this activity itself just *presumed* that you think about your life in these sorts of terms? If you think about the people who are important to you in your life now, does the word 'family' help to convey something significant about these people? Or has the activity that we have written for you here actually required you to try to 'fit' these relationships into a 'family' framework which is not really pertinent? Perhaps we, as authors, have ourselves imposed some particular assumptions on you, as reader?

The qualitative research evidence that we have available to us – some of which you will consider in more depth in Chapter 3 – suggests some broad general variations in people's everyday understandings of 'family':

■   Some people may think of 'family' in quite a clear-cut way: consisting of the people they live with, and to whom they are related by blood or marriage.

Figure 2.2
Do 'families'
mean
'children'?

Others may have a much looser sense of 'family': referring to networks of individuals who are spread out across different households and localities.

■ For those trying to establish their own 'new' ways of living (as with gay or lesbian households, for example), 'families of choice' may seem to be most relevant, with 'family' being something you make creatively from the people you care most about. In this sense, family may include friends as much as relatives, with friendships seen to be taking on 'family-like' qualities, sometimes even being regarded as 'more of a family' than the original kinship group.

■ Some might regard children as a key feature of 'family', as when pub signs state, 'Families are welcome', or people state that they want to 'start a family'; others might argue that a couple without children are still 'a family'.

■ For some people, it may be the household in which they grew up that gives them the strongest sense of 'family', as something they have left behind. For others, it may be that 'family' continues to be a strong force in their lives even if they live alone as adults (and we have new terms to express some of this, such as LAT families, which refers to Living Apart Together, or, in France, non-cohabiting couples). People who are single, living alone, and do not have a non-resident partner, may also have strong sense of family, in the sense of significant relationships or memories which have an important place in their lives, providing continuity over time and a sense of identity.

- Some people may associate family very strongly with the idea of particular places, as in 'the family home' or 'my home town', but for others, the sense of 'family' may stretch across continents and across periods of time. This may give rise to a sense of family as transnational, crossing boundaries, and working as a significant force in people's lives regardless of time and distance.

Taking all these different views into account, we also need to remember that, for each of us, ideas about 'family' may also seem, not only normal, but also natural, correct and proper, as well as evoking some strong feelings and memories, for both good and ill. For many of us, our emotional responses may well be very mixed, even while we may worry about whether our own 'family' lives up to what we think may be involved in being 'a proper family', or perhaps we may feel let down by earlier childhood experiences. So morality and emotions are closely entwined with all of this, and with each other, and can be very difficult to filter out. Furthermore, power relationships and dynamics within families may often be obscured within the moral and emotional rhetoric about families, so there are further questions about how far power, and related issues of conflict and abuse, is made more or less visible within family meanings.

Across this great variety of family meanings, then, we find question marks against all the key features of what may commonly be thought to define 'family': it need not necessarily involve co-residence (or even proximity), or parenting and children, or coupledom, or kinship. And all these sorts of issues become even more marked if we look back in history to consider what 'family' used to mean to people living in earlier times. (For example, the notion of 'family' would almost certainly have included non-kin relationships for many households prior to the twentieth century in the UK, and this is something you'll explore in Chapter 7 when we consider evidence of everyday family meanings in historical and global contexts.) The themes listed above can only provide us with some basic broad insights and pointers towards the variable ways in which 'family' may be imagined, and the features which define family on a personal level may not be bounded by location or membership in any definitive way at all. However, despite this, policy-makers and researchers do indeed attempt to impose family definitions on the population for various reasons, as you will discover in Chapters 4 and 8.

5   Overarching themes of family meanings

I now want to elaborate on our discussion of what it means to be 'family' by exploring evidence from contemporary qualitative research conducted in the UK. This evidence will help us to build some overarching themes of family meanings.

The extract you will read in the next activity is based on a study of parenting and step-parenting after divorce or separation that I undertook with Rosalind Edwards and Val Gillies (Ribbens McCarthy et al., 2003). In this extract, the authors offer a general and quite abstract discussion of what is involved in 'being a family'. Thus, what you will 'hear' in this extract is the composite voice of the authors, rather than those of the participants themselves. The extract will introduce you to some general processes by which people may treat 'family' *as if* it were a concrete entity in their lives – even if different people deal with these processes in variable ways. Developing the ideas from my earlier work (Ribbens, 1994, discussed in Section 2), the notion of 'boundary' is discussed as one important element by which 'family' as a unit may be constructed. Another important element concerns the internal cohesion of this social group.

Activity 2.3

As you read this extract, keep the following questions in mind:

1   What is meant by 'boundaries', and what different aspects of family boundaries are discussed?

2   What other issues are raised for what it means to 'be a family'?

3   What dilemmas are apparent for people trying to work out what it means to 'be a family'?

Reading 2.1   Jane Ribbens McCarthy, Rosalind Edwards and Val Gillies, 'Being a family: boundaries and cohesion'

In using the term 'boundary' we are drawing on anthropological definitions which refer to a symbolic social entity demarcated by various concrete criteria. Some of these may be quite obvious, such as a front door that may customarily be left open or shut, and some may be less obvious, such as appropriate forms of dress or language. Boundaries in this sense can also have important implications for more subtle aspects of social interactions, such as issues of identity, or forms of knowledge that are considered valid. There are also likely to be significant issues of power in relation to boundaries, such that the anthropologist Sandra Wallman (1978) suggests that boundaries are likely to signal areas of confusion, ambiguity and danger in social life.

... In our own usage of the notion, we are seeking to explore how individuals, as members of collectivities, may sometimes construct and experience clear boundaries, and at other times fudge or reject them. As Graham Allan and Graham Crow (2001: 155) comment:

Different boundaries are drawn around different sets of kin depending on the meaning 'family' has in the context in which it is being used. Like the boundaries of inclusion and exclusion constructed around different communities, these boundaries around families are not watertight or unchanging, although some formulations are more 'solidly' constructed than others.

People may vary as to how far they draw minimal or strong boundaries around their notion of their family unit, and how far they expect this to coincide with the physical boundaries of the residential unit. If they take a minimalist approach, they may see family almost as a loose assemblage of people. Within this approach, Western post-Enlightenment ideas of 'the individual' may be particularly strong ... If individuals take a strong approach to boundaries, they are likely to place a much greater stress on the family unit, and to expect this to be strongly reinforced by the significance of residential boundaries. This places considerable emphasis on the current time period, since this (step-) family unit is very much something that is being built in the present. In this formulation, children who have a biological parent living in another household represent a particular 'threat' to the strength and maintenance of the family boundaries. ...

Apart from issues of external boundaries, the family as a unit also raises issues of internal cohesion. Here we are faced with the significance of gender and generation as two fundamental axes of heterosexual family life, such that the 'family' unit is based on a fundamental social division between adults and children, cross-cut by gender expectations. Internal cohesion may be a particular source of concern for people living in changing households ...

Another relationship which may be seen as cutting across the internal cohesion of the unit is that of the couple. Understandings of coupledom may or may not be seen to be in conflict with the project of constructing a family unit. The couple may be seen as the foundation of family life, or alternatively, as constituting a separate element that is more to do with individual fulfilment and the pursuit of romantic happiness ...

There are thus a number of key relationships, which are shaped by people's ideas about how (far) to demarcate external boundaries, and how (far) to be concerned with the internal cohesion of the family unit. These have important consequences for people's notions of what it means to be a family and to undertake family practices.

Constructing 'family' is not just about identifying the relevant members. The quality of the relationships involved is also a key defining issue. A family is expected to be caring and nurturant of its members ... and there is a pervasive view of family life as involving something akin to a team effort ... Within the overall hierarchical division of adults and children, and in the context of expectations of appropriate gender identities, the distribution of resources and exertions is meant to be based around love rather than self-interest. There may thus be a core tension between an orientation towards communal needs and equitable but individualised principles (Clark and Chrisman, 1994). This raises issues about reciprocity, obligation and mutual support in the context of specific family-based identities and histories (Finch and Mason, 1993).

These various understandings are played out in everyday life in the context of mundane everyday issues, such as money or time ...

...

[Some interviewees, for example, highlighted] the shallow nature of lavishing money on children [and] often pointed to the 'real' work of responsible parenting as an effective contrast. The significance of spending time, as opposed to money, doing everyday family activities was emphasised as valuable and integral to developing relationships.

Reading source

Ribbens McCarthy et al., 2003, pp. 29–31 and p. 101

Comment

1   In this extract, I and colleagues discuss boundaries as symbolic meanings that may be concretely expressed through physical space, dress or language.

2   The other features of 'being a family' that are outlined concern issues of internal cohesion around differences of gender and generation, and the place of coupledom in a family context. The quality of relationships is also significant in defining family.

3   A balance between different needs is hard to achieve – between the common good of the group and equality between individuals. This often raises tensions around the importance of reciprocity, mutual support and love. These themes pose dilemmas about how to prioritise concrete practicalities such as time and money.

Between them, then, these various themes – of boundaries, cohesion, the quality of relationships, and the tensions between the individual and the common good – start to build towards a sense of what it means to 'be a family', and also introduce some of the complex issues that may be involved in working this out in daily lives.

6   Layers of meanings in variable settings

In the final section of this chapter you will continue your focus on family meanings in contemporary UK contexts by considering research evidence from interviews conducted in different localities. The extract you will look at here is from a

Figure 2.3
Swansea city

research study conducted in South Wales by Bettina Becker and Nickie Charles (2006). As you read this extended extract, you will begin to see how the themes we raised in the previous section may be found in interviews conducted in different localities.

An additional key issue is considered in the extract: how can we characterise differences between families in different localities and contexts, which relate to ethnicity, class (or material affluence), and household structures? As you read the extract I'd like you to think about how far you are building a sense of unique individuals and families, and how far you are developing a generalised image of families that follows the contours of ethnicity and class.

Such differences are very significant in understanding how family meanings are both individual and social creations: the outcome of individual reflections as well as social processes and interactions occurring in particular contexts. As we saw earlier, family meanings can also be understood as culturally systematised. So on what basis can we group meanings together (and the individuals, families and community networks who express them), and view them as demonstrations of particular cultural patterns – without creating stereotypes which fail to recognise diversity *within* these patterns as well as between them? We will return to this question in the discussion of

Activity 2.4. (It is also a key question for exploration across historical and global contexts in Chapter 7.)

Becker and Charles frame their analysis of these interviews in terms of layers of meaning, a notion by which they convey a sense of how far the language of 'family' may shift subtly and constantly in everyday talk. The notion of 'layers' also perhaps indicates how far there may be meanings hidden under other meanings, so that the analytic process may be one of constant discovery as the layers are uncovered. We present the following long extract in sections. You may like to make notes as you go and review them periodically.

Activity 2.4

Please read the following part of the Becker and Charles extract now.

Reading 2.2   Bettina Becker and Nickie Charles, 'Exploring family meanings in South Wales'

This paper discusses the meanings of the term 'family' as it is used by interviewees ... Three contrasting areas of Swansea were selected, an affluent, popular area, one of the most deprived council estates and an inner-city area with a relatively high proportion of minority ethnic families. In the paper we draw out differences and similarities in the meanings given to the term 'family' by interviewees in the three areas. Differing meanings emerge, but what is striking is the layering of meanings.
...

...

In all three areas interviewees tended to use the term 'family' in two main ways. It was used to describe those who counted as family and in this sense often varied within the same interview. It also had a moral dimension, indicating a normative ideal of what 'family' should be; this meaning was often invoked in relation to family practices ... Different meanings are layered within the interview so that the immediately obvious meaning might conceal other, alternative meanings. The first use of family emerged when we asked general questions about 'the family' or 'your family'. Thus 'family', as in 'having a family', often referred to 'children' with a heterosexual couple only assuming the status of family once they became parents. Interviewees also used 'family' to describe their family of origin; this usually included parents and siblings although people sometimes referred only to their parents when they spoke about family in this sense. They also used 'family' to describe a wider group of relatives and some referred to friends who were 'like family' which implied a particular quality of relationship. Thus family refers to different groups of kin and fictive kin at different points in each interview. The second, normative use of the term 'family' sometimes describes specific childrearing practices, and sometimes a special bond or relationship which carries certain expectations, such as 'being there for each other', providing support and maintaining contact.

Reading source

Becker and Charles, 2006, pp. 101 and 107

Comment

The study itself was structured around three 'contrasting areas', so our attention is immediately drawn to the ways in which these localities can be characterised, and the discussion that follows (below) is structured around these areas. Perhaps, then, we are led to understand that the interviewees are to be taken as, in some sense, 'typical' of those areas, or as representatives of particular cultures.

Two main meanings of family are identified at the outset:

1   Who counts as family – leading to the significance of children, of families of origin and other kin, and sometimes friends.

2   Family as a moral reference point – leading to ideals and moral standards with regard to family practices and the qualities of the relationships involved.

Activity 2.5

In the following sections of the Becker and Charles study, the analysis of family meanings is presented in the three different localities (Fairview, Pen–cwm and Parkfields). As you read the three sections you might like to structure your notes by reference to the following themes:

■ family structures (the question of who belongs, or who 'counts' as family)

■ the quality of the relationships involved

■ what is provided by family relationships

■ ideals of how families *ought* to be, and of how family members should behave

■ any personal reactions you are aware of as you read that you might like to reflect on. For example, do you find yourself identifying with the family experiences of some interviewees more than others? Are you irritated or offended by any of the discussion? Do you find yourself nodding in agreement with the views of any of the participants?

I will discuss various aspects of these themes after each section.

As you read, I would also like you to note how the interviews are painstakingly prised apart and puzzled over, in order to make the underlying family meanings explicit. This entails careful and detailed attention to both *what* is said, and *how* it is said. You may also be surprised to find the use of anthropological terms to describe some of the family structures or forms in ways that are unfamiliar to you. Examples of the terms you will encounter here include patrilocality and uxorilocality to describe whether newly married couples are expected to live with, or close to, the husband's or the wife's family of origin. How far do you think that such terms enable the discussion to 'stand outside' the taken-for-granted language of the interviews?

In the next section, then, we are introduced to some individual interviewees located in Fairview, which is 'one of the most sought after places to live in Swansea with the highest house prices' (Becker and Charles, 2006, p. 105). Rachel Morgan's discussion is used to explore who counts as family, while Sue and Richard Smith's interviews exemplify normative ideas of family, i.e. ideas of how families *ought* to be. See if you can identify what model of family underpins their discussion.

Fairview

Rachel [Morgan] is in her early 30s, is married and lives with her husband and their two preschool-age children. She and her husband are healthcare professionals, Rachel works part-time and both her parents and parents-in-law live nearby and help with childcare. The following exchange between her and the interviewer shows how different meanings of family emerge in the interview:

I: *Who would you count as family, who do you count as your family?*

R: *Immediately I would say, my husband and children. But I would involve my parents, and my brother and sister, but I quite happily leave out my in-laws, despite, (laughs) if someone said to me, you know if you were to take your family on holiday with you, I'd only take Ben [her husband] and the children, because I couldn't bear to have the in-laws.*

The definition of herself, husband and children as family is straightforward; she also includes her family of origin but is more hesitant about her in-laws. There is a suggestion here that she is thinking of her 'immediate' family (defined as 'one or both parents and their unmarried children living in one household' (Townsend, 1957, p. 108)) as she begins by saying 'immediately'; it is this which makes the connection with her in-laws different from the connection with both her family of origin and of procreation. She illustrates the difference by invoking a hypothetical situation of going on holiday; she would take her husband and children but not her in-laws (we assume that she is referring to her parents-in-law rather than any other in-laws). Note, however, that she would not take her parents either. This suggests a finely nuanced definition of who counts as family with her husband and children being most 'immediately' family, her parents and siblings coming next followed by her 'in-laws'. This definition of 'immediate' family was widespread amongst our interviewees, particularly amongst the women. Later in the interview when she talks about the support she receives from other members of her family she extends her definition of family to include other kin such as uncles, aunts and cousins whom she had not previously mentioned. Here it is their provision of support that leads to their inclusion as family. This suggests that providing support is an important way of 'doing' family.

...

Sue and Richard Smith, both in their 70s, develop similar meanings yet add other layers. They are both retired, Sue used to work as a teacher and Richard worked as a technical consultant. They have three adult children, two sons and a daughter, and four grandchildren. They speak about one of their sons in the following way.

R: *And he is very busy, working most peculiar hours, but they don't have a family because she is a modern mother, a modern woman, who wants a career.*

Here having a family means having children and there is an assumption that having children conflicts with the aspirations of the 'modern' woman who wants a career. ... A strong moral tone is evident during this interview and it becomes clear that the Smiths see 'family' as a specific normative practice of raising children within a heterosexual marriage.

R: *Well I think, we have talked about this a number of times, Sue and I, that when we got married, we knew we wanted to have a family. A family. It wasn't just having kids, it was having a family. And making a family, and that's what we wanted.*

S: *And do things with them.*

R: *And do things with them.*

S: *Not just to park them off with other people.*

...

S: *... Whereas these days, the modern generation, want to carry on, they seem to want to have children, but they want to continue with their activities they did before. They are not willing to give anything up, are they, with children.*

Having a family here means for Sue and Richard not only having children but bringing them up in a certain way and 'not parking them off on other people'. ... There seems to be an implied moral judgment of the 'modern family', and particularly the 'modern woman' who pursues a career at the expense of 'having a family'.

Reading source

Becker and Charles, 2006, pp. 108–9

Comment

Perhaps some of Rachel Morgan's discussion set you off thinking about the people you may feel comfortable to go on holiday with, and perhaps you wanted to engage with the Smiths' discussion to agree or disagree?

In the next section we meet people living in 'one of the most deprived council estates in Swansea [with a] reputation for crime and vandalism' (Becker and Charles, 2006, p. 106). In these interviews, can you see how the fairly clear (if implicit) model of the nuclear family underlying these Fairview interviews is 'replaced' (in Becker and Charles' terms) by a different family structure? Does this, perhaps, imply that the nuclear family is being used (in this academic article) as the point of reference by which we can 'place' other family meanings?

Pen-cwm

The layered meanings found in the Fairview interviews recur in the Pen-cwm interviews but with some differences. The male breadwinner family of parents and children (who may or may not still be living in the parental home) often seems to be replaced by mothers and children with fathers being marginal and the mother–child relationship being of primary importance. There are many close-knit families with family members living nearby, seeing each other every day, spending a lot of time together and supporting each other in a routine way with childcare or shopping. These networks tend to be women's networks and reflect the high proportion of lone mothers in Pen-cwm. Compared to the Fairview sample there are many more accounts of conflicts within families ending, at the worst, in family members being excluded from the family. This often applies to men who have failed to fulfil family responsibilities.

...

Margaret West, her 'sister-in-law' Helen Price (Margaret's partner's sister), and Margaret's partner's mother, three women who share much of everyday life and live in the same street, were interviewed together. Margaret West is in her early 30s and lives with her partner and their two school-age children. She went through a four-year period of separation from Helen's brother, who is the father of her children, during which time she maintained close contact with his mother and sister. After a recent traumatic incident the couple got back together and moved onto the same street as his mother and sisters. When Margaret introduced her family she mentioned first her children and then her parents and siblings; this is similar to Rachel with the difference that the father of her children is not included. However, in the following Helen suggests that Margaret's female 'in-laws' are also family and emphasizes her own inclusion of Margaret in family. While doing so, however, she talks in terms of her family which is, at one and the same time, distinguishable from and included as part of Margaret's family.

H: *I mean you class my family as your family as well, don't you? (to M) Even when Margaret and Robert split up for the four years, I still classed her as my sister-in-law.*

M: *Well you've seen me nearly every day, if you didn't, I was in the house.*

H: *Well I was closer to you than I was to Robert, wasn't I.*

Here it is daily contact and closeness that defines family for both Margaret and Helen.

Helen is in her late 20s, has three school-age children and is divorced. She moved a few miles away about four years ago but moved back close to her mother's after an accident when she needed care and help. Her mother clearly plays a key role in keeping the network together and helped her three children to find houses in her street ...

...

The women also make clear that their children come first, and that children and 'family', meaning the female network around them, are more permanent, more reliable and more important than their relationships with men. This is evident when Helen's mother talks about her youngest daughter who thought about moving away.

Mother: *The same with the youngest daughter, I can't let on with her moving away. But I mean his family [daughter's boyfriend] all live up in Oxford way, his two brothers, he is one of three, well he is on all the time about him getting a job away and them moving. And she told him flat out, no, she is not leaving her family. I mean at the end of the day, couples break up, marriages break up,*

M: *The family is always there.*

Mother: *The family is always there.*

A distinction is made here between couple relationships and the family, which is defined as a network of female kin: Relationships come and go unlike 'families' which are 'always there'.

Reading source

Becker and Charles, 2006, pp. 111–14

Comment

In these (related) interviews we can see a very different gendered pattern, with men (and coupledom) seen as less central to 'families' and childrearing. There is a vital basis of practical support between the women, creating long-standing networks (including the quasi-kin of 'in-laws' even without legal marriage). These 'family' networks spread across households, and so do the children's lives. Physical proximity is crucial and the older female (the grandmother) has worked actively to enable this to happen.

With the next interviews, we move on to Parkfields, which is 'a much more heterogeneous area in terms of ethnicity and social class' (Becker and Charles, 2006, p. 106). In the following extract the implied points of comparison are again apparent, when we hear that there is 'more variety' of household composition among minority-ethnic interviewees in this locality, such that the nuclear family model of Fairview is 'replaced' by something else.

Parkfields

The interviews conducted in Parkfields with minority ethnic respondents differ in significant ways from those conducted with the majority ethnic population and varying meanings of family emerge from the interview material. These meanings are rooted in social and cultural context and here we draw on our interviews with Bangladeshis. Amongst the Bangladeshi population there is more variety in household composition than amongst the majority ethnic population; most notably there are three-generation, patrilocal family-households or joint family-households. This can sometimes lead to conflict if it is not possible to follow culturally prescribed patterns of residence. ... Furthermore, men are central to families: they have financial responsibility for all family members and carry an obligation to ensure that their family is respected within the community. Patterns of authority within families are also very clear. Men are head of household and their authority is upheld and supported by the Bangladeshi community. Mothers-in-law have authority over their daughters-in-law and, as senior women, their advice and approval is sought by their sons and daughters in decision-making. Family is seen as crucial to cultural continuity through speaking Bengali at home and sometimes returning children to Bangladesh for education.

...

Aisha [Khatun] lives in a three-generation family-household where she is one of the daughters. She is in her 20s, has a job and is not married. She talks about living in an 'extended family' and defines the family in the following way.

A: *I would say, for me, it's not just my brothers and my mum, it's my uncles, their*
      children, my cousins from my father's side that are family. Immediate family. And
      then there's my mother's brothers and their children as immediate family. That's
      immediate family. These are the people you wouldn't have a wedding without. You
      wouldn't have any, your joys, sorrows, everything would be shared, these are the
      people.

...

She talks about her family as a traditional family which is different from families of the majority ethnic group and also involves different behaviour; family practices in this sense define cultural difference. She talks about this in relation to the hospitalization of a family member.

A: *In fact I think [name] hospital gets really annoyed with our family because one person in hospital, that's it! You are talking visitors around the clock. Because my brother [was recently in hospital] and it was like we couldn't keep the people away. It was quite funny because the hospital said only immediate family. And every family person came and said, I'm his cousin, I'm his brother, I'm his this. Then they thought we were lying, and I said, 'No, no this is his uncle, this is his auntie, this is etc.'. And they couldn't believe it. In fact they were shocked … My mother's generation don't even care what the hospital says. … They are quite funny my aunties because they'll say, 'It's not a British family, this is an Asian family. [laughter] I know British people don't visit their relatives that much but this is an Asian thing'.*

Reading source

Becker and Charles, 2006, pp. 114–5

Comment

Here we see another gender dynamic apparent again, with men very central to the authority and financial arrangements of families, and households centred around male kinship lines. In Aisha's discussion we find various layers by which families are identified. Nuclear family is distinguished from immediate family, which is identified in terms of the sharing quality of the relationships. And Asian families are distinguished from British families, a distinction which is used assertively in relation to expectations of hospital visiting. Aisha's family meanings thus move with explicit awareness between these different themes, and cultural patterns are identified in connection with family practices.

In the final extract, below, how do Becker and Charles consider the significance of their analysis?

The importance of social and cultural context in generating the meanings of family, together with the wide variation in meaning even within the same interview, point to the unspoken assumptions that enable people to understand what is being referred to by the term family. Thus a Bangladeshi woman may be talking about a wide range of relatives beyond her husband and children when she talks about her 'immediate' family but, at the same time and in recognition of the cultural norms of the majority population, she may be talking precisely about her husband and children. In contrast, a lone mother from Pen-cwm may be talking about her mother, sisters, partner's sisters and children. These differences are not usually made explicit and may lead to misunderstandings if outsiders, be they researchers or professionals working with families, assume that they know what family means to those with whom they are interacting. These different meanings of family are of practical relevance for those working with families and relate to the considerable diversity of family forms and family practices which characterize contemporary society. They also point to the importance of recognizing the way different socioeconomic and cultural contexts can give rise to different meanings of family and the possibility of misrecognition of the sets of relationships referred to by the term family.

Finally, there is no sign that this diversity of family forms and meanings is symptomatic of a lessening in the strength and importance of families, either practically or symbolically ... On the contrary, families (however defined) were extremely important to almost all our interviewees and the strength and durability of relationships was often symbolized by referring to people as family. Thus 'family' has continuing symbolic significance, in so far as it is used to identify relationships which have the characteristics of closeness and permanence associated with kinship, as well as being rooted in material practices and ways of 'doing' family which themselves constitute family.

Reading source

Becker and Charles, 2006, pp. 119–20

Comment

In their conclusions, Becker and Charles draw our attention to the importance of contexts for shared family meanings, as well as the subtle ways in which meanings can shift within the course of a single interview. These may include unspoken assumptions that may not be understood by 'outsiders' such as professionals and researchers. They also point to the continuing importance of families, both 'practically' and 'symbolically' across all these different localities.

Overall, this discussion provides a great deal of food for thought about individual understandings of family, and also about cultural variations that are described around differences of ethnicity and class. As always, however, there are some dilemmas in how to consider such cultural variations, since there is a danger of stereotyping and constructing too generalised an image of overarching cultural meanings of family that fails to encompass the diversity of family lives and meanings *within* ethnic and class groups. It is thus hard to convey both a sense of what is shared among people from particular ethnic or social class groups, and a sense of how far all families and all individuals need to be understood as specific and unique (and we return to such difficult issues in Chapter 7 when we look across cultures and contexts globally and historically). It is also a major dilemma for researchers, particularly when describing the family lives of people from more marginalised and vulnerable groups, who may feel a deep uneasiness and sense of exposure when differences and divisions within their communities are presented to, and discussed with, those who are perceived as outsiders.

7   Conclusions

This chapter introduced you to some of the ramifications of 'family meanings', for individuals, policy-makers, professionals, and social scientists, and considered the significance of what we mean by 'meaning' in the study of social lives.

We have also begun to open up some general themes around the diversity of what family means to people living in different contexts in contemporary European (particularly UK) and New World societies. Along the way, we have also introduced some difficult issues for researchers, including:

■ how to develop any language for describing and comparing people's lives and relationships that can accommodate both what is shared and what is variable, without creating stereotypes or models into which experience has to be shoehorned and by which it may be judged

■ how to study families when researchers are themselves implicated in the social contexts in which families occur and have their own taken-for-granted assumptions about what family means.

These issues point to the importance of recognising knowledge as partial and contingent, and the need for us to be as reflexive as possible about the ways in which our knowledge is shaped by our own particular social contexts. In the next chapter, we raise further issues about how qualitative research is undertaken, as we explore the taken-for-granted assumptions of family meanings and tease them apart in more detail across a broader range of research studies.

References

Becker, B. and Charles, N. (2006) 'Layered meanings: the construction of "the family" in the interview', *Community, Work and Family,* vol. 9, no. 2, pp. 101–22.

Bernardes, J. (1987) '"Doing things with words": Sociology and "Family Policy" debates', *Sociological Review,* vol. 35, no. 4, pp. 679–702.

HM Government, 'Humanitarian Assistance in Emergencies: Non-statutory guidance on establishing Humanitarian Assistance Centres', Department for Culture Media and Sport and the Association of Chief Police Officers, http://www.ukresilience.gov.uk/~/media/assets/www.ukresilience.info/hac_guidance%20pdf.ashx (Accessed 26 May 2008).

Lindley, B. (2007) UK Family Rights Group handout.

Ribbens, J. (1994) *Mothers and Their Children: A Sociology of Childrearing,* London, Sage.

Ribbens McCarthy, J., Edwards, R. and Gillies, V. (2003) *Making Families: Moral Tales of Parenting and Step-Parenting*, Durham, Sociology Press.

Rutter, M. (2000) 'Psychosocial influences: critiques, findings and research needs', *Development and Psychopathology*, vol. 12, no. 3, pp. 375–405.

Scott, J. (1997) 'Changing households in Britain: do families still matter?', *Sociological Review*, vol. 45, no. 4, pp. 590–620.

Walkover, B.C. (1992) 'The family as an overwrought object of desire' in Rosenwald, G.C. and Ochberg, R. (eds.) *Storied Lives: The Cultural Politics of Self-Understanding*, New Haven, CT, Yale University Press.

Chapter 3
Teasing threads apart

Jane Ribbens McCarthy

Contents

1   Introduction

In the last chapter we began to explore some overarching themes of family meanings arising from contemporary UK research. In the process, you were introduced to interviewees' detailed discussions of their everyday family lives. These included issues around:

■ the drawing of boundaries, and who 'counts' as 'family'

■ internal cohesion

■ normative ideas of 'family', i.e. what is seen as a normal or 'proper' family in particular contexts.

In this present chapter, we build on this discussion to elaborate these family meanings further, drawing out more detailed themes from qualitative research evidence of how many people talk about their families and relationships in open-ended interviews.

As you progress through the chapter, I suggest you try to read the research both thoughtfully and critically in order to listen to how interviewees themselves define and understand 'family'. You may find yourself drawn into the intricacies of different family meanings, and I certainly hope you will indeed find these engaging and fascinating. However, I would like you also to try to keep some additional focus on what is going on in this multi-faceted process of communication around families. The significance of talk is something you will explore in more detail in Chapter 5, particularly through the framework of family discourses, but you have already been introduced to this approach in Chapter 1, through Gubrium and Holstein's suggestion that we have to listen in order to know how to look. I hope this will have got you started on thinking about what may be involved in listening effectively to people's family meanings.

It should be clear, then, that there are no definitive answers to be found in the research interviews you will explore here. Rather, we are embarking on a journey of exploration, and hopefully deepening and extending our insights into family meanings along the way. But there may be some recurrent features in the landscapes through which we pass. By the end of the chapter, not only will we have explored some aspects of the shared and variable features of family meanings, but we will have also gained some sense of the power as well as the subtlety of the idea of 'family'.

2   Exploring qualitative research

2.1   Introducing the studies

In the previous chapter you were introduced to two extended general extracts from research publications, one which focused on step-parents living in various locations in Southern England (Ribbens McCarthy et al., 2003), and one which focused on three particular localities in Swansea (Becker and Charles, 2006). In this chapter, we sometimes draw on the studies you've already met, but also introduce some new ones. These include research conducted by:

- Virginia Morrow (1998), at the Institute of Education, of children of varying ethnic backgrounds, living in urban and rural areas of England

- Wendy Langford, Charlie Lewis, Yvette Solomon and Jo Warin (2001), at the University of Lancaster, of parents and younger teenagers (aged 11–16) – including both white- and Asian-British ethnic groups – living in cities in the North of England

- Val Gillies, Jane Ribbens McCarthy and Janet Holland (2001), at Oxford Brookes University, of parents and older teenagers aged 16–18, of varying ethnicities, living in various parts of the Midlands and Southern England

- Tracey Reynolds, at London South Bank University (2005), of Caribbean mothers living in London, and mothers involved in black-community organisations in other English cities.

Between them, such studies offer a variety of points of view from family members. You should note, however, that while these UK studies encompass a wide range of regions, localities, ethnicities, and social classes, these more structural dimensions of social context and inequalities are not, on the whole, brought strongly into the discussion – and some significant social dimensions (e.g. sexual orientation) are not included in the current discussion at all. Our concern in this chapter will be to focus on the intricacies and subtleties of family meanings as expressed by the individuals interviewed in these particular studies.

You may have noticed that these studies are all drawn from various parts of the UK, and it does seem to be the case that this particular form of in-depth qualitative research into the everyday meanings of 'family' has been particularly visible in British sociology. This is despite the importance and relevance here of the work by the US sociologists, Gubrium and Holstein (1990), whose discussion of 'what is family' you encountered in chapter 1. At the same time, there is a strong vein of US research around 'family stories', but these tend to be considered more for their place in child development and family interactions (including over generations) (e.g. Pratt and Fiese, 2004), than for what they reveal about people's everyday meanings and understandings of 'family'.

At the same time, however, there are some studies of family lives in European and New World societies that do point to the pervasiveness of some of the themes apparent in the UK studies which you will encounter later in this chapter. Some research from New World countries has centred on everyday experiences of family rituals, including, for example, family meal times, which point to some of the themes of 'togetherness' found so strongly in the context of the UK research we will consider later:

> It's comfy and nice to have the family all together. Having a family meal in the evening is very important to me because I get to talk to my family all together at the same time. (Australian teenager quoted by Gallegos et al., 2011, p. 253)

> In my family, dinner is a time when the family sits down together and talks about their day while we all listen attentively. This way we find out what is happening in each others' lives. For us, dinner is more than just eating food–it is about being together and sharing our thoughts. (South African young adult quoted by Smit, 2011, p. 360)

> ... watching TV together, eating meals together, making jokes about one another, celebrating birthdays–this keeps our family connected, because the more the family spends time together, the more we bond. (South African young adult quoted by Smit, 2011, p. 363)

Richards (1990) similarly found a widespread emphasis on 'togetherness' in her study of Australian suburban family lives, while Jallinoja (2008) found in her more quantitative research that an emphasis on family 'togetherness' has strikingly increased in Finland since the turn of the twenty-first century. Shaw's (2008) US research on leisure activities likewise found a strong emphasis on togetherness (Shaw's work is discussed further in chapter 5.) Further, some of the quality expected of family relationships can be seen in this quote from an interviewee in Gubrium and Holstein's US work, asserting the suitability of his living with his 'common-law wife's family':

> I got a whole family here, and family takes care of its own. I got my old lady and her sister and some cousin or somethin'. Name's Esther. That kind of family ain't gonna let nothin' happen to me. (Gubrium and Holstein, 1990, p. 60)

2.2 Reading critically

I hope you will explore these studies with a critical eye, and I set out here some issues to bear in mind as you read.

2.2.1 Who are we listening to?

Most of these studies were undertaken in order to understand family lives and relationships across the broad spectrum of contemporary UK society. They are thus focused on the family lives of people who were interviewed on some general basis, rather than because they were involved with professional services or interventions. Equally, the interviewees hadn't identified themselves, or been identified by the researchers, for inclusion in the studies on the basis of having particular difficulties. Instead, as you may notice, some of these studies are centred on particular localities and communities, others on particular age groups, ethnic groups, or changing household circumstances.

The way in which each study is focused around particular groups is apparent in the categories used to identify interviewees in the research reports, as you will see when you encounter quotes from individuals later in the chapter. In the research by Gillies and colleagues, quotes from individual speakers are identified by reference to their ethnicity, their social class, and their family position. In Reynolds' study, all her interviewees were mothers who identified themselves as African-Caribbean, some being first-generation migrants, and others who had been born in the UK. In this particular study by Reynolds, differences within the overall category of 'African-Caribbean' are not a feature of her analysis, so individuals are identified by their family and migration status. In the study by Langford and colleagues, a decision was made to analyse the interviews of white British and Asian British separately, and thereafter the quotes in the main report are from the white-British interviewees. In Morrow's study of children recruited through schools, a key distinction was made around schools based in rural and urban areas.

2.2.2   On what basis were they talking?

In all of these studies, participants were recruited on the basis that they were taking part in a study focused on their lives and personal relationships, often in a very open-ended way. So it is not surprising that the language of 'family' is recurrent. However, it is important here to consider at which points of the interviews the participants were talking quite spontaneously about their ideas of 'family', and at which points they were prompted by specific questions from the researcher.

2.2.3   Who are the researchers?

Besides such features of the study design, however, it is important to remember that the studies themselves have been conducted and written up by researchers who have their own histories, and who are working within the contexts of academic debates and institutions. Ribbens McCarthy and Edwards, for example, in other publications tentatively describe themselves as living in step-families.

2.2.4   Who are you, as the reader?

And last, but by no means least, what do you yourself bring to the process, as a reader, in terms of your personal biography and social characteristics? In reading these materials, you are actively adding in your own interpretations and frameworks of understanding, so you may like to attend to your own responses to what you are reading. Are there occasions

What? Do I want to knit a snake?

Figure 3.1

Listening is not always easy

when you would interpret the words of the interviewee rather differently from the discussion offered by the researcher? And, as you read, do you find that some family meanings surprise you or perhaps 'jar' a little? Do some quotes cause you to reflect on your own assumptions, or perhaps provoke particular emotional responses or evaluative judgements? Do you, for example, find yourself approving or disapproving of what some interviewees had to say? Building on the approach set out in previous chapters, I ask you to note any such responses. However, also try to set these thoughts to one side in order to be able to attend closely to the meanings of family as these are expressed by the interviewees themselves.

2.3 Framing questions

The discussion that follows, then, will introduce you to the possibility of 'teasing open' this intriguing – and perhaps endless – question of family meanings. This process is sometimes described as one of 'deconstructing' what is normally taken-for-granted about families. To do this, researchers analyse 'family' as something that is socially constructed rather than a natural and concrete object, so that it is shaped and produced by social forces and contexts. The processes by which this social construction occurs are often implicit and simply assumed by the people interviewed. The task of analysis, then, requires the researchers to 'de-construct' these processes and make them visible.

Building on our discussion in the previous chapter, where we considered broad themes of family meanings, below I suggest questions to bear in mind as you read the extracts from research interviews in this chapter. The suggestions I offer here are drawn primarily from research based in the UK and USA, and they offer a general starting point for analysing the participants' family meanings. But you may be able to think of more: there may be many issues that are not particularly touched upon by the questions below, or which could be expressed in more variable ways. At the end of the chapter, we will explore how the themes raised in these questions can be traced in the research interviews.

1   Who belongs, and how are people 'counted in' or 'counted out'? Here the notion of boundary becomes important, in terms of drawing up dividing lines; although the ways in which these boundaries are expressed may be very subtle – as in the notion of family jokes for example, where some shared memory or history gives rise to a sense of humour which others cannot fathom. Some people will draw such boundaries much more fluidly and contingently than others, with quite different implications for how far they see 'family' as a clearly defined unit. Many people seem to have some idea of a central core of what is sometimes referred to as 'immediate' family, with others drawn in or defined out in variable ways at different times and for different purposes. People also vary in terms of how far they see family members as autonomous individuals who have their own lives and concerns to pursue, or how far they see individuals as always bound up with their family relationships.

2   How far, and in what ways, is 'family' located in physical space? In the notion of the nuclear family household, 'family' is clearly located in the physical space of the home, although even here, there may still be variations – for example, if the father is working elsewhere. For some, 'family' may not only be spread across different residences but also across different countries or continents. Even so, there may often be an idea of 'family' that is attached to a particular physical locality, which may be seen as the ultimate place of 'home' – even if it is physically and temporally remote from current living arrangements.

3   What is 'family' membership based on? For some people, 'family' is categorically based on ties of blood or kinship, but for others, there may be a greater sense of family as something which is created and built painstakingly over time. Aspects of time are also likely to be important in other ways, with 'family' entailing a sense of shared history and traditions. This is apparent when people say, 'It's a family tradition that we always do x, y or z like this', or 'We always tend to be like that in my family'.

4   What qualities of relationships are involved? For some people, meanings of 'family' entail a strong sense of belonging and togetherness, perhaps amounting to a sense of shared identity. For others, there may be a sense of obligation and duty, which may be welcomed or resisted. Furthermore, 'family' may imply a sense of commitment. These qualities may be associated with quite idealised imagery and/or strong emotional desires and fears that go beyond the specifics of particular relationships in the here and now.

5   How do interviewees suggest that family relationships are evaluated? In one way or another, when we evaluate something, it has the effect of ranking it, so that we see some things as higher or lower, better or worse, by reference to a particular criterion. In the context of family meanings, such evaluations might, for example, invoke moral values, or beliefs about what may be thought to work or not to work, or to be appropriate or inappropriate. You may recall the older couple, Sue and Richard Smith from Swansea, for example, who evaluated their daughter-in-law as a 'modern woman', with the result that their son didn't have 'a family' in their particular normative version of a family with children and two parents who are prepared to 'give things up' for them. Evaluations of families thus often invoke particular values, so that there is then a sense of moral judgement. Consequently, it is hard to talk about family at all without there being some sense of moral or other evaluative judgements entailed. This makes it very difficult to consider differences, since these may be felt to involve a sense of judging the meanings of others according to values which might not be the same as our own. But, as discussed in Chapter 2, a hermeneutic approach to family meanings seeks to tease open such moral and evaluative judgements, and see how they are embedded within particular contexts, rather than to endorse or refute some meanings as right or wrong, better or worse.

6   What differences may be found both 'within' and between families? Differences around the dimensions of gender and generation are features of family meanings that may, on the one hand, be most taken-for-granted as part of the 'natural' order of things; on the other hand, these differences may be a major source of tension and dispute and a threat to family togetherness. While these are axes of difference that occur between family members themselves, differences may also be apparent at times – if perhaps less often articulated – in the ways in which people understand and 'place' their families by reference to their locality, neighbourhood, or society more generally.

These are some of the questions that we can begin to think about, then, as we explore family meanings, but this list is by no means definitive or exhaustive. And yet, for each individual, their particular 'take' on these different questions builds into a set of individual meanings that feels quite 'normal', to constitute an unremarkable way of living. I recommend that you keep this list to hand to refer to as you read on and encounter different examples of research evidence which will help us to tease apart some threads of family meanings.

3   Teasing threads apart

The discussion that follows is based on a close reading of the various studies that we are citing here, which I undertook in order to prepare this chapter. This has then led me to identify recurrent themes across the range of interviews and analyses reported in the different publications I was reading. So, in teasing the threads apart, I am continuing the process of 'de-constructing' the family meanings that are commonly found in these studies, leading to the four overall areas for discussion offered below. But besides looking for such commonalities of family meanings, when reading these different studies I was also looking at the tensions and variations that might be found – both between different interviewees, and also within the perspective of any one individual, as this is expressed at different points in the interview. Additionally, in the extracts that follow, you will hear from the researchers themselves as they develop their own discussion and analysis of family meanings, to consider common themes that are expressed, along with their subtle ambiguities, tensions and ambivalences.

(i)   The taken-for-granted quality of family

Some discussions in interviews are prompted by direct questions from the researchers about what 'family' means to people, and such questions can provoke some thoughtful responses. But sometimes people struggle to put into words what family means to them and this, in itself, says something important about the nature of family: family is taken-for-granted as a part of daily life to such an extent that its meaning can't be expressed.

I mean you just take it for granted really don't you that you're in a family. (Pat Burrows)

I take them for granted that they're there. (Ken Smith)

How can you put it? Just being there. Just being part of the family what's important. I don't know. It's hard to say really. No, I just can't think of anything to describe that one. It's just being here basically. Just being part of a family. (Sean Carlton)

(Langford et al., 2001, p. 13)

I can't describe what a family is. Everybody has one, you're just born into it. You argue sometimes, have fun, go on holiday, but I don't know what it is. I know you usually have mum, dad, brother, sister, gran, granddad, aunts, uncles, cousins. Families are so you're not lonely, they are also there to bring you to life. (13 year old girl)

(Morrow, 1998, p. 27)

This girl's reference to families helping to avoid loneliness leads us to another thread of family meaning that has arisen from research interviews: the idea of togetherness and belonging.

(ii) Family togetherness and belonging

While people may thus struggle to convey what 'family' actually is, the interviews also contain a pervasive language of family as 'togetherness', conveying a powerful sense of the family as a unit. This comes through strongly in the studies of teenagers' family lives.

Figure 3.2
People may value togetherness

The words 'closeness' and 'togetherness' recurred throughout interviewees' discussions of family. This emphasis on intimacy was often associated with particular bounded experiences such as 'living together', 'doing things together', 'going out together', 'sticking together' or 'pulling together'. Several people specifically referred to family as a unit:

A unit, to be together. You know, which I know a lot of people haven't got. (Susan, White, working-class mother)

A unit, a unit of people that pulls together. (Jim, White, working-class father)

(Gillies et al., 2001, p. 26)

Activity 3.1

As you read the following selection of quotes, which all concern aspects of belonging and togetherness, see if you can identify differences of emphasis between them about what it is that families 'share'.

A person is judged by their family, a person's evaluated by their family. (Somera, Pakistani, middle-class mother)

A sense of identity, belonging, I think that's very important. Em, shared values, shared things like humour that you have just in your family ... shared memories, the real sense of belonging really is the strongest I know. (Hugh, White, working-class father)

Family means to me speaking with one voice. You know, if you see one, the other will represent the same thing. And to me that's family. You have the similar sort of frame of mind. Like, if you see my brothers, and how they behave, and how they, their manners, will be similar to myself, you have a trait. Like your family has certain traits, you know, the conduct of your family. (Otis, African-Caribbean, middle-class father)

(Gillies et al., 2001, p. 27)

Comment

What I noticed here is that each quote refers to different aspects of what is shared. In Somera's quote, the emphasis is on being judged together. For Hugh, the emphasis is on shared attributes, like humour and memories, invoking a shared 'identity', while Otis suggests that the similarities are so strong (such as traits and frames of mind) that you share 'one voice' and represent 'the same thing'. Gillies et al. (2001) go on to suggest that this view of identity and social worth as being rooted in your family implies a particular version of the person. By this they mean that different cultures can have varying ideas of what it means to be a human being, with one particular version of the person being particularly predominant in white, masculine, middle-class culture in some European and New World countries. This particular westernised notion of the person stresses the individual as an autonomous, self-directing and rational being, rather than as a relational being who is intrinsically bound up with their significant relationships, family membership and wider networks. Such different assumptions of what it is to be a human being can be particularly hard to see as they are so taken-for-granted, but may be quite fundamental to the ways in which people understand their lives. In the quotes from Somera, Hugh and Otis we can see that the relational understanding of the person is being described, but these individuals might well have invoked different, more individualised ideas of the person in other parts of their interviews, since people may draw on different ideas at different times. We consider cultural variations in what it means to be a person further in Chapter 7.

Somewhat paradoxically, however, family togetherness may not necessarily be an entirely shared family meaning, as it may be experienced in different ways by different individuals within the household, with age and gender as significant sources of difference. As children grow, some parents may express a sense of nostalgia, and a gap begins to appear between the ideal and the lived experience of family. This is something that featured in the research by Langford and colleagues:

> Of particular interest ... are the contrasts between parents' and teenagers' perspectives. 'Togetherness' features more in parents' accounts of the importance of family than in teenagers'. This difference sets the scene for a major theme of this report: parents' investment in 'creating' the family as a unit and enacting family togetherness through such means as family outings and shared meals. Fathers in particular emphasised this aspect of the family and often this was linked to an understanding of their own role as the person who provides for the family ... This emphasis in parents' accounts is also linked to the more frequent appearance of 'self' where the family is understood as part of a personal history of achievement and as a means of endowing status, identity and role. Again this type of response was more present in parents' accounts, particularly fathers'.
>
> (Langford et al., 2001, pp. 16–7)

Activity 3.2

Consider what is meant by 'family' in the following two quotes from parents of teenagers. What meaning do you think 'family' holds for the speakers?

> You've got to let go of them. You can't keep them tied to your apron strings, can you? ... We always used to go the pantomime but we didn't go this year. Darren thinks he's getting too old for the pantomime but that was always a regular thing – we used to go as a family ... I don't like going out on my own, you know? It's not normal life. [Mandy Lawson, mother of Darren, 16]
>
> (Langford et al., 2001, p. 47)

[In the next quote] Peter is answering a question about what he most enjoys doing with David (14) and Daniel (12) ...

I wouldn't say anything in particular. I think just spending time with them really, whatever it is ... Whatever we do, as long as we're doing it together, I'm not bothered ... It can be anything really. I'm not bothered what it is. I just – as long as it's quality time really that you can talk together. Erm – working on the theory of families who play together stay together sort of thing really we're not likely to drift away totally in years to come like. I mean it does happen, doesn't it? And it might happen, you know?

(Langford et al., 2001, p. 48)

Comment

What I particularly noticed about Mandy's discussion is her reference to the regularity of the pantomime trip in times now past, and her account of 'normal' life as being about more than herself alone. So this is a look back to earlier times, with 'family' seen as involving regular events and a 'normal' sense of belonging with others. To be alone, without family relationships as part of everyday life, is not normal. In Peter's account, he is looking towards family as a (hoped for) feature of life in the future, which he hopes to secure through spending quality time in which family members talk together. In both cases, either looking back or forward, being a family is described as something much desired. But would it be difficult for people to talk in any other way about families?

Here's a flavour of how the researchers themselves discuss these accounts, emphasising the importance of parents' identifications with their families, and the strong evaluations and emotions attached to this.

> 'Family' events are often constructed as being 'for the children', but as teenagers lose their interest in 'doing the family' with mum and dad, it is the mums and dads who long for bright lights and pantomimes. Family life seems so precious yet so hard to grasp – just when you thought you had it, 'you find yourself drifting away'.

> The story is not, however, simply one of loss. Paradoxically, nostalgia for a lost family togetherness, visible in many parents' accounts, allows the construction – or perhaps the reconstruction – of the family as an ideal family. High days and holidays may in fact have always been exceptions to the normal pattern of family life. But they are significant because they evoke a time when the family really were all together ... a time when they really did do all those things they used to do together.

> ...

> Peter's desire to create opportunities for 'togetherness' appears to arise in response to his actual experience of a household where nobody in fact does anything together very much ... Peter's experience of the actual Jones 'family', then, is that it is hardly an observable entity at all. He lives in a 'hurly burly house' where

'everybody's going somewhere doing their own thing'. Only by deliberately creating opportunities for 'quality time' can Peter experience the togetherness that reassures him that his family is, and will continue to be, a family, and not fragment entirely in the face of 'all the other stresses that we've got'.

(Langford et al., 2001, p. 48)

Figure 3.3
The bright lights of the traditional pantomime

This study of families with teenagers thus conveys a strong sense of the changing experience of families over time – nothing stays the same, and change is a constant feature. And yet, even after the changes of divorce, separation and remarriage or re-partnering, the language of family togetherness may be undiminished, as found in the study by Ribbens McCarthy et al. (2003, p. 39).

> I always think of a proper family of people that all talk together and go out together ... (June – White, working class, mother)

For some mothers, the collective unit to which they express a sense of belonging is discussed in terms of community as much as family, as in Reynolds' study of Caribbean mothers:

> There's this saying 'it takes a community to raise a child' ... It means that we all have to take responsibility for them. They're our children. If we don't care then

how can we expect anyone else to care about them. We all have to play a part, no matter how big or small because they're our children. What happens to our children affects the community as a whole so it's all of our responsibility to get it right because they're the next generation. (Dolly, age 76, married, first generation)

(Reynolds, 2005, pp. 132)

In this case, then, boundaries may be drawn in terms of how communities are identified – so that the children become 'our children' – as much as with how families are demarcated. And, while some interviewees discussed the ways in which they might not experience such communities as entirely positive, the meanings of 'community' also carry important moral values, as we saw with 'family'. Some women thus suggested that formal organisations of support were becoming increasingly important, which is weakening the sense of 'family' in the face of what they saw as increasing 'selfishness' and lack of concern:

This time 30 or 40 years ago there wouldn't even have been a need for an organisation like ours. The family all pulled together and helped one another. I'm not just talking about your immediate family but uncles, aunts and cousins. They would all pull together and help. But now people are so busy. They say they haven't got time for you and that's not even your distant relations saying that but your own family. We've become selfish because people who only care about ourselves, about our own needs and we're not concerned with other people. (Janet, age 48, divorced, first generation)

(Reynolds, 2005, p. 123–4)

Togetherness may thus often be invoked through nostalgia, as something fragile that is under threat.

(iii) Physical proximity

Sometimes family togetherness can be experienced through being demonstrably together on a family outing, while another important symbol of family togetherness can be seen in the physical space of the 'family home' itself. So, is it possible for people to be members of one 'family' if they do not all live together, or live in different countries? This becomes relevant, for example, when parents live separately, whether for divorce or other reasons. This is what some lone mothers had to say:

Sometimes I want to rely more on [her daughter's father] – alright yeh, things didn't work out between us and he left. He's not here all the time but I still see him as family, as part of my family. (Jamilla, age 25, lone-mother, second generation)

...

T.R.: Do you see your son's father as part of your family?

Melanie: Well I'm stuck with him in my life, the same like a brother or sister because you know they're there, they're popping up in your life, always there. So because of that he's family in a way because I can't get rid of him [laughing]. (Melanie, age 29, lone-mother, second generation)

(Reynolds, 2005, p. 163)

So, in both these women's accounts, these men are 'like family' because they're 'stuck' with them. It is interesting to explore children's perspectives on this issue, since they may particularly want to feel a continuing tie to both parents, whether living with them or not.

Activity 3.3

The following group discussion comes from Morrow's study of children's understandings of family, and is centred on the question they were asked of whether or not a non-resident father 'counts' as family. What themes do you think the children draw on to decide this issue?

The large group of nine year olds had the following discussion:

No! Yes! Maybe! Shouts: They're not!

Keri: I think they are, because if they still see each other, at the weekends or in the school holidays, then yes, but if they don't then they might be, but not as much as they used to be, because they were family at one point, and they can still carry on being a family, even if they are divorced ...

Sam: Well, no, because this family won't be living together.

Kevin: But if you're family, 'cos you've got aunts and uncles and you don't live together, you don't live in the same house as them ...

Betty: I think they are a family because even if the mum and dad don't love each other, the dad and the child, or the mum and the child, love each other. If the child thinks it's a family, it's gonna make them happier.

...

Emily: Well, I think they're sort of like a family, because if Karin goes to see her dad, then they are still a family, they're sort of like a family in one way, and sort of not like a family because they don't live with each other.

...

... One girl mentioned that 'some of your family can be in Pakistan but they are still your family', and this came up in other groups too, for example, a group of four boys said the following: 'Yeah, yes, maybe ... it doesn't matter, he's always [her] father, no matter where they were'; 'you're still a family like my dad goes somewhere else, we're still a family though ...' In another group of boys, one asked 'are they separated?' Another boy answered: 'No, they only live apart'. Another boy said: 'he might be going for a job somewhere, Miss, if he is gone for a job then that is family, but if he's slipped up with his wife, then that isn't a family ... If they both love each other than it's still a family. If they're somewhere else and you're somewhere else, you're still a family'.

(Morrow, 1998, pp. 15–16)

Comment

It is apparent that the children found this quite a difficult issue to agree upon, and they drew on various themes to help them decide whether or not the father belongs to 'the family'. These include: having a shared history; time spent together; living together; loving relationships between parents and children; the reason for the father's absence. At times this led them to develop a qualified notion of family, i.e. the possibility of being 'more or less' of a family, 'sort of like a family ... and sort of not like a family'.

A significant dimension, then, in what can make you 'more or less' of a family, is the nature and quality of the relationships involved.

(iv) Family support and commitment

Categorical criteria for identifying 'family' in everyday lives can thus be ambiguous and indeterminate. Other criteria can come into play: often issues of the quality, emotion and commitment of the relationships involved. Family meanings may thus implicate issues of support as well as love and care, themes which may be closely intertwined. We consider such meanings here within their own terms of reference, although I will raise the question of whether or not these qualities actually relate to lived experiences and realities, and what happens when they don't, later on in the chapter.

For younger children, physical care was particularly important as a key indicator of family meanings, as with some of the older interviewees discussed in other sections of the Swansea study (Becker and Charles, 2006, discussed in Chapter 2). This draws our attention to the theme of family as defined by support, which may be particularly relevant to individuals, of whatever age, who feel vulnerable and in need of care.

A family is people who care for you. Families are for looking after you. (Kyle, 8)

... families are for you, so if your mum and dad go to Pakistan or another country, the other half or the other quarter or something can like look after you. (Tahir, 8)

(Morrow, 1998, p. 20 and p. 22)

While the sense of 'being looked after' may be less relevant for older children, the notion of family as 'being there' for you can still be strong, as with these teenagers – even alongside the significance of peer relationships. Consider here how John Field (aged 14) thoughtfully distinguishes between the qualities of his family and friendship relationships.

> I think that if I didn't have like um, a stable family, like I've got, then you know, I've got a wide circle of friends and I've got um, other people ... especially with my Theatre Company that I'm very involved with ... I'm very close to some of them. I feel like I'd always, they'd always be there and everything and sort of act like a family but it wouldn't be the same ... they never would actually be a real family ... it's like right at the back of your mind all the time, this family that I've got now is always there ... I always know that someone is going to be there for me whatever is happening ... but with like the other people that I'm close to it's not the same it's um, I'll always feel they'd back me up and stuff but they wouldn't go to the end of the world for me whereas the family I've got here would do – through thick and thin the family I've got here, but other people, although they stand over you and see you alright and everything, it's not quite as far stretched.
>
> (Langford et al., 2001, pp. 13–4)

This issue of the quality of relationships as a key feature of family is particularly important with regard to family ideals and morality. This raises the possibility that, if these qualities are not fulfilled, there is a sense in which family is invalidated even if there are biological or legal ties in place. Conversely, for some people, it is the demonstration of these qualities, over time, that creates the very foundation of family from a group of people who come together.

Activity 3.4

If you compare the quotes below, what different bases do they suggest for the foundation of family life? The first set of quotes is taken from a study of parents and older teenagers.

> I think if you cohabit for 20 years then you're a family. If you're still friends at the end of that time you've probably done a good many things right, I don't think family is just mum, dad and two kids, it's the end result. I think it's four adults who like each other, and are quite keen to be associated under the same name. (Andy, White, middle-class father)
>
> ...
>
> Family means there's me, myself, my wife, my children, that's it, that's the family. (Ahmed, Pakistani, middle-class father)

I've often said to people, you can choose your friends but you can't choose your family. (Michelle, White, working-class mother)

They're sort of the people you're stuck with. (Emma, White, working-class young woman)

(Gillies et al., 2001, p. 26)

The next set of quotes come from the study of re-partnered parents, and in the first one Mark is discussing whether or not he and his expectant wife constitute a family, together with her child from a previous marriage:

I don't know, I see blood relatives more as family ... it may be different when the baby's born. Then we're more of a unit. We're bound by something more than love. (Mark – White, middle class, step-father and expectant father)

...

Family is blood ties more I think, you know. So your actual birth family. That can be separate from the household structure. (Sue – White, middle class, half-weekly resident mother)

If you're tied together by blood or marriage, it's your family. Your history and everything. (Karen – African-Caribbean, working class, mother)

...

It doesn't matter what shape or form it is as long as all the love's still there. (Louise – White, working class, mother)

You just ensure that they're safe and well looked after, and that there's a strong loving bond that blends it all together. (Pete – White, middle class, father and step-father)

(Ribbens McCarthy et al., 2003, pp. 41–2)

Comment

These different speakers express quite different views of the foundations of family life, in terms of whether or not this is something fixed or achieved. Andy's view, for example, states that biological or legal ties are not enough to make you 'a family', but others take quite the opposite view. Others suggest, like the lone mothers quoted earlier, that family consists of people you are 'stuck with'. Biological links are invoked here as an idea around which to categorically define fixed and unalterable relationships. Paradoxically, however, sometimes it seems it is precisely this 'fixed' nature of family relationships which gives them a distinctive quality of enduring and persisting despite anything – being bound by something 'more than love'.

Activity 3.5

In the following quotes, speakers draw on similar notions of family relationships based on enduring ties and commitment. But can you identify variations in how far they see this as something to be valued and desired?

> I think what's important about family is that, as I was saying, they were really, really supportive. I could abuse them. You can do that with families. You can muck them about and piss them off, and they still come back for more. You can be forgiven all these horrendous things you put them through and you can expect it all back from them too. (Tina – White, middle class, mother)
>
> ...
>
> Having children means you have to give up being selfish, I think, to a certain extent, and um, by taking on a relationship which has got children in, you have to be less self-centred. I mean I can't sort of do all the things that I would like to do, erm, because I can't just say to Sue, 'Oh, do you fancy going to Paris this weekend?' or something. (John White, middle class, half-weekly resident father)
>
> And my feeling of entrapment, if you like, in the [work] field and the [geographical] location and so on, which weren't actually what I'd been aiming for. I'd much rather have been elsewhere in the country. (Jonathan – White, middle class, resident father)
>
> ...
>
> Well, it just means sort of like a bit of a haven, where you can be as relaxed and uncaring about pressure as you like ... and it's sort of like security as well. When you feel low, you can be built up and you're sort of cosseted. (Jo – White, middle class, father and step-father)
>
> Security, stability. Um, loyalty. Not necessarily getting on all the time but knowing that you've got family who are there for you. Yeah, security and, er, somewhere to go when all else fails. (Paula – White, middle class, mother and non-resident step-mother)
>
> (Ribbens McCarthy et al., 2003, pp. 39–40)

Comment

For some of these interviewees, the enduring quality of family relationships means that they see family as providing 'goods', such as support, security, and stability, 'somewhere to go when all else fails', 'a haven'. But for others there are expressions of such ties as requiring 'giving something up', not being able to do what you like, and 'entrapment'. These are quite starkly polarised emotional evaluations.

Summary

So far, then, we have explored in some detail various significant themes of family meanings, including: their taken-for-granted nature; how boundaries are drawn to include or exclude particular people; the significance of location and physical space; and the quality and evaluation of relationships which form the basis of family. Overall, in terms of the potential emotional resonances of families, we see a potent blend apparent in these quotes, around categorical and enduring ties, mutual support, and emotional connections of love. Where these different threads coincide, then such ideals may hold together in people's family meanings, but these different themes could also be in tension with one another. In the next section we will tackle more directly the question of family as ideal, and what happens when realities fail to live up to it.

4   Ideals and daily experiences – living up to 'family'

We have thus seen some common threads around which people weave various patterns in their family meanings, but there can be tensions where the different threads sometimes pull against each other, and there can be much ambiguity and variation about exactly what may 'count' as family. If the quality of the relationships does not match up to the expectations of 'family', then maybe it doesn't count as 'family' at all. In this way we can start to see the extent to which moral evaluations and positive and negative feelings about 'family' are not extra 'layers on the cake', but are deeply and inextricably at the core of the idea of 'family' itself. To invoke 'family' is thus to draw upon a moral language. 'A family is the be-all and end-all of life ... family life is, er – just the top priority and everything should go into that'. (Paul Sanderson, quoted in Langford et al., 2001, p. 12.)

Figure 3.4
Family life
can create
tensions

In this final section, I want to focus on this issue more directly, to consider just what is at stake – morally and also emotionally – in family meanings, what happens when daily experiences do not match up to these family expectations, and how people manage these tensions. Sometimes it is hard to see this happening in research interviews, since such tensions may be apparent as much through what is *not* said, as what *is*. Sometimes, then, researchers pay attention to what is absent.

To introduce this discussion, we draw on one further study with rather a different focus from those you've considered so far. In the studies cited earlier, the research was set up to explore the family lives and understandings of a wide range of people living their lives together in an apparently unremarkable way. In this next study, however, undertaken in Scotland by Marina Barnard, people were interviewed precisely because there was something very difficult happening in their family lives, namely the very serious abuse of drugs by at least one family member to an extent that significantly affected their understandings and experiences of family. In these circumstances, interviewees may be quite explicit about the gaps between family ideals and lived experiences, but the issues raised may also point to the fragility of family ideals more generally.

In this next quote, then, a mother and a grandmother suggest that 'family' can in fact be destroyed by experiences of severe drug abuse.

> I: What's the worst thing about drugs for you?
>
> R: The destruction it does to your family and the destruction it does to yourself. I always say drugs took me to places that I didn't want to go to, you know, mentally, physically and spiritually. They're a killer, even for the families and for the people that's looking on ... (Parent: Mrs Cameron)
>
> (Barnard, 2007, p. 26)

This raises the question of what family means if it can be destroyed in this way – what is this 'it' that is under such threat of annihilation? We have seen throughout these explorations of the research evidence that the idea of 'family' can raise a number of key themes, including the idea of a cohesive and bounded unit, an idealised moral standard, and a set of relationships that embody certain qualities. In saying that the family is destroyed by drugs, it is not clear whether the speaker is referring to any one of these in particular – maybe it is indeed the potent combination of them all that is being destroyed.

Activity 3.6

As you read the following quotes, what themes can you identify that are 'destroying the family'?

> Drugs ... it destroys a family, so it does. I mean ... it destroys their parents' life. It can split them up. You know, the weans [children] suffer, the grand weans suffer terrible because they've no' got their parents any more and the grandparents suffer all the time because it's their weans that are on the drugs and it's their weans that are coming into their house and stealing off them right, left and centre, you know and it's just ... it's ... it's just like a spiral thing, I mean it just goes round and round all the time, you know? (Parent: Mrs Blackie)
>
> (Barnard, 2007, p. 28)

...

> We got invited to weddings... you know, family affairs and that and they [sons]
> would get turned out for that under dire threat, you know, to behave themselves,
> not be looking drunk or full of it and then of course we would be half way
> through the night and they'd been to the toilet a few times [to do drugs] and
> suddenly they were fucking stoned out their boxes, you know, and it was that, all
> that kind of pressure and all. (Parent: Mr Merrick)
>
> (Barnard, 2007, p. 30)

Comment

The quote from Mrs Blackie points to several different dimensions: destruction of
the parents' lives (the parents being on drugs); splitting up of relationships; children's
loss of their parents; violation of the home by theft. Mr Merrick's quote points to
the precariousness of the family reputation that may be at stake in such 'family affairs'
as weddings – which in itself points to layers of secrecy and public display among
different 'family' relationships. Between them, it appears, such issues can 'destroy' a
family.

As Barnard goes on to explain, however, while these features of these parents'
experiences meant their ideas of family were seriously undermined, a sense of family
might, nevertheless, still prevent parents from taking actions that might otherwise be seen
as appropriate and effective. In the following discussion, she refers to a parent whose
daughter had stolen money by forging her father's signature on his bank account:

> As this parent, like others, went on to explain, the only real route to recovering the
> money was to involve police and have their child legally charged with fraud.
> However, to do so was so humiliating and shameful and so far at odds with their
> notion of being a family, that most parents would resist this course of action ...
> Nothing about this situation sits easily with the commonly held idea of the family
> home as a place of some respite and relaxation. Having locks placed on doors to
> bedrooms and hiding valuables away, monitoring behaviour and assuming always
> the worst of your child or sibling was deeply at odds with this notion. As a site of
> endemic conflict the home became for many, a source of distress, rather than respite
> from the outside world.
>
> (Barnard, 2007, p. 34)

We can thus see how the quality of relationships can potentially undermine 'family'
to such an extent that it can hardly be said to 'exist' at all. And yet, *at the same time*,
ideas of family appear to maintain (or to be expected to maintain) relationships over
time and in the face of great stresses, as people hold onto their sense of 'family'
against all odds. Similar tensions are seen in the research conducted in the US by
Gubrium and Holstein, with support groups for people caught up in the difficulties
of coping with a relative with Alzheimer's disease. In the first quote, John suggests

he is actually thinking better of how he and his relations were coping, after hearing someone else speaking in this context:

> I hadn't thought about how we were all, really, in this together... [when I heard someone else speaking in the support group about his own experience]... Something he said really brought it together for me. I'll never forget it. He said, 'you never know what a family is until something like this happens'. That's when I started to think that, by God, we're the type of family he's talking about.
>
> (Gubrium and Holstein, 1990, p. 64)

On the other hand, Adele reconsiders her relations less favourably as a result of their distancing responses to her mother's dementia, when her siblings were not seen to be supportive:

> To make a long story short, we moved her in and, as you might guess, it wasn't easy. We start having 'those family problems'. You know the scene – 'grandma griping' I call it. ... I remember [my husband] saying something that really hurt, when things were going pretty awful. He said 'What kind of family do you have anyway, putting the whole thing on you?'...It started to really sink in: what kind of family were we anyway?
>
> (ibid, p. 65)

In the context of such difficult experience as drug abuse and dementia, such issues may be writ large, but we can also see links with threads and tensions that run through other accounts as well, although the threat to 'family' existence may be less stark.

Thus, in the study by Langford et al., of the family lives of younger teenagers, the researchers point first to the idealism apparent in some interviewees' version of 'family', but then go on to explore how people may manage the tensions around experiences that don't quite match up to the ideal.

Activity 3.7

What tensions can you identify in the following quote from a father, Ed Finch?

> Susan is starting to break away from the family side of it. She's now coming up to 16 and she's after independence so we're tending to lose a bit of family there which is understandable. We understand it. She wants to go with her friends ... She doesn't want her mum and dad hanging around with her does she? ... [But] we stayed together all weekend this weekend as a family ... we decided as a family we'd do a full weekend together. So ... we went bowling and then ... just generally messed around for the afternoon, had a take away in the evening, watched a bit of er television ... Er Sunday we had a nice lie in. Er and then we went for a ride on Sunday lunchtime, you know, for a couple of hours ... So that was what we did this weekend. But as I say, it's starting to break down a little bit, purely and simply because of them now wanting independence.
>
> (Langford et al., 2001, p. 48)

Comment

Here's how the authors of the report teased open Ed Finch's family meanings:

> Ed's account of how the Finch family came to spend the weekend together constructs this decision as a democratic agreement: 'we decided as a family we'd do a whole weekend together'. Yet the fact that the family members do not have an equal investment in group bonding is at once revealed in his statements that 'she' and 'they' are wanting independence, 'breaking away from the family side of it', causing things to 'break down', causing them to 'lose a bit of family'.
>
> The existence of this contradiction does not necessarily mean, however, that teenagers simply submit to family togetherness in order to meet parental expectations. On the contrary, there were several ways in which teenagers' own 'investments' were visible. ... while parents emphasised togetherness and identity, teenagers placed more emphasis on the receipt of benefits such as care, attention and material provision. Teenagers might thus be happy to 'do things together' with their parents to the extent that they experience these benefits. For example, we found that shopping was commonly referred to as a focus for parents and teenagers spending time together. In teenagers' accounts, however, there was more direct reference to what they themselves were going to obtain during these outings, with hopes expressed that the company of their parents would be for their benefit in this respect. Parents on the other hand were more likely to stress the fact that 'we go as a family' or refer to aspects of leisure activities which provided a focus for parental identities. Fathers in particular, for example, were likely to refer to their 'taking' the family on trips and outings or to refer to paying for things. While all members of a family may agree to spend time together, then, each person may have a quite different motivation in respect of togetherness and enjoy it for different reasons.
>
> (Langford et al., 2001, pp. 48–9)

Layers of shifting meanings may enable people to manage such tensions and ambivalences, and avoid confronting the gaps around ideals and lived experiences. They may also enable people to maintain generalised images of other people's families alongside their own direct experiences of the messiness of personal relationships (as we saw in the discussion of Bernardes' work in Chapter 1).

Interviews with young children also reveal a capacity to shift between different family meanings according to the context of talk, with some meanings being more categorical, some more idealistic, and some more subtle. In Morrow's (1998) study of children's understandings of family, the researchers used two different approaches to explore children's understandings: the first was based on brief outlines of a series of different household types or relationships, asking children if these groupings constitute 'family'; the second approach drew in a much more open-ended way on data obtained via a variety of methods, including drawings and group discussions. With regard to the first method, children's views varied greatly as to whether or not they regarded different sorts of households or relationships as being 'a family', with only the intact married nuclear household with children gaining consensus that this does indeed unequivocally 'count' as a family. So this data alone would suggest that the nuclear family definition is still very strong. But in their other discussions and responses, children's views were far more subtle and inflected with all sorts of other considerations of what counted as family, with older children especially stressing issues concerning the quality of relationships in making family. Indeed, overall Morrow concluded that roles and relationships were more important than household structures in defining family for children. Many children, Morrow tells us, thus defined family in terms of love and happiness:

> Some ... children defined family only in terms of the quality of relationships, and the love and affection that family members provide to each other, for example:

> A family is loving people. Families are for telling people secrets and they care about you. (Georgina, 9)

> Families are for helping each other and loving each other. (Inzaman, 10)

> A family is people you love. Families are for love and looking after each other. (Max, 11)

> The youngest children of Pakistani origin defined families in very similar ways to the Village children, though there were differences in vocabulary. They tended not to use the word 'love' for example:

> A family is someone who you live with, and who you really like, you do everything with, you live round their house and everything like that. (Shareen, 8)
> (Morrow, 1998, p. 23 and p. 25)

But, while some children stressed happiness as a defining element of family, Morrow also describes other children as expressing a 'more realistic view that families can still be families even if they don't always get on together' (1998, p. 27). Morrow summarises the children's views overall in these terms:

> Generally, children's definitions of family reflected their descriptions of who is important to them ... When they said what they thought a family is and what families are for, it was clear that love, care and mutual respect and support were the key characteristics for them of 'family', and this was the case regardless of gender, ethnic background and location. Overall, children's definitions did not centre around the 'nuclear norm'. For many children, 'family' consists of a wide range of people, and it is the roles that these people perform, and the quality of the relationships, that define them as 'family'.
> (Morrow, 1998, p. 28)

For many people, then, and apparently regardless of age, gender, class or ethnic background, 'family' is intrinsically understood as something positive and desirable. These next two quotes were expressed by mothers of older teenagers:

Family is the most important thing – the most important thing in the world you know. (Somera, Pakistani, middle-class mother)

You're close, and you got a closeness, and there's a nice atmosphere, and you've got a nice home and you're happy. (Hilary, White, working-class mother)

(Gillies et al., 2001, p. 27)

So how far can the term be used to accommodate experiences and relationships that don't exhibit such necessary qualities?

Activity 3.8

Faced with disappointments, and a gap between ideals and experiences, how do you think people might respond? How would their meanings of family be affected? Gillies et al. discuss this in relation to their interviews with parents and teenagers aged 16–18. What clues can be gained from the following quotes from this study?

I suppose I've been totally disillusioned with it … I suppose it's not all as sweet as it's supposed to be. It's been the opposite. (Howard, White, working-class father)

…

I suppose there's two ways – one is my perception of the family and the way I think it should, thought it should have been. And the reality of the family, of what I've experienced, I suppose they're two different things. I've always thought a family should be partnership, then a child or children … I just thought a family should be cosy and comfortable. I don't remember my family being particularly cosy and comfortable but I thought that's the way it should be … But the reality of it was different to that. Em, it, unfortunately for my marriage and family, it was a bit of a power struggle thing, it was about duties, perceived duties, responsibilities and things like that. Not comfortable a lot of the time. (Moira, White, middle-class mother)

…

… (family) doesn't mean nothing to me any more, 'cos as far as I'm concerned I ain't got no family. (Alyx, White, working-class young woman)

(Gillies et al., 2001, p. 28)

Comment

We see here themes of disillusion, the tension between comfort and duties that have been imposed, and a categorical denial of the term as relevant to the lived experience. The last quote above comes from Alyx, who was homeless after experiencing a particularly unhappy childhood. But, as the researchers go on to comment:

Nevertheless, a mismatch between family as an ideal and family as reality was often interpreted in terms of deficiencies and mistakes, as opposed to 'family' being an ideological construct based upon an unattainable ideal. Significantly, Alyx's major ambition for the future was to build her own family and provide her future children with a more authentic experience.

(Gillies et al., 2001, pp. 27–8)

In these ways, then, we can see just how deep are the ambiguities and ambivalences as to whether family meanings are intrinsically idealised, and the depth of the desires that may be associated with the achievement of 'family'.

5   Conclusions

In this chapter you have seen how researchers seek to uncover some of the variable assumptions that may be associated with everyday family experiences, as these are expressed through in-depth qualitative research. And we have also gained some sense of the power of family meanings in people's everyday lives, in terms of the moral and emotional investments family holds for people, and the implications for their family practices and identities.

These issues also have significant implications for others who are concerned to understand, or work with, family members, whether researchers, policy-makers, or professionals. The subtleties and shifting content of family meanings mean it is only too easy to misunderstand others' family lives. I hope I have conveyed here some sense of the thoughtfulness and sensitivity that is required for anyone to get past their own family meanings and assumptions to begin to gain insight into the family meanings of others. And yet the evaluative content of 'family' means that moral identities and moral frameworks are almost inevitably features of such processes of understanding. Furthermore, morality implicates emotions, not just behaviours – having the 'right' feelings, as well as doing 'the right thing'. Thus, at an emotional level, people may look to 'family' as the place where they should be able to share their joys and sorrows (as Aisha from Swansea put it). And at a moral level, tensions can arise, most centrally, between notions of individual happiness alongside commitment to the common 'family' good. When individuality is understood to entail autonomy rather then connection to others, then, this tension can be expressed in terms of moral obligations to avoid being 'selfish', on the one hand, and being prepared 'to give things up' for the sake of 'the family' on the other. We return to such themes in later chapters.

You may have been struck particularly by certain quotes and themes as you have been reading these studies, depending on your own background and family meanings. However, if we return to some of the general questions raised early in this chapter, here are some brief indications of how they might be seen to be relevant to some of the issues raised by these research studies:

1   Who belongs, and how are people 'counted in' or 'counted out'?

In terms of 'who counts' and who 'belongs', we have seen how boundaries may shift in varying contexts of talking, giving rise to variable layers of family invoked for different reasons. Thus for many people family refers to a 'unit', although the position of some individuals in relation to this unit may not always be clear. However, it can also refer to demonstrable family ties that are broader than this, which might or might not, for example, be the case for transnational families.

2   How far, and in what ways, is 'family' located in physical space?

Physical space can be very important at times, but not necessarily in terms of the household unit – which is quite striking when we consider how prominently academic definitions of 'family', as discussed in Chapter 1, emphasise co-residence as a key defining feature. For example, children might not see living together as a necessary element of 'being family', while for the women in Pen-cwm in Swansea (who we discussed in Chapter 2), living nearby was a key feature of family ties, with women and children living their lives across various houses in the same road or close by. In this context, any idea of moving away was seen to threaten the security that could be provided by such female 'family' networks. For the Bengali families in Swansea, by contrast, family was symbolised by linguistic and cultural ties to the country of origin, even while this is physically very distant.

3   What is 'family' membership based on?

Biological ties might be an unequivocal element of family meanings for many people, but not for all, and the quality of relationships is stressed by many. There are some quite different points of view here. If these desirable and defining qualities are absent, perhaps there is no family either. Alternatively, whatever the qualities of the relationships, perhaps the family ties are always there, and this is indeed the most significant quality of the relationships. Sharing lives over time was also very important, giving rise to a remembered family of shared histories and memories.

4   What qualities of relationships are involved?

The key quality of relationships that recurs prominently across many studies is the sense of togetherness that is said to characterise family. What is more, doing family 'properly' for some interviewees means more than living together under one roof, requiring individuals to 'put the family first' in order to make 'family' real. Nevertheless, togetherness could mean different things to different family members, particularly across the generations, and is always also subject to change. Togetherness could be manifested in all sorts of ways, including both shared activities and contributing to the common good.

5   How do interviewees suggest that family relationships are evaluated?

Family meanings are suffused with moral values. Very predominantly, family is seen in highly positive terms, with expectations that it can provide security and a sense of belonging that can survive through 'thick and thin'. However, there are also hints of other evaluations at times, including the potential for power struggles and loss of freedom, and the very real possibility that family may be found to let you down, or that individuals may fail to live up to these expectations.

6   What differences may be found both 'within' and between families?

We have also seen differences of gender and generation played out throughout these studies, often in ways that are seen as altogether unremarkable, but sometimes constituting sources of anxieties and tensions. In some of the interviews by Langford and colleagues with parents with younger teenaged children, there might thus be considerable effort to maintain the sense of 'family' against the daily experience of disconnected lives that only meet in passing. And the position of men in relation to 'family' featured very differently in different interviews: sometimes as central authority figures, sometimes quite marginal, and sometimes as people you are 'stuck with', whether or not they are co-resident. Differences between families are also alluded to in passing, and such processes of comparison with others is a general feature of social lives as people seek to understand how they 'fit' into the world. You will return to these issues in relation to family meanings in Chapter 7.

These brief thoughts can hardly do justice to the richness and complexity of the variable family meanings we have been exploring in this chapter. But one overall conclusion does seem to be possible, which is the profound and powerful emotional and moral significance of the language of 'family'. Consequently, any claim to 'being a family' is almost intrinsically making a claim to something worthwhile and desirable. This then centralises the issue of how professionals and social scientists can use the concept without inevitably implicating these emotional and moral evaluations. You will turn to professional and policy issues later, in Chapter 8, but in the next chapter you will consider a very different approach to social research on families, by which social scientists seek to understand families in terms of large-scale statistical data.

References

Barnard, M. (2007) *Drug Addiction and Families*, London, Jessica Kingsley.

Becker, B., and Charles, N. (2006) 'Layered meanings: the construction of 'the family' in the interview', *Community, Work and Family*, vol. 9, no. 2, pp. 101–22.

Gallegos, D., Dziurawiec, S., Fozdar, F. and Abernethie, L. (2011) 'Adolescent experiences of 'family meals' in Australia', *Journal of Sociology*, 47.

Gillies, V., Ribbens McCarthy, J. and Holland, J. (2001) *'Pulling Together: Pulling Apart': The Family Lives of Young People Aged 16–18*, London, Family Policy Studies Centre/Joseph Rowntree Foundation.

Jallinoja, R. (2008) 'Togetherness and being together: family configurations in the making' in Widmer, E.D. and Jallinoja, R. (eds.) *Beyond the Nuclear Family: Families in a Configurational Perspective*, Bern, Peter Lang.

Langford, W., Lewis, C., Solomon, Y. and Warin, J. (2001) *Family Understandings: Closeness, Authority and Independence in Families with Teenagers*, London, Family Policy Studies Centre/Joseph Rowntree Foundation.

Morrow, V. (1998) *Understanding Families: Children's Perspectives*, London, National Children's Bureau/Joseph Rowntree Foundation.

Pratt, M.W. and Fiese, B.H. (2004) 'Families, stories and the life course: an ecological context' in Pratt, M.W. and Fiese, B.H. (eds.) *Family Stories and the Life Course: Across Time and Generations*, Mahwah New Jersey, Lawrence Erlbaum Associates.

Reynolds, T. (2005) *Caribbean Mothers: Identity and Experience in the U.K.*, London, Tufnell Press.

Ribbens McCarthy, J., Edwards, R. and Gillies, V. (2003) *Making Families: Moral Tales of Parenting and Step-Parenting*, Abingdon, Routledge.

Richards, L. (1990) *Nobody's Home: Dreams and Realities in a New Suburb*, Melbourne, Oxford University Press.

Shaw, S. (2008) 'Family leisure and changing ideologies of parenthood', *Sociology Compass*, 2: 1–16.

Smit, R. (2011) 'Maintaining family memories through symbolic action: young adults' perceptions of family rituals in their families of origin', *Journal of Comparative Family Studies*, 42 May/June: pp. 355-67.

Chapter 4

Understanding 'family' and household through quantitative evidence

Megan Doolittle

Contents

1   Introduction

In this chapter you will continue to explore family meanings by focusing on research evidence, mainly from the UK. In particular, you will focus on evidence from quantitative data in order to see what this can tell us about families, and how this kind of data has itself influenced and shaped contemporary meanings of family. What we know about families is very strongly influenced by the gathering and publication of statistics about families and households which have been routinely and extensively collected by governments and social researchers for the last two centuries. In this chapter, you will look at how these processes have an effect on the way families are defined. In order to do this you will learn to read, interpret and critically assess some straightforward quantitative data about families. You will focus on the historical development of the census, on some more recent data about families, and then explore the intersecting meanings of household and family. In doing so, we build on and extend discussions that you were introduced to in Chapter 1, regarding how evidence about families is produced and how to interpret it. As you will see, even in quantitative data which appears to show 'family' as a clear and fixed category, the concept of family remains elusive and difficult to pin down.

2   Categories, boundaries and counting families

Quantitative data is research evidence which is analysed and presented in numerical form. Researchers count, measure and categorise social phenomena which can then be analysed using statistical techniques. Data is often presented as tables, graphs or other visual forms. When data is collected on a large scale, it can be used to develop a generalised picture of what is being studied, and if collected over time, predictions can be made about likely changes or continuities in the future – for example, how quickly the population might grow or decline. Different features of data can also be combined and compared. An example might be to compare the number of men and women who fall into different age groups in the population in a particular year. The detailed and specific methods for gathering, collating, categorising and testing the validity of quantitative data are not our concern here. Rather, we will be reading and interpreting some quantitative evidence about families and examining the strengths and weaknesses of this kind of evidence. In this process, we will see that such data is socially created through the research process, just as the qualitative interviews were that you encountered in Chapters 2 and 3.

Quantitative data about families is widely available from government statistics, which can also form the evidence base for social researchers. Many of the most commonly used statistics about UK society and the economy are freely available through National Statistics Online. In this chapter, we will be looking in depth at the national census, and drawing on the General Household Survey and survey results from other agencies. However there are other important sources available: for example, Eurostat provides social statistics from the European Union, and the UK Data Archive holds an extensive range of economic and social data from official agencies, international statistical agencies, market research agencies, and academic researchers.

2.1   Strengths and weaknesses of quantitative research

Before we examine what quantitative evidence can tell us about families, it is important to assess how useful this kind of evidence is. The following extract by Janet Parr and Elizabeth Silva will give you an idea of the general strengths and weaknesses of quantitative research:

Reading 4.1   Janet Parr and Elizabeth Silva

Strengths of quantitative research

- Quantitative research belongs to a powerful and recognized research tradition which is perceived to be valid. It provides a sound basis for claiming that one knows something.

- Quantification provides useful knowledge to permit the examination of the patterns and distribution of social processes ...

- Quantitative approaches are especially efficient for exploring the large-scale, 'structural' features of social life.

- Quantitative methods readily allow researchers to establish relationships among variables.

- Quantitative methods enable researchers to make generalizing claims and sound arguments about the social world.

Weaknesses of quantitative research

- Quantitative data are usually produced by someone other than the researcher and are often produced for purposes that are not always easy to assess.

- Quantitative research is often expensive to undertake.

- Quantitative approaches are usually driven by the concerns of funding agencies and the researchers, leaving no room for the expression of the concerns of research participants.

- Quantitative methods risk imposing the researcher's values on those being researched and often fail to capture the participant's point of view.

- Quantitative methods are weak in exploring the reasons for relationships between variables.

Reading source

Parr and Silva, 2005, Chapter 3

From this we can see that data relating to families which can be quantified can be very useful: it can be gathered and analysed on a large scale, although this is expensive; it can be used to identify change and continuities over time; it can be used to compare a number of variables – i.e. different aspects of families – and there are a well-tested range of techniques available to assess the data's representativeness, reliability and comparability.

When thinking about quantitative data in relation to families, one of the central problems we will be examining is the difficulty of creating and maintaining categories relating to families. As you have already seen in Chapters 2 and 3, the personal experiences and understandings of family are difficult to pin down, even between quite small groups of people. When looking at a large and diverse group, such as we find in a region or a nation, researchers must develop robust and manageable ways of categorising their data. In the process, they *impose* an order on the lived experience of the lives they represent, and create particular meanings of family.

2.2 Geographical boundaries

Even defining the geographic location of families presents issues of boundaries and categories. Most of the statistics we will look at in this chapter are from the United Kingdom, although some are from the United States. Statistics are gathered and organised around geographical entities, often nations or parts of nations, and this can create complexities for those countries like the UK which are a federation or union of nation states. You will focus on these kinds of complexities in more detail in Chapter 7, when we compare statistics about families between European nations. It is important to clarify to which nation, region or state each set of data refers, to avoid the very common confusions between the terms for Britain, the United Kingdom and the nations of England, Wales, Northern Ireland and Scotland which have arisen from various historical movements relating to identity, sovereignty and citizenship. For our purposes in discussing family meanings, it is important to highlight these issues, because, although these four can be considered separate nations, there are some overlapping, and some very different, legal and political elements.

Great Britain and Northern Ireland together make up the *United Kingdom*, with Great Britain comprising England, Wales and Scotland. 'Great Britain' is both a geographical term referring to the island on which the greater parts of these three nations are situated, and a legal one referring to those three territories considered together. This defines the area represented in the UK Parliament and for which that Parliament normally makes laws. It is also a citizenship unit. It does not define the whole area for which the UK government is responsible in international law, which also includes the Channel Islands and the Isle of Man. Scotland, Wales, and Northern Ireland each has a devolved legislature and its own government or executive, led by a First Minister. England, despite being the largest country of the United Kingdom, has no devolved executive or legislature and is ruled and legislated for directly by the UK government and Parliament. Each of these entities produces statistics relating to its population.

What we mean when we say 'England and Wales' however, is somewhat different. This unit does not even have its own name, but it is important because it defines the jurisdiction of the English courts, usually just called 'the jurisdiction' in legal terminology. It is the area of application of English law, which strictly should be called the law of England and Wales but rarely is. There is no such thing as British or United Kingdom law, because there are no British or United Kingdom courts. Therefore family matters which arise through the legal system can be categorised differently from population statistics, depending on the particular legal jurisdiction for any matter. The key point to bear in mind here is that when you read statistics from Britain, or any particular geographical area, you need to be clear about what region, nation or legal entity is being considered.

2.3 Families and categories

In Chapter 1 you were introduced to the difficulty of pinning down the 'slippery' concept of family. This also creates a problem for researchers using quantitative data about families. In thinking about broader questions facing researchers using quantitative data about families, Linda Hantrais sets out a fundamental problem:

> Family is a shifting concept. What it means to be a member of a family and what is expected of family relationships, as well as the language used to describe them ... vary over time and place, at both individual and societal levels. Although the term 'the family' continues to be widely used to refer to an enduring core, or fundamental social unit, it is difficult, if not impossible, to find a universally agreed definition that can be applied across or within societies. Families and households, a more meaningful and tractable umbrella term for demographers, were initially defined for national census purposes in the 19th century. Definitions have subsequently been refined, adapted and extended to achieve international standardisation and to take account of the changing socio-demographic scene.
>
> (Hantrais, 2004, p. 38)

Researchers have had to find ways of categorising and measuring families in order to count, compare and aggregate them, and to do this, they grapple with the complexities of establishing boundaries for family units. The reading below will give you an idea of some of the issues involved.

Reading 4.2   Helen Sweeting and Peter Seaman, 'Family boundaries'

Quantitative researchers with an interest in family life are a ... group for whom the fluid nature of family boundaries is an issue, since they generally wish to define various family characteristics within a narrow range of predetermined categories for analytical purposes. For example, studies that focus on the family structure of children and young people usually ask respondents to tick a number of boxes ('mother', 'father', 'stepmother', 'father's girlfriend', and so on) in order to indicate which adults they live with. These responses are then used to divide their sample into two (those with two resident parents compared with those with one ...) or three groups, ... (those residing with two birth parents, compared with those with one birth parent plus a new partner forming a 'step' or 'reconstituted' household ...). ...

...

A second issue raised by the 'who do you live with' tickbox approach is that researchers' predefined categories may be quite different from those perceived by individual respondents. An illustration of this can be found in the way that the great majority of those with an interest in family structure restrict themselves to relationships between members who are co-resident in the same household. In this they are like almost all censuses and surveys in assuming that 'family' and 'household' can be treated as interchangeable because they coincide. However, the greater variety and changeability of modern family life means that for increasing numbers of research participants the fact is that they do not ... Accompanying this is the growing recognition that by compiling information only on family members living in the same household, some potentially important players may be being excluded. For instance, a 'one parent household' may for many purposes be a 'two parent family' via the involvement of a parent figure absent from the household.

Reading source

Sweeting and Seaman, 2005, pp. 96–9

3   The census and the household

Sweeting and Seaman imply that difficulties in establishing clear boundaries around families is a new phenomenon but, as you will see below, families were just as difficult to pin down in the past. The household is a social category which has been

used as a common way of 'fixing' people in particular places at particular times for
the purposes of counting and categorising the population, but it is important to be
clear that the category of 'household' is not exactly the same as 'family'. Household
boundaries may appear to be more tangible, but they are still not entirely
straightforward. (Historical changes in the relationship between definitions of
household and family is something you will explore in more detail in Chapter 7.)
Thus the household has been a fundamental unit for social statistics from the very
beginnings of the collection of social data, in particular through the national census
which had its origins in records used for taxation based on where people lived, i.e. on
residence. In early local censuses, household data was grouped under a 'head of
household', and every other person present was listed according to their relationship to
this head. The practice of counting the population by recording data from every
household continues to this day.

Activity 4.1

You may have researched your family tree, and in the process you are very likely to
have looked at census records. In particular, the Census Enumerator Books show the
ways that people were recorded as part of households. These books were compiled
by people employed as census enumerators to collect, compile and report the
information gathered about the population in a particular district, according to a set
of rules and guidelines.

I would now like you to look at Figure 4.1, which is an example of a page from the
1891 census from the Gorbals district of Glasgow, an inner-city area with a wide
range of industrial workplaces and dense urban housing.

This page is quite difficult to read, not least because handwriting styles of the period
are unfamiliar to us now – as are the language and specialist terms used in describing
occupations and relationships, for instance. For example, 'daur' is short for Daughter,
and the abbreviation 'do' means 'ditto'. The first thing to notice on this page is that
there are a large number of households at a single address: 58 Brown Street. On the
previous and subsequent pages there were more households listed at the same
address. This indicates that this building was a tenement: a common form of
working-class housing in Glasgow at this time, containing a large number of people
in various combinations of rooms within the building.

1   For the five complete households on this page (marked 68 to 72 in the first
    column), can you identify the various family and household relationships? Each
    household was separated out by the enumerators by drawing a dark line above
    and below the household group in the 'Name' column.

2   Can you summarise the similarities and differences between these households?

3   Would these families fit into the stereotype of the 'traditional' nineteenth-
    century family?

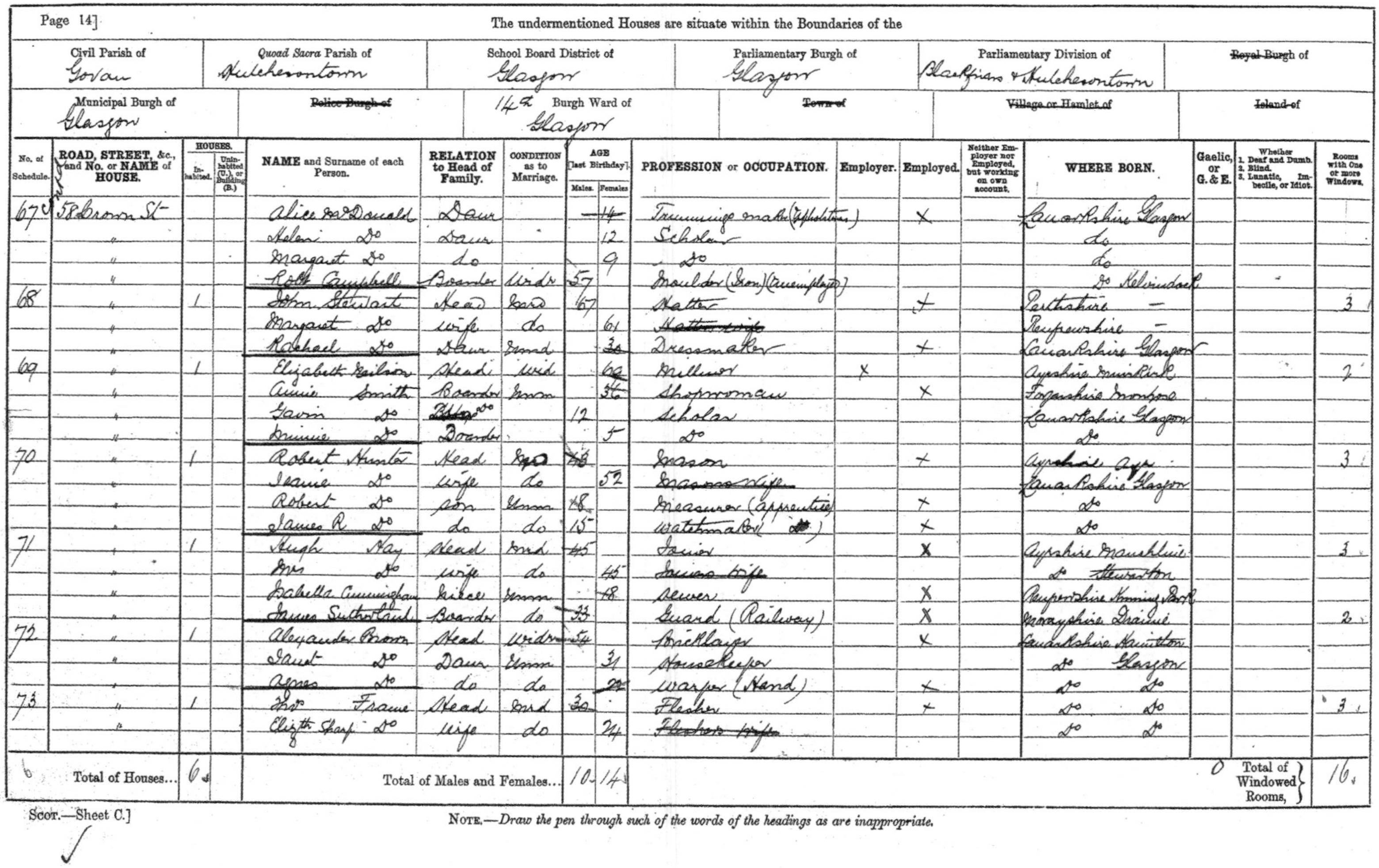

Page 14]

The undermentioned Houses are situate within the Boundaries of the

Civil Parish of	*Quoad Sacra* Parish of	School Board District of	Parliamentary Burgh of	Parliamentary Division of	~~Royal Burgh~~ of
Govan	Hutchesontown	Glasgow	Glasgow	Blackfriars & Hutchesontown	

Municipal Burgh of	~~Police Burgh of~~	14th Burgh Ward of	~~Town of~~	~~Village or Hamlet of~~	~~Island of~~
Glasgow		Glasgow			

No. of Schedule.	ROAD, STREET, &c., and No. or NAME of HOUSE.	HOUSES. In-habited.	HOUSES. Unin-habited (U.), or Building (B.)	NAME and Surname of each Person.	RELATION to Head of Family.	CONDITION as to Marriage.	AGE [last Birthday]. Males.	AGE [last Birthday]. Females.	PROFESSION or OCCUPATION.	Employer.	Employed.	Neither Employer nor Employed, but working on own account.	WHERE BORN.	Gaelic, or G. & E.	Whether 1. Deaf and Dumb. 2. Blind. 3. Lunatic, Imbecile, or Idiot.	Rooms with One or more Windows.
67	58 Crown St			Alice McDonald	Daur			14	Trimmings maker (Upholsterer)		X		Lanarkshire Glasgow			
	"			Helen Do	Daur			12	Scholar				do			
	"			Margaret Do	do			9	Do				do			
	"			Robt Campbell	Boarder	Widr	57		Moulder (Iron) (unemployed)				Do Kelvindock			
68	"	1		John Stewart	Head	Mard	67		Hatter		+		Perthshire —			3
	"			Margaret Do	wife	do		61	~~Hatter's wife~~				Renfrewshire —			
	"			Rachael Do	Daur	Unm		30	Dressmaker		+		Lanarkshire Glasgow			
69	"	1		Elizabeth Neilson	Head	Wid		62	Milliner	X			Ayrshire Kilmarnock			2
	"			Annie Smith	Boarder	Unm		36	Shopwoman		X		Forfarshire Montrose			
	"			Gavin Do	Do		12		Scholar				Lanarkshire Glasgow			
	"			Minnie Do	Boarder			5	Do				Do			
70	"	1		Robert Hunter	Head	Mard	53		Mason		+		Ayrshire Ayr			3
	"			Jeanie Do	wife	do		52	~~Mason's wife~~				Lanarkshire Glasgow			
	"			Robert Do	son	Unm	18		Measurer (apprentice)		+		Do			
	"			James R Do	do	do	15		Watchmaker (do)		+		Do			
71	"	1		Hugh Hay	Head	Mard	45		Joiner		X		Ayrshire Mauchline			3
	"			Mrs Do	wife	do		45	~~Joiner's wife~~				Do Stewarton			
	"			Isabella Cunningham	Niece	Unm		18	Sewer		X		Renfrewshire Kinning Park			
	"			James Sutherland	Boarder	do	33		Guard (Railway)		X		Morayshire Drainie			2
72	"	1		Alexander Brown	Head	Widr	54		Bricklayer		X		Lanarkshire Hamilton			
	"			Janet Do	Daur	Unm		31	Housekeeper				Do Glasgow			
	"			Agnes Do	do	do		22	Warper (Hand)		+		Do Do			
73	"	1		Thos Frame	Head	Mard	30		Flesher		+		Do Do			3
	"			Elizth Sharp Do	wife	do		24	~~Flesher's wife~~				Do Do			
	Total of Houses...	6		Total of Males and Females...			10	14						0	Total of Windowed Rooms,	16

Scot.—Sheet C.]

NOTE.—*Draw the pen through such of the words of the headings as are inappropriate.*

Figure 4.1
Page from Census Enumerator's Book for the 1891 census of the Gorbals district of Glasgow

Figure 4.2
Nineteenth-
century
tenement
buildings in
Glasgow

Comment

1   I hope you didn't struggle too much with the nineteenth-century handwriting and terminology. In my reading I found:

(a)   Household one contains two parents and one adult child.

(b)   Household two is headed by a widow with three boarders, an unmarried woman and her two children.

(c)   Household three has two parents and their two teenaged children, already out at work.

(d)   Household four has a married couple, their adult niece and a boarder.

(e)   Household five consists of a widower with his two adult daughters.

2   In general, each of these households was quite small in size, but they were very diverse. There were a significant number of boarders even within such small households, and two lone-parent families, one of whom included an unmarried mother. There were four families which included adult or nearly adult children living with their parents. We can also note that these census records show that 'household' and 'family' are not always the same.

3   There did not appear to be any households containing more than two generations; in particular grandparents were not found. With such a very small number of households it is impossible to make any generalisations, but it is clear

that census records demonstrate that families and households could be diverse and complex, and did not always conform to stereotypes of the 'traditional family'.

You can see from this example just how the census was compiled by painstakingly recording every single person in residence at every household in the country on the same night. You might also imagine the kinds of errors that were commonly made, and the difficulties that enumerators might have had in fitting the people they found into the limited number of categories provided by the forms they filled in. The enumerators needed clear definitions of what they were recording, and the extract I'd like you to read in the next activity will give you an idea of the way in which the household came to be defined as the census was developed throughout the nineteenth century. The details of these definitions are not as important as the underlying point that household and family are categories which were difficult to define and have changed over time.

Activity 4.2

While you read this extract, consider the ways that family and household were nevertheless considered to be 'natural' categories with certain fixed characteristics.

Reading 4.3   Megan Doolittle, 'Defining family in the nineteenth-century census'

We can locate some of the mid-nineteenth century definitions of head of household through the census reports, which ... required the development of specific parameters to guide enumerators and to enforce completion of census returns. Those who designed and supervised the censuses were profoundly influenced by ideas ... which sharply separated the family from the public world, and struggled to fit the population of Britain into this ... with varying degrees of success. Defining the family and household were central to these attempts.

The 1831 census was the last to be taken without listing individuals, but rather counted the numbers of families and individuals within them in each parish. The difficulties of collecting data on families in this way were acute, and this is most clearly seen in the attempt to record the occupations of families, rather than individuals. The census report complained that great inaccuracies arose:

> from the impossibility of deciding whether females of the family, children and servants were to be classed as if of no occupation, or of the occupation of the adult males of the family'

(1831 Census Report, p. 3)

...

Under the regime established in 1841 of requiring every household to complete a census return, the instructions to enumerators were to ask every occupier to act as an agent by completing the form for himself, or less often herself, and any dependants. ... A court decision in 1847 defined an occupier as one who could: 'retain his quality of master, reserving to himself the general control and dominion over the whole house.' ... Thus the headship of a household was defined as a combination of two elements of control: over dependants, as 'master', and physical space, 'the whole house'.

In the 1851 census, more serious attempts were made to define household and family. A householder or occupier was again defined in terms of control over space: as owner or paying rent as a tenant of a whole house, or a distinct part of a house. ...

The definition of a family was much more concerned with relationships, ...

> the family (is) not considered as the children of one parent, but as the persons under one head; who is the occupier of the house, the householder, master, husband or father; while the other members of the family are, the wife, children, servants, relatives, visitors, and persons constantly or accidentally in the house. The head of the family supports and rules the family, – occupies the house. ... (possession of a house) throws a sharp, well-defined circle round his family and hearth the shrine of his sorrow, joys and mediations. This feeling, as it is natural, is universal ...
>
> (1851 Census Report, Vol. LXXXV, p. xxxv)

...

In 1861 attempts were made to clarify what constituted the difference between a lodger and a distinct family where living space was shared, and dependent lodgers were defined as those who ate with the rest of the household, paying for food with their lodging. ...

By 1871, a shift in definitions of the family had occurred. The nuclear family was becoming synonymous with the household, consisting of a husband, wife and children, with other dependants no longer specifically mentioned:

> The natural family is founded by marriage, and consists, in its complete state, of husband, wife and children. Family is generally held also in England to be synonymous with household, as a family occupies a house; and the particulars of each family were enumerated in Householders' Schedules. ... family is not easily defined for the practical purposes of the Census. ... So the family of the census may be said to consist always of a head, with generally dependent members, living together in the same dwelling.
>
> (1871 Census Report Vol. LXXI, p. xx–xxi)

...

These particular definitions of household, family and occupier developed for the censuses were not necessarily those adopted or understood by everyone, but they ... reveal a historical shift in one of the dominant understandings of what defined family and household over these decades, a shift from families as working units, to families containing various types of dependants, and by 1871, to the conjugal family.

Reading source

Doolittle, 1996, pp. 88–92

Comment

From this extract we can see that apparently straightforward definitions have deep historical roots. By categorising men, women and children according to a single relationship to the head of household, the census both reflected social norms of the time and also helped to legitimise understandings of domestic relationships as being hierarchical, with husbands and fathers likely to have a more dominant position. We can also see that these relationships were seen as natural, not as socially determined. The census was recording practices which appeared to be shaped by 'natural' ties and obligations, but the evidence from these reports shows that these categories were in fact constantly being changed by those who determined the policy and procedures for gathering census data. As people were questioned about their households, who lived within them, and what their relationships were with each other, they had to provide answers which would fit the questions being asked and the categories which the census demanded. The census was thus not only a powerful tool for gathering information about the population; it also had a very significant role in shaping how people thought about their families at the time.

The census remains a set of data that is socially constructed and historically specific, an attempt to count and categorise populations by the state. There is an argument that the growth of social statistics in the nineteenth century was part of a movement by modernising nation states to influence and control populations by generating knowledge about them. Concerns about the size of the population certainly drove the censuses in the early 1800s in Britain, as debates raged as to whether the population was growing or declining during the period of rapid social change and widespread unrest in the wake of industrial development and political unrest sparked off by the French Revolution. A century later, in the early 1900s, as it was becoming clear that growing numbers of families were limiting their fertility, social statistics were central in debates about the strength of the nation as it competed with other developing economies. Families were seen as important sites of social change, either because they were failing to maintain social cohesion or because they could offer solutions to social problems. Defining and categorising families was an essential task for nations seeking to understand and strengthen the stability of society.

This may sound familiar to us today, as we face a constant barrage of research which seems to show that families are undergoing drastic changes. Attempts to refine the definitions used in the census to count and categorise the population have also continued. By 2001, there was no attempt to relate being in a household to being in a family. Households are no longer described as 'natural' units but rather as bounded spaces that are shared by a distinct group of people. What are clearly more difficult to categorise are people who are more mobile, who may have a 'base' but also have somewhere else to live, such as young people in the transition to adulthood and those with holiday homes. Another group which continue to complicate definitions of household are those living within another household as boarders.

From these exceptions to the norm, it is clear that there are people in the population who cannot easily 'fit' into the census, and may find themselves defined by it in ways which do not reflect their day-to-day experiences. One example of this might be children whose parents have separated who spend an equal amount of time with each parent, therefore living in two households. The census will be unable to capture this experience, and such children will either be counted twice, or be inaccurately recorded as living with only one parent. By their very nature, such ways of living will not appear in evidence collected through the census.

Summary

- The census has been a means for collecting data every ten years about families and households in Britain for two centuries. In order to collect this data, definitions of family and household have had to be clarified, refined and altered from time to time to reflect wider social changes.

- Household and family are closely related concepts, but are not the same. The household has been the main way of categorising the population through the census because it is related to where people live on the particular day that the census is taken.

- Data from the census has always included information about families and relationships as well as individuals and household groups.

- The assumptions and requirements of those designing the census have shaped the ways families and households are defined, and this has influenced the knowledge produced by the census data. It is very difficult to design ways to accurately record those families and household relationships which are different from the usual census categories and definitions.

4   Reading and interpreting quantitative data

Activity 4.3

In the graph below we can see an example of how census and other national data have been used to show an important trend in family life in England and Wales: the increase in the number of households which are not defined as families in the years 1971–2006.

As you 'read' this graph, think about what it can tell you and what it is less good at telling you. You can begin with these questions:

1   What was the general growth trend of all households in the UK overall from 1971? Were households increasing, decreasing or staying the same?

2   Was there a greater or lesser number of one-person households than 'families' in 2006?

3   What were the overall changes in the proportions of family and one-person households in relation to the proportion of all households from 1971 to 2006?

4   What was the overall growth trend for one-person households since 1971?

(Source: Office for National Statistics, 2007)

Figure 4.3

Households and families 1971 to 2006

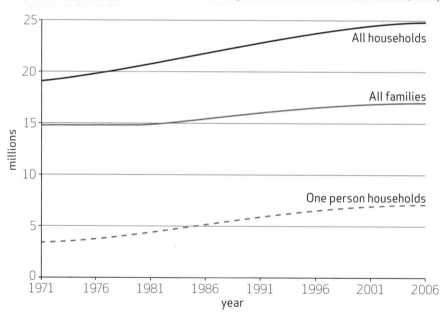

(Data sourced from: Censuses, Labour Force Survey, Office for National Statistics; Censuses, General Register Office for Scotland; Household estimates, Communities and Local Government; Household estimates, Scottish Executive.)

Comment

1   The number of households in the UK grew from about 19 million in 1971 to 25 million in 2006.

2   The number of one-person households in 2006 (about 7 million) was much less than the number of family households (about 17 million). But the number of *family* households has not grown as fast as the *overall* number of households.

3   The data shows that the proportion of family households in relation to all households decreased slightly between 1991 and 2001, and that this decrease was offset by an increase in the proportion of one-person households over the same period. We can see from this that it is important to be clear whether we are discussing the actual numbers of family households, which is increasing, or the proportion of family households compared to households as a whole, which is declining. Sometimes percentages are used to indicate proportion; if used in this case, about 71% of all households in 1991 were family households, while in 2006 the percentage was about 67% – a slight decrease of about 4 percentage points.

4   The number of people living alone has steadily increased since 1971; the growing trend in people living alone accounted for much of the increase in the overall number of households and, as a result, the average household size has decreased. However, the rate of increase in single-person households has slowed down in the years 2001–2006, as indicated in the slight flattening of the bottom line; thus while the number of households is still increasing, it is not increasing as fast as in the previous 30 years. The rate of change is thus another aspect of looking at trends over time.

4.1 Reading statistics with a critical eye

When reading graphs such as the one we have used in this activity, it is important to be critical of the information presented. The following points can be used as a 'check list' of important information to consider when presented with such data.

(a) Where does the data in the graph come from? What organisation produces the data, and for what purpose? When was it prepared? What might its source tell us about the data?

The data in the graph was collected by the Office for National Statistics (ONS) for the census, with additional data from other official sources. It was collated specifically for *Social Trends,* a statistical report produced every year by the ONS to provide a picture of how life in the UK is changing. It is important to note the ONS is a government office that officially defines families and households in ways that may be different from how members of the public experience their lives. Thinking about why these particular variables in this data were chosen is another way of examining its purposes. Here we see data which relates to a wide range of social policies – for example housing and the provision of care for the elderly who live alone – but also perhaps reflecting deeper concerns about social cohesion when more people live by themselves than in the past.

(b) How is the data presented? Is it a bar chart, graph, pie chart, or table?

The data is presented as a line graph, which is useful for comparing how one value changes in proportion to another value or values.

(c) What numerical form does the data take? Does it show actual numbers, or is it in the form of percentages or rates?

The vertical axis on the graph shows households, in millions, while the horizontal axis shows years. The graph itself doesn't show actual numbers, but the lines instead indicate a trend.

(d) What information is being presented? What is the data about overall?

The title is usually a good indication – here it is about the numbers of different kinds of households between 1971 and 2006.

(e) Is there more than one type of information being presented?

The information is segmented into 'all households', 'families' and 'one-person households'.

(f) What are the limitations of the data? What is not shown?

The line graph above is limited in respect of the multitude of forms of households and family that can be found in the UK. It masks the variety of ways that families and households are formed and reconstituted. Therefore, it is important to understand that in this case, although government definitions are used to capture some very broad trends in family and household structure, families (and households), are more diverse than this.

(g) What is the overall story being told by the data that is presented?

Changes in 'all households' are compared to changes in one-person households and all families. As we saw above, there are three stories here: the *number* of households is increasing; the *proportion* of households which consist of families is slightly decreasing; and one-person households are increasing both proportionally and in the actual numbers of households.

4.2 Trends and time frames

The graph above shows what can be done by putting a series of snapshots about families together to demonstrate trends over time. Such information is invaluable to governments planning services for the population, as it provides assistance in predicting the kinds of changes which can be expected in the future. For example, knowing the number of children in different age groups in the population will help determine the number of school places which will be needed. However, identifying trends is not always straightforward, because there may be data from the period before or after the graph which does not follow the trend. The longer time period that a graph or table covers, the clearer the trends will be.

Activity 4.4

In the next extract, Susan McRae shows how changing the time frame for data about families can completely alter our perception of trends in family life. The extract includes a table to demonstrate McRae's argument, which will give you an opportunity to practise your skills in reading statistical data. Do keep in mind the points listed above when interpreting the table.

Reading 4.4 Susan McRae, 'Changing the time frame'

Much of what we are seeing in Britain today is the continuation of trends briefly interrupted by the 'ideal family' of the 1950s and 1960s. The first two columns of [Table 4.1] indicate the extent of change from the mid-sixties to the mid-nineties in a range of family and demographic indicators including, for women, age at first marriage and first birth, total fertility rate, and proportion remaining childless, as well as showing the rising incidence of divorce, births outside marriage, cohabitation, and lone-parent families. [Table 4.1] paints a familiar picture of the changing British family over the post-war period: as age at marriage and first motherhood has risen, family size has fallen and childlessness has increased. Cohabitation has become common, both before marriage and between marriages. With rising cohabitation has come a sharp increase in births outside marriage; rising divorce rates, in their turn, have been accompanied by a near-trebling in the number of lone-parent families. These changes are frequently cited to demonstrate the decline of traditional family life.

Table 4.1 Family change in Britain: mid-thirties to mid-nineties

	Mid-1960s	Mid-1990s	Mid-1930s
Mean age at first marriage	22	26	26
Mean age at first birth	23.9	26.5	26.7
Fertility rate (TFR)	2.93	1.8	1.8
Childlessness (%)	10	20	23
Divorces per 1,000 marriages	2	13	
Births outside marriage (%)	5	35	
Cohabitation before marriage (%)	5	70	
Lone-parent families	570 000	1 500 000	

The third column of [Table 4.1] steps back from women born just after the Second World War to focus on those born before the first war, and presents a rather different picture of contemporary family change – one that signals the existence of long-term trends in demographic behaviour and reminds us that, in many respects, it is the sixties family that stands out, not the nineties one. Precise historical data on the incidence of divorce, cohabitation, births outside marriage, and lone-parent families are not presented in [Table 4.1]; although indications of their frequency may be gleaned from many sources. For example, prior to 1850, which marked the beginning of the long period of divorce reform, there were at least five ways to end a legal marriage: Parliamentary divorce for the rich; judicial separation for the middle classes; wife sales or desertion for the working classes; and private separation for everyone. And these avenues were used ... Moreover, death ended marriage: it has been calculated that prior to the nineteenth century, 17 per cent of children in England were fatherless by age 10, and 27 per cent by age 15 (Gillis 1997: 9). For women born in the 1930s, almost one in ten experienced the death of a parent before age 16, and it was not until the cohorts born in the 1950s that children under 16 were more likely to live in one-parent families because of divorce than the death of a parent (Lewis and Kiernan 1996: 382, table 6).

Nor were unmarried pregnancies, illegitimacy, or living together outside marriage uncommon in earlier periods ... It has been estimated that between the mid-eighteenth and mid-nineteenth centuries, as much as one-fifth of the population in England and Wales may have cohabited unlawfully for some period, either as a prelude to legal marriage or as a substitute for it (Gillis 1985: 219). Moreover, the men and women who defied both church and state in this manner were not, as in earlier centuries, vagabonds, ne'er-do-wells, or the disinherited. Rather, common-law marriage practices were found throughout Britain, in whole communities, rural and urban, and often where small farming mixed with new manufacturing. ...

These comments are not made to suggest that nothing has changed. Families and households have altered substantially since the early nineteenth century and, indeed, the early twentieth century, when divorce, for example, could be described as 'expensive, demeaning and often sordid' and divorce legislation as 'encouraging adultery and perjury' (McKibbin 1997: 302). Childlessness in the last century existed for different reasons than it does today. The consequences of a parent's death for children are different to those following divorce. What was once the behaviour of the marginal or the eccentric has become normal – as the large majority cohabit before marriage; as one in three babies are born outside legal marriage; as it becomes increasingly common for children to have more than one set of parents or two sets of grandparents. Nonetheless, in order to explain the changes captured in [Table 4.1], it is prudent to look backwards in time to beyond the immediate post-war period.

Reading source

McRae, 1999 pp. 2–3

Comment

McRae uses a range of statistical data here to make a striking point about the continuities and changes which can be traced across a shorter or longer period. She goes on to draw on other kinds of social data from histories of family life to build a more complex argument. It is interesting to note that the statistics about family breakups in the 1930s might be similar to those of the 1990s, but the underlying reasons are very different. Broad demographic and social changes relating to fertility, mortality, religious belief and social mores have all affected families profoundly, and these are not always visible in statistical data.

This reveals a more general point: quantitative data is, by its very nature, descriptive. It can show us evidence about many aspects of families and households, but it cannot explore the processes by which they have occurred. Why do women in the 1990s marry later than the 1960s? Why has cohabitation increased so dramatically? Are these trends related to each other? The data in these tables cannot tell us the answers to such questions. We would need to draw on more complex statistical techniques to build explanatory frameworks involving comparisons of variables and modelling the possible relationships between them, which we will not be learning about here. And we would need to do more detailed research which does not simply count particular living arrangements at specific points in time.

5   Beyond the official statistics: other quantitative research about families

Social researchers have found that the definitions used by the census and other large-scale surveys such as the General Household Survey are inadequate for studying families in any depth and have sought to develop more sophisticated ways of categorising and analysing families using quantitative methods.

In the following activity, you will look at a sample of the data produced by researchers for the Families and Children Study, which is based on a survey undertaken in 2003 by the National Centre for Social Research. This research was carried out on behalf of the Department for Work and Pensions, a government office which requires strict definitions of family to administer a range of benefits and services. The survey was first undertaken in 1999 to provide a picture of low-income families in Britain. Since then, it has been expanded to look at all families with dependent children. It is a longitudinal study, which means that each year the survey is repeated on as many of the same people as possible each time in order to gain a picture of year-on-year family change.

The researchers defined a 'couple' family as a household with dependent children that was headed by one natural or adoptive parent, and a partner. A 'lone parent' family was one with dependent children headed by one natural or adoptive parent only. Lone parents could be male or female. The researchers designated the 'mother figure' as the adult with the main responsibility for looking after the children in the family. In the vast majority of couple families, this person was female. In lone parent families, this person was either the lone mother or the lone father.

Activity 4.5

Answer the following questions based on Table 4.2 (overleaf).

1   As you read the table, keep in mind the earlier points about critical reading and interpretation of statistics.

2   How many couples were there where both parents were working more than 16 hours per week, how many where one parent was working more than 16 hours per week, and how many lone parents were working more than 16 hours per week?

3   What percentage of lone fathers had four or more dependent children? Was this figure higher or lower than any of the other categories of family listed as having four or more children?

4   Which lone-parent family type had the highest percentage of children aged 0–4 years?

5   What types of family are left out of this table?

Comment

1   A critical reading of the table might include the following points:

(a)   Where does the data in the graph come from? What organisation produces the data, and for what purpose? When was it prepared? What might its source tell us about the data?

The table was extracted from the report 'Family Life in Britain: Findings from the 2003 Families and Children Study', published in 2005 and comes from a survey undertaken in 2003. This survey started from a concern with low-income families with children, and the data it collects relates to issues which affect the material resources available to families. The purposes of this research are complex, as they involve the need for information to better administer and plan for state benefits and services, but they also encompass a social concern for children living in poverty which was a significant element of government policy under New Labour between 1997–2010.

(b)   How is the data presented? Is it a bar chart, graph, pie chart, or table?

The data is presented in table format.

Table 4.2 Family characteristics by family type

Family characteristic	Lone parent		Lone mother		Lone father		Couple		All	
	%	Unweighted base	%	Unweighted base	%	Unweighted base	%	Unweighted base	%	Unweighted base
Family unit work status										
Lone parent: 16+ hours	48	961	48	925	45	36	–	–	12	961
Lone parent: 0–15 hours	52	1099	52	1052	55	47	–	–	13	1099
Couple: both 16+ hours	–	–	–	–	–	–	56	2901	42	2901
Couple: one 16+ hours	–	–	–	–	–	–	38	1964	28	1964
Couple: both 0–15 hours	–	–	–	–	–	–	6	325	4	325
Age of youngest child										
0–4 years	33	731	34	723	10	8	41	2273	39	3004
5–10 years	35	715	35	684	36	31	29	1497	31	2212
11–15 years	26	494	25	464	38	30	23	1098	23	1592
16–18 years	7	120	6	106	16	14	7	322	7	442
Number of dependent children										
1	55	1073	54	1026	58	47	40	1991	44	3064
2	30	661	31	638	26	23	42	2270	39	2931
3	11	245	11	238	9	7	13	697	12	942
4 or more	4	81	4	75	7	6	4	232	4	313

Unweighted base refers to the actual number of people who filled out a survey.

(Source: Department of Work and Pensions (2005) *Family Life in Britian: Findings from the 2003 Families and Children Survey (FACS)* [online], http://www.dwp.gov. uk/asd/asd5/rports2005–2006/rrep250.pdf (Accessed 2 June 2008), London, HMSO).

(c) What numerical form does the data take? Does it show actual numbers, or is it in the form of percentages or rates?

It shows the percentages of the variable 'family type' against three different family characteristics. It also shows the numbers of people who completed the survey in each category.

(d) What information is being presented? What is the data about overall?

The data in the table highlights which family characteristics are associated with particular family types.

(e) Is there more than one type of information being presented?

There are breakdowns of the different types of family having three different kinds of family characteristics: family unit work status; age of youngest child; and number of dependent children. The types of family are defined by the number and gender of parents that children are living with.

(f) What are the limitations of the data? What is not shown?

For the purposes of this research, the data is limited to very specific and particular types of family which include dependent children. This necessarily leaves out many other kinds of families and many other variables between families which are not related to work, or the numbers and ages of children.

(g) What is the overall story being told by the data that is presented?

The overall story of the data is quite complex – there is a lot of information here. By focusing on the number of hours worked by parents in different types of families, it is able to identify issues of inequalities relating to paid employment. It also shows the distribution of ages of children and numbers of children in different types of family, both of which are important considerations for parents in the labour market. By separating out lone mothers and lone fathers, it can show differences in work, age and number of children between these two types of family.

2   There are 2901 families where both parents work more than 16 hours per week, 1964 couple families where one parent works more than 16 hours per week, and 961 lone parents working more than 16 hours per week. If we look at the percentages, we can see that for couple families, 56% have two adults working more than 16 hours and 38% have one adult working more than 16 hours, while 48% of lone parents work more than 16 hours. This means that more than half of couple families have two substantial incomes, an option which is not available to any lone parent. This data thus suggests that 'couples' generally fare better – with both adults able to work more than 16 hours, and where they may also be able to share childcare responsibilities. It does not, however, tell us about all the forms of financial resources available to both types of families which are not

based on earnings in formal employment, such as benefits, payments from absent partners, and help from family and friends.

Figure 4.4

Campaigning against child poverty in 2005

3   The percentage of lone fathers who have four or more dependent children is 7% of all lone fathers. This figure is higher than both lone mothers and couple families – both are at 4%.

4   Lone mothers are more likely to have very young children (0–4) with 34% having a youngest child in this age group. This is similar to couple families at 41%, whereas only 10% of lone fathers have their youngest child in this age range.

5   These are all families which are comprised of parents and their children, and only particular types of these. Perhaps you know other kinds of families which would not fit the types used in this survey. A few examples might be: couples with grown-up children; families where children live with grandparents or other relatives, rather than parents; families where parents do not live together but share the care of their children; foster families.

This kind of quantitative study is trying to get at a wider range of relationships and practices than the census or General Household Survey. However, it is still categorising families, and in this process, it shapes the kinds of results it can produce. In its choice of what to show about families, it reflects particular concerns about families at the time it was produced and develops particular family meanings. More complicated questions about how families might define themselves are not obvious from this data, and we will explore some of these complexities in the following section.

Summary

■   Quantitative data about families is produced by a wide range of public agencies and academic researchers. It is used by governments, policy-makers, and voluntary social agencies as evidence on which to base decisions relating to resources and services. It is also used in the media, by politicians and by social campaigners to reinforce arguments for social change.

■   Like all research evidence, it requires careful reading to make sense of what it says – and what it cannot say.

■   A critical approach to quantitative data will assist us in understanding its strengths and limitations.

6 Comparing households and families

We have seen that 'household' is a central category for census data, and has been for a long time. Other large-scale research also relies on residence as a way of categorising families, attempting to capture the great variety of living arrangements which arise in practice. However, as you have seen in the previous chapters, many people do not define 'family' exclusively or even primarily in terms of who they live with. Family relationships extend between households and even across continents. And looked at from the other direction, households can include people such as friends, paid domestic workers or lodgers who are not imagined as part of the family, although to a much lesser extent than in earlier centuries. And there are households which are not categorised as families at all, with the majority of these containing a single person even though most single people would see themselves as part of a family in some other way.

There is a second crucial side of family life for which such surveys are not as good at providing evidence. This is the way that families change size and shape over time, over the life cycle as children are born and grow up, as adults grow older, and as couples start living together or are separated through divorce or death. Other changes can also be missed in the kind of 'snapshot' approach that a survey necessarily involves. For example, financial or health crises can bring about drastic rearrangements of both household and family situations over shorter or longer periods of time.

Martha Hill discusses these two issues in the context of the United States. She provides a quantitative comparison between relationships defined by residence (household) and by 'relatedness' (family) based on a large scale research survey undertaken every year in the US called the Panel Study of Income Dynamics (PSID). The PSID contains a broad range of relational and co-residency information following a sizable sample of the US population for more than 20 years. Family structure was not one of its initial interests, but it began to supplement residency data with birth, marriage and adoption histories to create the PSID Relationship File, used as the source for Table 4.3 below.

Activity 4.6

This will give you another opportunity to use your skills in reading and interpreting quantitative data. Hill also provides us with some key points which emerged from this data from her perspective. See if you can summarise them after reading the extract.

Reading 4.5   Martha Hill, 'Residence, relatedness and the life cycle'

Relationships between persons living apart are central to issues such as support of children by noncustodial parents or support of frail parents in nursing homes. Because of high rates of divorce and a large proportion of births occurring out of wedlock, many young children live apart from at least one parent. Once they reach adulthood, most children live apart from their parents, thus family ties involving adult children tend to span multiple households. The structure of and linkages connecting nonresident family members have received considerably less attention than coresident family structures, despite the potential for strong economic ties based on relational rather than coresidency ties.

Identifying key nonresident as well as coresident ties requires additional relational information. Comprehensive data on marital, fertility, and adoption ... aid in the identification of key relatives whether they live together or apart. But marital, fertility, and adoption histories ... gathered from all eligible coresidents will not identify both parents of a child, for example, if the child was born out of wedlock and one parent is absent from the child's household. Fertility histories of relatives absent from the household may be needed to determine the full parentage of children. This information is rarely collected in surveys.

...

Assessments of the fit of actual American families to the model of a coresident nuclear family should take account of life-course variation in an individual's set of nuclear families. Life begins as a child in one nuclear family (the family of birth) and then shifts to a different nuclear family (the procreative family) in adulthood when marriage and procreation occur. Hence the relatives who are key to a nuclear family tend to vary with age. For young individuals the family of birth is most relevant, and the presence of both of the individual's parents in the household is a requisite of a coresident nuclear family. For adults their procreative family is most relevant, and the presence of all children and a spouse is key in designating the family as a nuclear family living together under one roof.

How prevalent are nuclear families? Figures under the heading 'Household Structure' in [Table 4.3] indicate that, even taking account of both forms of nuclear family, the model of a coresident nuclear family does not fit most age groups of adults. The coresident nuclear family, identified for young children by the presence of both parents (see the right-most column of [Table 4.3]), is the model family situation of U.S. children (individuals under age 20) but does not characterize the family situation of about one-quarter of them. It is a poor characterization of the family situation of adults, for whom the key identifying characteristic is presence of a spouse and all children. Adults are rarely in a coresident nuclear family of birth, and only among those aged 30–39 is the norm to be in a procreative nuclear family living together under one roof (fourth column of figures under the heading 'Household Structure'). Adults aged 50 or older are rarely in a coresident nuclear family with the full complement of members.

These data suggest that the coresident nuclear family should be considered a model, but not the only one, for policy design. This is especially applicable to policies pertaining to older adults, but it applies to most age groups of adults and to children as well.

Table 4.3 Family structure vs. household structure, 1985

Age and sex	Sample size	Family structure				Household structure						
		Percentage who have:				Percentage who live with:						
		Child	Spouse	Child + spouse	No child + No spouse	Some or all children	All children	Spouse	All children + spouse	Mother	Father	Both parents
Males												
0–9	1 262	0.0	0.0	0.0	100.0	0.0	0.0	0.0	0.0	94.6	74.1	71.0
10–19	1 229	1.2	1.7	1.1	98.2	1.1	1.1	1.6	1.1	92.9	76.9	75.0
20–29	1 535	35.1	46.7	29.2	47.4	28.6	26.8	44.8	25.2			22.6
30–39	1 300	76.2	79.4	70.0	14.5	64.9	56.6	75.0	55.4			3.5
40–49	598	91.8	82.8	80.3	5.7	74.1	45.1	79.8	43.0			0.6
50–59	545	94.8	92.4	89.9	2.6	58.0	12.1	90.5	12.1			0.9
60–69	426	90.0	88.4	83.1	4.7	27.8	2.2	86.8	2.2			0.1
70–101	299	77.2	76.3	65.5	12.0	8.7	1.3	75.2	0.1			0.0
Females												
0–9	1 236	0.0	0.0	0.0	100.0	0.0	0.0	0.0	0.0	98.6	76.3	75.8
10–19	1 217	4.1	3.6	1.9	94.1	4.1	4.1	3.4	1.8	90.1	69.4	67.4
20–29	1 698	49.3	56.1	37.7	32.2	47.1	45.1	53.0	32.6			17.0
30–39	1 416	82.0	74.7	69.0	12.3	79.0	70.5	70.1	58.4			3.0
40–49	711	94.1	80.7	79.1	4.3	80.2	39.7	77.3	33.6			1.4
50–59	744	93.8	73.6	72.7	5.3	50.3	7.1	70.6	6.3			0.3
60–69	565	86.9	63.7	59.1	8.6	22.1	2.0	61.9	0.4			0.0
70–101	527	81.6	34.7	29.6	13.3	12.0	7.6	32.1	0.6			0.0
All	15 458											

Source: PSID sample members in interviewed family units in 1985.

Focusing again on the nuclear family, [Table 4.3] provides evidence about the extent to which major relational ties are unobserved when only the relatives in the household are identified (an approach taken in many surveys and public programs). This table illustrates the differences in family structure based on blood, marriage, and adoption ties (labeled 'Family Structure') and those based on coresidency (labeled 'Household Structure'). The 'Family Structure' figures show the prevalence of those with nuclear family relational ties, and the 'Household Structure' figures show the prevalence of those residing with nuclear family members. A comparison of the patterns for the two structures shows the extent to which household structure is an accurate representation of family structure as defined by relational ties.

For children under age 20, the data mostly allow us to view coresidency ties with incomplete knowledge about whether key relatives are still living, and living elsewhere. (As is true of most data sets, the PSID does not always indicate if the missing father is still living and hence a genuine part of the children's relational ties. Parenting ties to a father are missed in the PSID if the father never lived with the child during the period 1968–1985, if the father was not in an interviewed family unit in 1985, or if the child was not reported in the father's fertility history as of 1985).

For many children, a key nuclear family member – the father – lives apart from them. Only about three-quarters of the children in the age groups 0–9 and 10–19 were living with a father, whereas at least 9 in 10 were residing with a mother. A restriction of parental ties to biological ones would yield lower counts, [because step-parents would be excluded].

For the adult ages, the focus is more on the procreative nuclear family, and the data are better suited to comparing the relational ties with the coresidency ties. Procreative nuclear families tend to be formed by adults in their twenties and thirties (as indicated by the sharp drop in the percentage with no children and no spouse in the fourth column of [Table 4.3]). From that point onward through most of their adult life they tend to have relational ties that bind them to a procreative nuclear family (note the high percentages with both children and a spouse in the third column of figures from ages 30–39 through 70–101). An exception is elderly women, who are likely to have lost a spouse to death but still have living children.

A comparison of the percentage with current spousal relational ties versus current spousal coresidency ties indicates that ties to a current spouse are, for the most, accurately reflected by household structure. At all adult ages only a small percentage of those with a current spouse are not residing with that spouse.

The overall pattern regarding presence of children is quite different. The thirties are the only age range during which the majority of adults coreside with their entire complement of procreative nuclear family members. From their thirties onward (for men from their twenties onward), there is considerable disbursement of children to other locations (compare the first and sixth columns of figures). In their forties only about 40% of adults coreside with all their children. And the percentage drops to well under 10% from age 60 onward. This is not to say that all children are absent from the household. Adults in their thirties, forties, and fifties tend to have at least one child present in the household. Hence throughout adulthood, even though a household will often contain at least one child, there is a good chance, especially after middle age, that at least one child will be absent.

... Sizable segments – about one in five – of adult men in their thirties and forties have young children living elsewhere and, hence, obligations that go beyond their own households. Three-quarters of the adults aged 70 and older have adult children who do not live with them, this is a potential source of assistance that does not show up in a household listing of family members.

...

Although policies and researchers often implicitly assume an unchanging family structure over time, families and households are highly subject to change. Concepts such as "family" and "household" are difficult to define in a dynamic context, and different approaches have been used to trace the changes that occur over time ... One approach is to define families and households in a way that allows distinctions between units remaining intact versus discontinuing or forming. Another approach is to trace individuals as they move from one family or household to another and delineate the differences in their family or household circumstances. But whether the fluidity in families and households is measured from the perspective of the family/household unit or from the perspective of individuals who are members of the units, the evidence shows considerable change.

Assessing change from the perspective of longitudinal household units yields a finding that over a one-year period 9.0% of the households that had existed at the start of the year were no longer in the same category by the end of the year. Over a two-year period the percentage of initial households subsequently discontinuing rose to 15.6% (U.S. Bureau of the Census, 1992b, Table A).

Reading source

Hill, 1995, pp. 58–62

Summary

■ It is difficult to capture the depth and breadth of family relationships using surveys based on residence or household. Surveys which ask about relationships are more likely to reveal family connections between people who do not live together.

■ Family forms and types change over the life cycle so people only live in such families (if at all) at particular stages in their lives, either as children or as parents.

■ Both these factors show the fluidity and variation in family life and it requires sophisticated quantitative methods to capture their complexity.

7   Conclusions

In this chapter we have looked at both the strengths of quantitative research for family studies, and the necessity for a critical approach to the evidence it produces. To do this, we have posed questions about the boundaries and categories of family and household which have been central to the ways in which quantitative data has been produced and analysed. We looked in some depth at the historical construction of the census and how it has shaped meanings of family and household over a long period of time. In doing so, we saw how the methods of categorising and representing 'the people' have never fully captured the diversity and complexities of family life as people and families adapted themselves to periods of social change. The purposes of governments in collecting and counting the population were also examined, highlighting the importance of knowledge about the population both in practical ways in planning for services but also in terms of how the nation imagines its people.

In order to understand these processes, you saw how a 'checklist' can help us to interpret a range of quantitative data about families. Quantitative data can be very densely presented in numerical or graphical forms, but by taking the time to unpick a table or graph we can learn a great deal. In this chapter, I have emphasised the importance of adopting a critical stance by carefully interrogating the data. An awareness of when and by whom the research was carried out, and for what purpose, is of fundamental importance in this process. Furthermore, when analysing data, is it important to bear in mind the difficulties of those collecting the data in making it 'fit' the requirements of the research, such as the problems that census enumerators faced in the nineteenth century. If we also consider what such research leaves out, what it does not include, and the ways that families do not fit its particular categories, we can begin to recognise the limitations of a piece of quantitative evidence. We also saw how selective presentation of data can obscure the wider picture, particularly when looking at trends over time. What appears to be a crisis in families today can look rather different if a longer timescale is used. Finally, quantitative data can point to possible relationships between social phenomena, but it cannot directly explain how families have come to be the way they are. The kinds of qualitative research you explored in Chapters 2 and 3 are likely to be more helpful in this regard.

The fluidity of family life within and between households and across the world is particularly difficult to capture in large scale surveys of national populations which underpin a great deal of quantitative research and analysis. The shifts and changes in family life as people grow up and grow old, and as crises and happy events shape everyday life and relationships, are not readily amenable to research which captures a single moment when data is fixed into categories. But to gain an overview or more general picture, quantitative data is invaluable to the researcher and to those making policies relating to families.

The production and representation of quantitative data is not only useful in providing us with information about families: it also shapes the ways that 'family' is defined. Its limitations will restrict the ways that we can 'see' families, but they will also limit what 'family' means in society. A key example of this are the ways that family and household are often conflated, which can be traced to quantitative data based on residence such as the census. Families that do not fit generalised categories, which are fluid in terms of space and time, or are in the process of shaping new kinds of family lives, will find their experiences are not always visible in large-scale survey research. Thus, many families can be marginalised or even disappear from the picture presented by quantitative evidence. In these ways, then, quantitative studies can shape the notions of 'family' that people hold.

Quantitative research will continue to be highly influential in shaping our images and understandings of family lives. It enables us to look beyond our own immediate families and experiences and place them in the context of wider and more general patterns and trends. The findings of quantitative researchers have particular authority in our society which values what can be measured, counted and presented in what appears to be unassailable facts, and they have been crucial in shaping family meanings in many different directions. But as we have seen, they are not just simple descriptions of a pre-existing reality; they are the result of complex social processes and decisions.

References

Doolittle, M. (1996) 'Missing Fathers: Assembling a History of Fatherhood in Mid-Nineteenth Century England', unpublished PhD thesis, University of Essex.

Hantrais, L. (2004) *Family Policy Matters: Responding to Family Change in Europe*, Bristol, Policy Press.

Hill, M.S. (1995) 'When is a family a family? Evidence from survey data and implications for family policy', *Journal of Family and Economic Issues*, vol. 16, no. 1, pp. 35–64.

Office for National Statistics (2007) '*Focus on Families*, Smallwood, S. and Wilson, B. (eds) Basingstoke, Palgrave Macmillan, p. 3.

Parr, J. and Silva, E.B. (2005) 'Quantitative social research' in The Open University *The Uses of Sociology: Traditions, Methods and Practices* (eds P. Redman, E.B. Silva and S. Watson), Milton Keynes, The Open University.

McRae, S. (1999) 'Introduction: family and household change in Britain' in McRae, S. (ed.) *Changing Britain: Families and Households in the 1990s*, Oxford, Oxford University Press, pp. 1–33.

Sweeting, H. and Seaman, P. (2005), 'Family within and beyond the household boundary: children's constructions of who they live with' in McKie, L. and Cunningham-Burley, S. (eds) *Families in Society: Boundaries and Relationships*, Bristol, Policy Press, pp. 95–110.

Part 2
Theories and concepts

Introduction to Part 2

Shelley Day Sclater

In Part 1 of this book, you explored family meanings that have arisen from research evidence. You looked in some detail at different types of data and learned how research both draws upon and helps to construct and re-present family meanings. In Part 2 of the book we introduce two theoretical approaches to the study of 'family' – family as discourse and family as practice (Chapter 5), and two key concepts – 'intimacy' and 'personal life' (Chapter 6).

Theories are important because they provide us with frameworks within which meanings of 'family' may be explored systematically. Theorising is something we all do every day, although mostly we will not be aware that we are doing it! Every time we invoke ideas or memories to make sense of something, we are also constructing a theory about it. Similarly, in social science, theorising enables us to organise our ideas and to make sense of the social world. Even to *describe* the social world without recourse to theory would be difficult and, without theory, we certainly wouldn't be able to *analyse* what we see, let alone *explain* it.

Different theoretical approaches bring different issues into the frame, and have different implications for family research. Theories enable us to move between the general and the particular, as we use them to make sense of our evidence, to guide our thinking and inform our analysis. In Chapter 5 we discuss two linked theoretical approaches to the study of family meanings: family as discourse, and family as practice. We have chosen these particular frameworks because they are currently the most used and most widely debated.

Family as discourse

Discourse theory is widely used in social science and is well suited as a theoretical tool to approach our study of family meanings. Discourse theory emphasises the fundamental importance of language and representation – in talk, text and image – in organising and structuring the world. Discourses are not only words, but are closely linked to practices – indeed, talking, or writing and reading text, or making and viewing images, are themselves material social practices. This is why it is helpful to view the two theoretical approaches alongside each other. Discourse theory can seem a little complex at first, and you might find it helpful to begin your study of Chapter 5 with a working definition that you can modify as you deepen your understanding of the theory. A useful shorthand definition to start off with is: *discourses are frameworks of meaning*.

The most crucial point to grasp at this stage is that ideas and images are *represented* in discourse, but there is a sense in which they are also *constructed* in discourse. This is important because as we *construct ideas* in discourse – for example, particular ideas of family in policy debates about 'hardworking families' – so we also *construct meanings*, and those meanings have *values* attached to them. As discourses invoke certain values, so they can reinforce ideas about what families *should* be like, rather than what families actually *are* like. So, in our example of 'hardworking families' – an idea that often appears in policy documents and political speeches – the discourse invokes an idea that families *should* be 'hardworking'; families *should* contribute to the economy; they *should* pay their own way (i.e. they *should not* live on state benefits); and so on. These associations to 'hardworking families' are set in train by the systematised meanings in the discourse. Thus, discourse theory helps us see how certain family meanings can become the dominant meanings and be linked to moral judgements. Those moral evaluations approve certain family meanings whilst marginalising or excluding others.

Discourse theory will enable you to think more critically about what is going on below the surface in talk, text and images of 'family'. You might, for example, notice new dimensions to representations that you read about in the newspaper, or that you see on TV, or even when your friend tells you about her family holiday. As you begin to think in terms of discourse of family, you will find yourself analysing what you see and hear; you may be surprised to discover discourses everywhere! When you do encounter them, try to think about how they shape sets of often competing family meanings. You might focus too on the less obvious aspects of discourse; for example, how we make implicit value judgements simply through talking about 'family' in a particular way – such as 'family time is very important to me' or 'blood is thicker than water'. Each of these phrases says something significant about how families ought to be.

Family practices

If discourse theory emphasises the significance of representation through text and images, the theory of family practices draws our attention to what people *do* to 'make family'. On this theory, people are seen as actively shaping 'family' through the things that they do – through their everyday 'family practices'. We might sum up this approach with a sentence: 'families are as families do'.

Examples of family practices include things like the weekly grocery shop, doing the laundry, brushing a child's hair, family holidays, and so on. In Chapter 5 we discuss family leisure as family practice and demonstrate how something as ordinary as playing Monopoly helps to construct 'family' as a cohesive unit. Family leisure also constitutes a set of family practices that helps construct 'mothers' and 'fathers' as 'good' parents; it provides a setting for the enactment of socially approved parent–child relationships.

Once you start thinking in terms of family practices, ordinary things like breakfast time, or TV ads, or a birthday party, or even the washing up, will begin to take on something of a strange quality – they're ordinary family practices that you'll see have a deep significance for family and what families mean to us. Think about how those everyday practices actually shape what family is and what family means, and the range of feelings that family carries which are played out in those ordinary practices.

Family as discourse and family as practice are linked theoretical approaches to the study of what 'family' means. We discuss them separately in Chapter 5 but once you have a grasp of both, you will see how putting them together will deepen your understanding. For example, if you put discourses and practices together in relation to family leisure, you will see how the family practices take on their meanings within discourses, as well as how discourses are realised in practice. Together, the discourses and practices of family leisure help to construct not only 'family', but also identity positions within family, including mothers, fathers and children.

When we bring family discourses and practices together in this way, we see that discourses are highly influential in structuring family meanings, but they do not have the last word. It is in the everyday activities and family practices of people that the struggles over family meanings are played out.

Two key concepts: 'intimacy' and 'personal life'

In Chapter 6, we discuss two key concepts in family studies: 'intimacy' and 'personal life'. Our discussion builds on the theories of discourse and practice that we explored in Chapter 5. Concepts can't ever stand alone, but always borrow their meanings from the theories in which they are embedded (and which are not always made explicit).

Discourse theory reminds us that ideas of 'family' can serve to normalise some living arrangements and relationships whilst marginalising, stigmatising or excluding others. This raises some important questions in Family Studies: is the concept of 'family' possibly too morally loaded? Might there be other more flexible – or less emotive – concepts we can use to capture significant aspects of our lives and relationships without becoming bogged down in the trappings of 'family'?

In Chapter 6 we explore two such concepts – 'intimacy' and 'personal life'. We explore how far the use of these concepts shifts our focus away from 'family', and ask whether a focus on either intimacies or personal lives can be used to enrich, or alternatively to replace, the term 'family'. In other words, if we use a different language to alter our focus and move our image of 'family' from centre stage, perhaps we can get a different perspective, or see new things waiting in the wings; perhaps we will notice features or dimensions of families that have not stood out before. Or perhaps the way will be more open to think about alternatives to 'family'.

Where 'family' suggests a social unit, 'intimacy' draws attention to a range of significant relationships, and emphasises the quality of those relationships rather than their structural aspects. The concept of intimacy thus does more, and less, than 'family'. Like 'family', 'intimacy' is a fluid concept with multiple meanings that depend on context. The context includes the discourses that frame the range of meanings for intimacy as well as the concrete social practices where those meanings are played out.

There is, of course, a danger that the concept of 'intimacy', like 'family', will become too politically or morally loaded, or fixed in discourses that limit its usefulness as an alternative to 'family'. There may be signs that this is already happening – for example, in the way that 'intimacy' connotes a sexual relationship. In Chapter 6 we address this issue by exploring a range of intimate practices that decentre the sexual relationship. In the second part of the chapter, the concept of 'personal life' goes one step further towards capturing those living arrangements and significant relationships (for example, friendships) that neither 'family' nor 'intimacy' encompasses.

Drawing on our explorations of concepts of 'intimacy' and 'personal life' we conclude Part 2 of the book with a discussion about the advantages and disadvantages of the different concepts and ask whether or not the concept of 'family' continues to have any usefulness in social science.

The two chapters in this part equip you with two theoretical approaches, and two key concepts, with which to further your quest for family meanings. It will undoubtedly be helpful if you can use the ideas from this section of the book to interrogate your own experiences of family – your own, and those of others that you know. Do the theories and concepts capture important elements of your experience? Do they help you explore family meanings?

Chapter 5
Family discourses and family practices

Shelley Day Sclater

Contents

1   Introduction

In this chapter, we continue our quest to understand family meanings. We consider how social scientists have sought to move beyond the language of 'family' as too limiting, to explore 'family' in terms of discourse (as something that takes shape in talk, text and images) and as everyday practices (as something that people 'do'). In these two theoretical approaches, 'family' is conceptualised, not as a static 'thing', but in terms of dynamic social processes. In this chapter we explore how 'family' is produced and reproduced through the interacting discourses and practices of everyday life.

A discourse perspective explains how 'family' is constructed through language, whilst a focus on family practices highlights the human activities that are involved in 'doing family'. Although we discuss them separately for the sake of clarity, family discourses and family practices are not mutually exclusive but are, as we shall see, profoundly interdependent.

You will notice how a dual focus on discourses and practices represent two different, though linked, routes into understanding 'family'; both help us move away from 'family' as a noun, and move towards a more fluid conception of 'family' as an adjective or verb, as discussed in the extract from David Morgan (Reading 1.1) in Chapter 1. 'Discourse' draws attention to the *systems of meaning* that are enacted and expressed in everyday lives. They can be found in media representations, or in expert knowledges and are expressed through professional practices. Such discourses are found in a wide range of settings – for example, in law and policy. Through these discourses, as we shall see, 'family' is constructed in particular ways.

A focus on family 'practices' highlights the importance of everyday activities that involve social actors in 'doing family'. Those practices may be routinised (as, for example, in doing the laundry on a certain day, or taking the children to school), or ritualised (as in weddings, or birthday parties, or in 'Sunday lunch'), or they may simply be taken for granted (as in doing the weekly shopping). The hallmark of such practices is that 'family' comes into being through the 'doing' of these activities.

It is important to note that 'family' can be constructed, not only through discourses and practices that refer directly to 'family' (for example, government polices directed at 'hardworking families') but also through more peripheral discourses and practices that relate to family matters and where 'family' may only be implicit. For example, as Megan Doolittle discusses in Chapter 8, 'family' as an important locus for the education of children is implicitly constructed through a school's homework policy (a discourse and a practice – or a 'discursive practice'). Or 'family' as a social unit responsible for care may be invoked by a local authority's provisions for care of the elderly. In each case, there are underlying assumptions about the nature and functions of 'family' that inform policy and practice and that link to particular discursive constructions of 'family'. No doubt you will be able to think of many more examples where 'family' is similarly constructed in broader discourses and practices.

We begin our discussion with a consideration of discourses and, in Section 3 of the chapter, we look in some detail at family practices.

2   Discourses of family

As was suggested in Chapter 1, if we 'listen in order to know how to look', we highlight issues of language and representation in our quest for family meanings. One such approach is to regard 'family' as something which is constructed through discourse. Before we discuss examples of discourses in which particular images of family are constructed, it will be helpful to consider, more generally, what is meant by 'discourse'.

2.1   What is discourse?

The term 'discourse' has a range of meanings depending upon the theoretical or methodological framework within which social scientists use the term, and there are ongoing debates on these issues. At a broad level, however, I think that most would agree that discourses may usefully be defined as *frameworks of meaning that organise the social world and make a difference to it.*

You will notice that I have referred to 'meaning' here, so it is important to make clear the difference between 'meaning' and 'discourse'. As you discovered in Chapter 2, meanings may be either 'individualised' – where a particular interpretation belongs to an individual – or they can be 'culturally systematised' – where they are shared amongst members of a social group. It may be helpful to think of discourses as *systematised meanings* that are *available in a culture as resources for sense-making.* There are two main ways in which meanings may become systematised: first, through everyday usages and interactions as, for example, over generations within a family; secondly, through becoming embedded in institutional or professional contexts. In both cases, the systematisation of meanings leads to the implicit privileging of certain meanings over others. In making sense of their lives, people habitually draw on a wide range of discourses and personal meanings.

To familiarise yourself with the general concept, let us briefly consider the workings of a routinely encountered discourse – a medical discourse.

2.1.1   An example of the workings of discourse

Activity 5.1

Read the vignette below and then answer these questions.

1   At what point does the medical discourse become important in structuring Naheed's experience?

2   At what point does Naheed 'position' herself in the medical discourse? Why does she do this?

3   What are the consequences for Naheed of positioning herself as 'sick' or as 'a patient'?

4   What alternative discourses are available? Are they all equally available, equally viable or equally powerful?

Naheed comes home early from work one day with a pain in her abdominal area. She takes some painkillers and goes to bed. She doesn't sleep well, and is still troubled by the pain the following morning. She rings into work sick and goes to see her GP. The doctor examines her, takes her temperature, pulse and blood pressure, and asks about the history of the symptoms and how Naheed is feeling. The doctor is not sure exactly what the trouble is – it could be a few things, possibly just a virus – but is sufficiently worried to arrange for Naheed to see a specialist and attend at the hospital for further tests. At the hospital, Naheed is given an ultrasound scan and talks to the specialist about the results. There is some suggestion that she might need an operation, but Naheed is first referred to a nutritionist to see whether a radical change in diet and some targeted medication might relieve her symptoms. Back at home, Naheed rings her friend who suggests that a homeopath might be able to help; she advises Naheed that medications can have unwanted side effects and surgery can carry unacceptable risks. Another friend suggests that Naheed has been quite stressed lately and that lifestyle changes and possibly counselling might be what is needed. After talking to her friends, Naheed is thrown into a quandary; she is not quite sure what to do and does not know whom to trust.

Comment

1   As soon as Naheed experiences the pain, the medical discourse clicks in. It is immediately important in structuring Naheed's experience because it is a dominant one in many Western industrialised societies. It is generally available and likely to be a primary resource used by people to make sense of experience. Ordinarily we draw on discourses without being aware that we are doing any such thing. In the medical discourse, a pain becomes a 'symptom' of an underlying illness or condition. Medical expertise is needed for 'diagnosis' and 'treatment'.

2   Naheed 'positions' herself in the medical discourse as soon as she experiences an unusual pain. This immediately makes her think in terms of the medical discourse – perhaps she might be poorly. Naheed thinks in these terms because of the dominance of the medical discourse in the society where she lives. If she

lived in another time or another place, different discourses might be available to her.

3   Positioning herself as 'sick' in this way immediately puts Naheed into the framework of a medical discourse, which has certain consequences for her thoughts ('I wonder what's wrong with me, I hope it's not serious'), her actions ('I'd better make an appointment at the doctor's') and also her feelings (uncertainty, fear, hope that the doctor will put it right). It also has consequences, for what happens to her in the short and longer term: the doctor has privileged access to the patient's body; during a diagnostic examination, a medical professional may touch the patient in ways that, in other circumstances, may be intimate or even forbidden. 'Trust' is an important aspect of the relationship between the patient and the professional who has had a specialised training and who has access to specialised knowledge whose esoteric language patients are unlikely to understand. In this way, Naheed becomes subject to the power of the doctor (and the medical profession), implicitly accepting new norms and rules.

4   Naheed's friends suggest alternative discourses (homeopathy, lifestyle and counselling) that are less dominant than the medical discourse, but nevertheless are available to compete with it and to challenge its dominance. Naheed has a 'choice' about how she makes sense of her pain, but that choice is constrained to the extent that the medical discourse is the dominant one. The medical discourse is dominant partly for historical reasons, but partly also because it has institutional power (the NHS, for example, in the UK) and even legal power behind it (in some cases courts can override consent and impose treatments).

From this brief example, do you notice how a focus on discourse draws attention to how language can be organised in ways that privilege certain meanings over others? Some meanings are relegated to the marginal, the undesirable or even the unacceptable. Discourses, therefore, are ways of seeing and thinking – ways of organising the world – that are not neutral: they are always underpinned by moral and political concerns.

A discourse approach suggests that, as we *describe* the social world, so also do we *structure* that world, *categorise* it and, crucially, also *evaluate* it. In this way, we can say that discourses are linked to power. In the medical example, the power lies with the professionals (their expert knowledge derives from an apparently unassailable science as well as a long tradition) and is backed up by institutions and law.

Discourses can thus reflect power differentials, such as those between doctor and patient, as well as broader social inequalities, such as those of social class, gender, ethnicity, sexuality, disability, age, and so on. For example, there are many commonly encountered discourses that advocate behaviours that cost money, or require time, that many people simply do not have. 'Healthy eating', for example, or regular exercise, or the value of family leisure activities, have become very dominant ideas that are deemed to be morally right, yet many people lack the resources to be able to participate. These discourses thus reflect inequalities relating to the availability of resources. In this way, even discourses that are not obviously discriminatory can support or reproduce inequalities and oppressions or reinforce stereotypes. But conversely, as you will see in this chapter, people often find ways to negotiate around the strictures of discourse, and new discourses can and do emerge to disrupt, resist or challenge the dominant ones.

The idea of discourse is a complex one, but I hope that by the end of this chapter, you will share with me the belief that this approach is well worth pursuing, as it allows us to look below the surface of things and to identify features and patterns that are not otherwise immediately obvious.

Key points to note about discourse

From the brief example of a commonly available medical discourse, there are a few key general points that you will find useful to bear in mind as we focus more specifically on discourses of family:

- Discourses are *systematised meanings* that we draw on to help us make sense of the world and our experiences.

- As we draw on available discourses to *describe* the world, so do we also *categorise it* and *evaluate* it.

- Discourses transmit *moral* views, and often contain *prescriptions* for behaviour (e.g. they suggest what is desirable, or unacceptable).

- Discourses are linked to *social power* and, as such, can reinforce or reproduce *inequalities* (e.g. gender, class, ethnicity) as well as challenge them.

- Some discourses are more *dominant* than others, particularly when they are linked to expertise (for example, child-development expertise which borrows its authority from its location in a broader dominant scientific discourse) or institutional power (such as the law).

- Discourses can be *challenged*, for example by reference to other discourses (e.g. medical discourse vs 'alternative' medicine).

- Discourses have *consequences* for our identities, and for how we think, how we feel, and what we do. We make *personal investments* every time we engage with a discourse.

2.2   Family discourse and social power

In the following activity, I would like you to read an extract by Nikolas Rose, a social theorist, who has applied discourse theory to understanding 'family'. Rose shows how the personal investments that people habitually make in family – their desire to be 'good' parents, for example – locks them into discourse and so contributes to broader systems of management and control, systems he calls 'governance'.

Rose's starting point is that the vast majority of people, in domestic settings, do not have to be forced into doing what is regarded as socially desirable. On the contrary, most want to do what seems 'right', and their personal aspirations are linked in important ways to discourses. For example, as regards education and childcare, most parents will want to be 'good' parents, and to do what is best for their children. Parental identities and practices thus take shape against a backdrop of discourses of family – what Rose refers to as 'familial' discourses – that are purveyed by the media and in schools and are backed up by a body of child-development expertise and institutional power (including, ultimately, the power of law).

The next stage of Rose's argument (which you will focus on now) is that the personal commitments and aspirations that take shape in familial discourses have social effects as well as personal significance: they are the crucial link between 'family' and systems of governance.

Activity 5.2

Study the reading carefully.

1   What do you understand by Rose's idea of 'familialising projects'?

2   In what ways do people's emotional investments in family contribute to the furtherance of social objectives?

Reading 5.1   Nikolas Rose, 'Familialising projects'

Of course, the construction of subjective values and assessments was the aim of many **familialising projects** of the nineteenth and twentieth centuries. It was an explicit rationale in the moralising philanthropy of the nineteenth century, and in the arguments for universal education. It was also evident in the concern for the health and welfare of children in the early twentieth century. This certainly sought to utilise 'the family' and the relations within it as a kind of social or socialising machine in order to fulfil various objectives: military, industrial and moral. But this was to be done not through the coercive enforcement of control under threat of sanction, but through the construction of mothers who would want their homes and children to be governed according to hygienic norms. The promotion of hygiene and welfare could only be successful to the extent that it managed to solicit the active engagement of individuals in the promotion of their own bodily efficiency. ...

If the family came to serve social objectives, it was not in spite of the wishes of women and men, but because it came to work as a private, voluntary and responsible agency for the rearing and moralising of children and promoting their physical and mental welfare. Domestic, conjugal and parental conduct is increasingly regulated not by obedience compelled by threat of sanction but through the activation of individual guilt, personal anxiety and private disappointment. Husbands and wives, mothers and fathers themselves regulate their feelings, desires, wishes and emotions and think themselves through the potent images of parenthood, sexual pleasure and quality of life. In the necessary gap between expectation and realisation, between desires and satisfaction, anxiety and disappointment fuel the search for expert assistance. It is this pleasure/anxiety relation that drives the government of personal life.

Reading source

Rose, 1987, p. 73

Comment

1   In his concept of 'familialisation' Rose is conveying a sense of how ordinary domestic life is part and parcel of broader systems of governance. The crucial linkages are the discourses of family that help to shape people's own deep-felt desires for themselves and their families against a backdrop of expertise and insitutionalised power.

Thus, ordinarily, people will feel the effects of the dominant familial discourses in their lives. They will aspire to and derive pleasure from doing things the *right* way, and will suffer anxieties and guilt when they cannot meet their own high standards. Thus, Rose's concept of 'familialisation' is intended to capture the ways in which societies govern their citizens *through* discursively constructing family relationships and meanings in particular ways.

2   Rose's argument is that domestic life is regulated, not by coerced adherence to externally imposed norms, but by reference to individual emotions and internal states: desire, pleasure, aspiration, anxiety and guilt. These feelings are routinely activated by engagement with dominant discourses of family and managed in family practices (which we discuss in Section 3 of this chapter). Such is the power of discourse that citizens commonly strive to position themselves so as to maximise pleasure and minimise anxiety.

2.3 Competing discourses

As Rose indicates, discourses can be very powerful. But as you saw in the medical example, it is important to recognise that discourses are not determining, and so outcomes cannot easily be predicted.

There are two main reasons for this. First, there are several competing discourses, although some will be more dominant than others. Secondly, people do not passively accept the strictures of discourse: they are active agents who create, choose, negotiate, challenge and resist. Or people may subvert the power of a discourse by using it for their own ends, or they may choose to invoke a particular discourse to draw on its moral or emotional authority.

People can create discourses too, as they interact with one another in their everyday lives. But these new discourses are unlikely to be widely recognised, or to become institutionally dominant unless they also represent the meanings of powerful groups. For example, working men's clubs might express and formulate particular sorts of discourse (e.g. around masculinity), but these may not become widely recognised nor embedded into policy or professional expertise, unless perhaps through trade union activities.

In the next two activities, we explore how people actively negotiate their way among competing discourses of parenting, against the backdrop of the institutional power of family law.

Activity 5.3

Read the extract below and focus first of all on the two competing discourses. In this extract, Rosalind Edwards and her co-workers discuss the tensions between two competing discourses in their research on step-parenting.

1   Can you identify the two competing discourses?

2   Which discourse do you think is the dominant one, and why?

3   What are the consequences of dominance?

Reading 5.2   Rosalind Edwards et al., 'Biological parents and social families'

In recent years the British legal discourse has shifted clearly in favour of the view that children need biological parents, and that the tie with biological parents is for life ... The thrust of the contemporary legal discourse is therefore towards maintaining the biological links and supporting notions of 'shared parenting' after divorce or separation which ... in effect re-emphasizes the patriarchal rights of the (biological) father. ... Within this British legal discourse, there is no notion of 'children need (social) families'. ...

In analysing our data ... [i]t ... became apparent that the complexity in interviewees' views about the legal position of step-parents is largely centred on a clash of moralities concerning whether children need (biological) parents or whether they need (social) families. ...

On the one hand, there is a discourse in these interviews that suggests that parenting is supposed to be a natural phenomenon, based on biological ties, the sentiments of which are largely beyond rational planning and control. This 'children need biological parents' discourse is most compatible with the legal prescription, and similarly involves quite a clear cut notion of where power is vested – in biological parenthood. In some interviews, blood ties between parents and children were regarded as resulting in more intense and enduring emotional relationships, being characterized by absolute commitment and loyalty. Biological parents were regarded as 'naturally' more protective of their own children. This was most apparent in relation to the issue of disciplining children. ....

On the other hand, there is another moral discourse very apparent, that centres on ideas of equity, family-defined social positions, and tolerance, sometimes associated with planning. This discourse comes close to the idea that rational planning and thought, and/or 'natural' feelings for children, can overcome inequities of biology, and that a form of personalized social engineering or construction can lead to the formation of a new social (family) unit that will meet children's needs. This 'children need families' discourse is tied in with a view that children need stability, and they need to feel they 'belong' to a clear-cut social unit, which can be provided by a 'family'. The ability to forge close emotional relationships was not regarded as dependent on biological status – indeed, a sustained, caring relationship with a step-parent who deliberately and thoughtfully treats his step-children 'as his own', or carefully nurtures the relationship over time, can outweigh the relatively insignificant contribution some biological parents can make. The 'natural' cohesiveness of a family unit based on biology, with application and commitment, can be recreated. ... The primary emphasis is that adults and children all occupy socially-defined positions within a family unit. ...

The British legal discourse ... does not recognize the complexities of these everyday views, and it does this by largely ignoring the notion that children need 'families', and that these families are social units created by living together and relating together in the everyday business of caring for children.

Reading source

Edwards et al., 1999, pp. 309, 311–12, 325

Comment

1   The two competing discourses the authors discuss are:

   (a)   the legal discourse that embodies a 'biological' view of parenthood, and

   (b)   the competing everyday discourse of step-parents that emphasises instead 'social' ties in the creation of a 'family' unit.

2   The legal discourse is dominant, because it is backed up by the institutional power of the law (which ultimately can force or coerce by imposing sanctions) and also because of its links to a prominent branch of child-welfare science.

3   The consequences are:

(a)   the 'social' discourse that tended to dominate some parents' accounts, particularly among working-class interviewees, was likely to be much less visible in any court proceedings, and

(b)   the experiences and values of such step-parents are marginalised as of little or no consequence, or rendered invisible.

Thus, some voices are heard whilst others are silenced. In this way, discourses can perpetuate inequalities, such as those of social class.

In this extract, did you notice how the 'everyday' discourses could be eclipsed by the legal ones? Did you also notice that the legal discourse focuses on (biological) parenthood and refers to a dyadic (i.e. consisting of only two parts) relationship between a parent and a child. By contrast, the 'everyday' discourses invoke more of a notion of family as a social unit to which parents, step-parents and children alike all belong.

Importantly, both the legal and the everyday discourses of step-parenting invoke competing versions of 'family': 'family' may be implicit, but is nevertheless present. The legal discourse uses a language of parenthood and so displaces 'family' from centre stage, whereas 'family' is more central – though still only implied – in the everyday discourses. In this extract, there is a clear conflict between the priorities of some step-parents and those of the law and policy. One can only speculate as to the likely consequences of policy provisions being so far at a distance from people's everyday meanings and concerns!

2.4 Discourse, power, negotiation and the patterning of meaning

Returning to the theme that discourses construct 'family' but do not have the last word, we now explore what can happen when people are confronted with a discourse that is too much at odds with their own understandings and desires. In this example – also from empirical research on family law – we see parents not only resisting a dominant discourse, but actually transforming it and using it for their own ends. Thus, 'family' is not straightforwardly constructed in discourse, but is an outcome of complex negotiations, and people can, and often do, subvert the dominance of a discourse.

In this second example of how family meanings take shape in discourse, you should also look closely for the patterning of meanings and how inequalities are managed.

The inequalities addressed here concern gender: look out for how they are negotiated by individual men and women.

Gender represents only one example of a wider range of inequalities that are supported, reproduced, or challenged, or resisted in discourses of family. Owing to limitations of space, we cannot discuss the full range here. Inequalities that you are likely to find in family discourses also include sexuality (where, for example, gay or lesbian families are portrayed as 'unnatural'), ethnicity (seen, for example, in the stereotyping of minority ethnic families), and social class. The perpetuation of inequalities of class in UK social policy discourses and practices has been consistently demonstrated in research. For example, Val Gillies, a social researcher, analysed policy discourse about 'support' for parents. She showed that although those ideas were intended to apply equally to all, a close analysis revealed a 'class specific concern with disadvantaged or "socially excluded" families' (Gillies, 2003, p. 71). She argued that the government's commitment to 'supporting' parents was driven by a moral agenda that sought to control the behaviour of marginalised families.

To explore further how 'family' takes shape in discourse, we now consider an example from family law where a very powerful discourse of 'children's welfare' structures post-divorce family arrangements. Look closely for the patterning of meanings and how gender issues are managed.

Activity 5.4

Read the first part of the following extract and write some brief notes about the dominant discourse.

1   What do you see as its main feature?

2   Why might it be difficult to challenge the dominant discourse directly?

In this example, a direct challenge to the dominant discourse is hardly possible, yet the parents in this study still manage to resist its power and, in fact, harness that power to express their own deeply felt meanings.

Reading 5.3 Felicity Kaganas and Shelley Day Sclater, 'Subverting the dominant discourse'

Children's welfare ... remains key to the decision-making process and judicial constructions of welfare remain ... crucial. And while this brief discussion ... reveals some important shifts in judicial interpretations of the welfare discourse, courts as well as professionals continue to stress the importance of contact as well as conflict-free and co-operative decision-making and parenting.

It is in the context of these norms and assumptions that we will now consider the results of our research, a study that focused on the accounts given by mothers and fathers of their experiences of contact disputes. Our concern was to uncover disputing parents' own perspectives on their involvement in protracted disputes. It is immediately apparent that the welfare discourse embodied in law and espoused by professionals has entered parents' vocabularies; it is routinely used by parents as a framework for understanding and talking about their experiences. But the myriad ways in which parents invoke the discourse suggest that, although they accept it in the abstract, they are actively interpreting it according to their own criteria. Law's prescriptions become matters not for passive acceptance but for active, often critical, negotiation. For instance, contact, despite the law's gender-neutral approach to parenting, remains very much a gender issue.

Reading source

Kaganas and Day Sclater, 2004, pp. 15–16

Comment

1   The main feature of the dominant discourse is that the interests of children should come first. The children's 'welfare' is key to judicial decision-making where there are disputes between separated parents. In fact, the law states that it should be the main ('paramount') consideration, and should take precedence over everything else, including the wishes and feelings of the disputing parents.

2   The discourse is difficult to challenge directly because it is extremely powerful. This is partly because it seems to accord with common-sense thinking – a good indicator that the discourse has become a dominant one. It's the power of discourse that makes certain social arrangements appear, not socially constructed, but as 'natural' and obvious. It is also difficult to challenge because it is based on an established body of child-welfare science, and it has the institutional power of the law behind it. Other dominant discourses that position 'science' as unassailable, and 'law' as the final arbiter contextualise the welfare discourse and add to its power.

Figure 5.1
An idealised version of the nuclear family

Thus there really is very little room for manoeuvre if you are a parent engaged in a legal dispute. But it is clear that parents are not passive even in the face of such a dominant discourse: we are told that mothers and fathers use the idea that children's needs must come first to support their own side of the story. In appropriating the discourse in this way, mothers and fathers are bringing their own meanings to bear, as they take up identity positions as 'good parents' in the discourse.

Central to parents' own meanings is a strong conviction that, contrary to the provisions of law, parenting is *a gendered activity*: mothering and fathering are not the same.

Activity 5.5

Read the second part of the extract and answer the questions:

1   Why do you think parents regard legal disputes over children as a 'battle of the sexes'?

2   How do mothers and fathers resolve the tensions between their own gendered family meanings and the prescriptions of the dominant welfare discourse?

Reading 5.4   Felicity Kaganas and Shelley Day Sclater, 'A battle of the sexes'

Both mothers and fathers frequently framed the meaning of the dispute in terms of a battle of the sexes. The legal system was perceived to be colluding with the opposite sex; respondents of both sexes expressed a strong sense of injustice, which they talked about in terms of gender bias. Gina, for example, saw the system as favouring men: 'It seems to me with the legal system, ... there doesn't seem to be any protection for the woman, or for the children. But as long as they all pander to the man's rights. ... His 'right' to see the children.' Gina's indignant talk of the apparent dominance of men's 'rights' challenges law to fulfil its own stated objective of putting children first.

That contact disputes are seen as battles in a sex war should perhaps not be surprising because contact is seen by parents of both sexes as being about parenting, and parenting remains a strongly gendered activity. The law's gender neutrality ascribes equal value to mothering and fathering, and thereby effectively silences talk about gender politics in the legal arena. ...

Mothers often feel that the legal system favours fathers, but fathers feel equally aggrieved. James, for example, averred that 'the whole judiciary is biased in favour of women'. Welfare professionals too were seen as biased. Harry asserted that the Court Welfare Officers were 'only interested in the mother's point of view'. And in Charlie's opinion, 'the politics of social work is about abusing men'.

...

Good mothers

For some mothers, resistance to contact presents them with a dilemma: how can they be seen by the courts and professionals to be 'good' mothers, 'doing the right thing', whilst at the same time opposing contact? Such is the power of the welfare discourse that many mothers appear to accept that contact can, in principle, be good for children. But practice is a very different matter from principle. Some mothers find that the emphasis on contact exists in profound and continual tension with their own need to break free altogether from the past, from a failed or even abusive relationship, and from the former partner. For these mothers, the meaning of the welfare discourse takes shape against a background of their own practical and emotional needs. The tension thus created can be resolved in creative ways, for example, by reconceptualising the child's interests. Cora, for example, re-phrased what she wanted in terms of her child's interests: 'I want to go forward. I don't want to go backward. For my child's sake, I don't want to go back to that kind of life any more'. By framing her preferences for the future in the language of welfare, Cora positioned herself as a good mother whilst actually resisting contact.

...

These mothers were acknowledging the dominance of the welfare discourse whilst they simultaneously challenged it. ... While they subscribed to these general tenets of welfare, these mothers conceived of their particular children's welfare in ways that precluded contact. Their resistance to contact was achieved by invoking the welfare discourse, but making their own interpretations of it.

Distinguishing the 'bad' father

Fathers, too, positioned themselves as 'good' parents by acknowledging dominant norms and by operating within the welfare discourse. But, in contrast with mothers, they tended to find – as we might expect – that those norms supported their arguments. Within the dominant discourse, contact between non-resident fathers and children is seen to be crucial to children's well-being. To warrant description as 'bad', fathers must have behaved in exceptionally callous or irresponsible ways. On the other hand, the qualifications for being a 'good' father are not very onerous.

The fathers in our study held views consistent with the dominant discourse; they felt that, provided they had not conducted themselves badly, their standing as good fathers should be accorded recognition in the form of contact orders. Those who had been accused of acting in ways that they knew might be open to criticism were careful to deny the allegations or to minimise or normalise their conduct.

...

These fathers, then, seek to position themselves as good parents by normalising and minimising their conduct, so distancing themselves from images of cruel abusers or deadbeat dads.

Reading source

Kaganas and Day Sclater, 2004, pp. 16–20

Comment

1   Mothers and fathers commonly construct legal disputes over children following divorce or separation in terms of a 'battle of the sexes', though for different reasons. Mothers are convinced that parenting remains a deeply gendered practice, and that the practices of motherhood and fatherhood are not equivalent. The authors go on to discuss how mothers feel that the gender-neutral stance on parenting taken by the courts ignores their gendered experiences of pre- and post-divorce family life. Research suggests that, for mothers, the gendering of family occurs in relation to caregiving activities, for which women continue to assume a primary role. Fathers also think that gender is a salient layer of meaning in parental disputes, and many feel that the legal discourse favours women and marginalises men. Research suggests that, for men, issues of gender touch not on 'care', but on questions of 'justice and rights', including a discourse that emphasises children's 'rights' to see their fathers.

2   Mothers and fathers seek to resolve the tensions between their own gendered meanings and the prescriptions of the gender-neutral discourse by appropriating the terms of that discourse to their own ends. They each seek to convince the court that they are a 'good' parent by couching their own desires in terms of the 'best interests of the child'.

You will have noticed in this example, as in the earlier extract relating to step-families, that the dynamic discursive activity around parenting and parent–child relationships often occurs to the exclusion of a broader concept of 'family'. Indeed, it is interesting to note how discourses of parenting can become detached from more general discourses of family yet, at the same time, reinforce notions of family through ideas and images that are implicit in the discourse. In the two examples that we have discussed in some detail, powerful images and ideas of family may be discernible even where the discourse in question does not specifically refer to 'family'. On the other hand, discourses of parenting can encompass diverse sets of relationships and household formations, and such discourses may thus challenge implicit meanings of family, thus framing parenting in ways that do not necessarily tie it into a discourse of 'family'.

The dominant welfare discourse in family law prescribes how 'good' parents ought to behave: they should be amicable with each other, even when separated, and must put their own feelings aside 'for the sake of the children'. Further, both biological parents should be involved in active parenting. But these prescriptions for parenting are underpinned by ideas about what families should be doing: families ideally are bastions of morality and bulwarks against a range of worrying social ills. In social policy, families can be seen as the arena where social ills germinate – and hence where they can be put right. Discourses and practices of parenting, therefore, derive from and feed into those of 'family' that, in turn, derive their meanings from wider social concerns about morality, social cohesion, social exclusion, youth, and crime. But as individual mothers and fathers appropriate the dominant discourse for their own ends, we can see a range of alternative discourses embodying different images of family under construction.

Thus discourses of welfare, parenting, and family are linked, and can be mutually reinforcing, but they are not the same. 'Family' constitutes another whole dimension beyond parenthood, and the discourses and practices that shape each are different. But beyond that difference, is an interdependence – an *intertextuality* – whereby talk and activities around parenthood can set in train broader images of family, and vice versa. In this way, discourses and practices of any aspect of family have implications for the variable meanings of family we construct in different contexts.

Our analysis of family discourse has highlighted the crucial significance of language, but discourses are also highly significant for concrete practices, shaping and expressing the meanings that material objects, bodies, physical spaces, and technologies hold for people. Family as discourse is deeply interrelated with material experiences, and in the next section, we focus more specifically on family practices.

3 Family practices

3.1 Why family practices?

In the previous section, we saw how a focus on discourse can provide insights into the ways in which family meanings are produced and reproduced, or resisted and challenged. Crucially, we saw that discourses would remain just words unless people engaged with them. This recognition that it is breathing, passionate, embodied human agents that continually make and remake families leads to the notion that it is 'family practices' that are crucially important.

This concept was developed by the family sociologist David H.J. Morgan in 1996 to address the limitations of earlier social scientific approaches that portrayed 'the family' as a static category. The concept draws attention to activities and processes of interaction and sees 'family' as continually created and recreated through everyday practices. Val Gillies (2003, p. 8) summarises Morgan's contribution succinctly: 'Morgan drew attention to the way everyday activities constitute family experience, reframing family as something you do rather than something you are'.

In the extract you will focus on in the next activity, David Morgan outlines his theory of family practices.

Activity 5.6

Read the extract below and answer these questions:

1   Can you suggest a definition of family practices, based on Morgan's discussion?

2   Can you explain why Morgan seems to shy away from the idea that we abandon talk of 'family' altogether?

Reading 5.5   David Morgan, 'Family practices'

In place of an approach which defined a clear object of study – 'the family' – ... I [have] argued for something much more open. In this alternative approach, family was seen as less of a noun and more of an adjective or, possibly, a verb. 'Family' represents a constructed quality of human interaction or an active process rather than a thing-like object of detached social investigation. ... My approach was to see 'family' as being rather like a primary colour, interesting in itself in a somewhat limited way, but achieving its real significance in combination, undergoing repeated variation, with other colours. ...

At the same time, the continuing use of the word 'family', albeit in a somewhat transformed way, recognises the fact that 'family', however conceived, is still a matter of some importance for large sections of the population. ... To abandon talk of 'family' altogether would be to deny the realities of these experiences and the importance which social actors assigned to them.

In very general terms the use of the term 'practices' is intended to convey a range of related themes:

1   A sense of interplay between the perspectives of the social actor, the individual whose actions are being described and accounted for, and the perspectives of the observer. The addition of the latter to the former serves as a reminder that there are, potentially, a range of different perspectives, interpretations or understandings available. ...

2   A sense of the active rather than the passive or static. Whatever the topic, the emphasis is upon doing class, doing gender, doing family. ...

3   A focus on the everyday. With practices we are concerned with the relatively routine or trivial, not necessarily to the exclusion of more weighty matters but rather in the realisation that it is often in the routine or the trivial that some of the wider concerns are understood or constructed. ...

4   A stress on regularities. ... [M]any of the regularities with which we are concerned constitute part of the everyday taken-for-granted worlds of the social actors concerned. ...

5   A sense of fluidity. Practices ... flow into other practices of the same kind or mix with other practices that might be differently described. Thus a family outing might consist of a variety of different family practices while also blending with gendered practices, leisure practices and so on.

6   An interplay between history and biography. ... [P]ractices have a societal and an historical dimension ... For example, 'family outings' are part of the interwoven life courses of individuals but are also located in a wider historical framework to do with the development of leisure, transportation and shifting constructions of parenthood and childhood.

Reading source

Morgan, 1999, pp. 16–21

Comment

1   Definitions of family practices, based on Morgan's discussion, might include 'family practices are what make family' or 'families are as families do'.

2   Morgan stops short of abandoning talk of 'family' altogether because he recognises that it has a continuing significance for many people. For example, as you discovered in Chapter 3, 'family' tends to have connotations of belonging and entitlement as well as, for better or worse, an emotional significance that other ideas (such as 'intimacy' or 'personal life' that we discuss in the next chapter) do not seem fully to capture.

In the chapter from which I have taken the reading, Morgan goes on to ask what work the word 'family' does in 'family practices'. What is a 'family practice'? What makes it 'family'?

Family practices, he says, are wide ranging and includes all those practices that are constructed as being about family, which of course will differ according to each individual standpoint.

If you pause for a moment to reflect on your own life you might easily bring to mind the sorts of things that count for you as family practices. For me, family practices include family holidays; when the children were small we went 'as a family' to a remote Welsh farmhouse. Family holidays were 'family time' and the only rule was that we all did things together. We played Monopoly and made Welshcakes and trudged, heads down, wellies on, across hillsides of horizontal rain, determined to have a good time. The possibilities for learning from reflection about what counts to you as a family practice are limitless.

Figure 5.2
Birthday
celebrations
are family
practices

Morgan identifies three sources for the construction of family practices: first, the social actors themselves – the parents, spouses, children and kin – who see their activities as having something to do with family. Secondly, there are institutions and agencies – including professionals, journalists, legislators and policy-makers, TV producers and film makers, and religious leaders – who provide the cultural resources upon which family members may draw. Finally, the construction of family practices also involves an observer – in Morgan's case, a sociologist – who observes, describes and theorises family practices and whose meanings may filter back reflexively into the social world she or he is observing.

Morgan (1999, p. 19) also reminds us that ideas and practices relating to family carry emotional 'baggage': 'family practices are not just any old practices; they are also practices which matter to the persons concerned and which are seen in some way as being 'special' ... [I]n family matters ... we are dealing with love and hate, attraction and repulsion, approval and disapproval'. You will, no doubt encounter a range of emotions when exploring your own personal reflections on family!

In 2011, in *Rethinking Family Practices*, Morgan revisits the idea of 'family practices'. He explores its range of meanings and discusses how the idea might be developed to enhance our understanding of family life and its place within wider social settings. He locates family practices within a broader sociological discussion and considers how other researchers have used, extended and critiqued the idea.

Morgan addresses four main areas of criticism: First, the benefits and limitations of the continued use of the term 'family'; for example, whether it implies and therefore normalises heterosexuality. Secondly, whether the idea of family practices underplays the influence of broader social factors, such as structural constraint and historical context. Thirdly, whether the original idea of family practices sufficiently emphasises the importance of discourse. Finally, the need to acknowledge the darker sides of family life and to recognise that some family practices are harmful, or even lethal. We will return to this point in Chapter 9.

Morgan also explores some emergent themes in sociological inquiry – Time and Space; the Body; Emotion; the 'Ethical Turn' – that he finds especially helpful in developing the idea of family practices. What emerges from Morgan's new discussion is a greater emphasis on social context; family practices have particular meanings in specific socio-cultural milieux, and, as has been suggested in this chapter, practices both shape and are shaped by their dynamic relationships with discourses.

3.2 Families are what families do: the example of family leisure

In this section, we consider family leisure as an example of 'family practices'. Research by Jane Ribbens (1994) into childrearing practices indicates that family leisure is not just 'fun' but has a wider significance: it contributes to the creation of 'family' as a cohesive group. Parents imbue family leisure pursuits – whether theme-park outings, restaurant meals, or playing board games at home – with a deep significance, seeing them as constitutive of a desired 'family life'. Such is the moral and emotional significance with which parents invest these practices, that not having the time, the inclination or the energy to pursue them can seem tantamount to being a 'bad' parent. These moral evaluations indicate there are discourses of family at work framing the context for the family practices.

In the next reading, Susan Shaw discusses how discourses and practices of family leisure are informed by, and contribute to, dominant discourses of parenthood and, ultimately, of 'family'.

Activity 5.7

Read the extract. Pay particular attention to the two-way relationships between discourses and practices. How do family leisure practices contribute to the production and reproduction of normative discourses of parenthood and of family?

Reading 5.6   Susan Shaw, 'Family leisure and "good" parenting'

Parents are clearly the targets of the public scrutiny and recipients of the media messages about 'good' parenting behaviours. Thus, the experiences and meanings of parenthood will be influenced by these discourses. At the same time, parental practices and patterns of daily life, including caregiving practices and responsibilities, family time and patterns of interaction among family members, also contribute to changing ideas and beliefs about motherhood and fatherhood. One area of family life that has received relatively little attention in the academic literature is that of family leisure, including everyday activities, as well as special events such as family vacations. Family leisure, though, may be an increasingly important part of family life that both reflects and contributes to changing ideas and beliefs about parenthood, about the gendered nature of parenthood and about the meaning of family. ...

...

It is evident from several studies ... that many parents take their responsibility for family leisure very seriously. Whereas parents in previous generations might have told their children to 'go outside and play' on weekends, school holidays or during the early evening hours, today's parents take on a much more active, and deliberate parenting role. For them, family time is something that needs to be planned, organised and 'constructed' so that it has a particular value or quality. ... Both mothers and fathers talk about the 'critical importance' of children spending time with their parents and doing activities together such as playing games, going for walks or bike rides or going out for dinner as a family. ...

...

The initial commitment to family leisure for parents, and the importance parents attach to family activities, relates to the benefits that these activities are seen to provide for the children ... Activities, outings and vacations are typically selected, organised and managed for the sake of the children. However, this is done not simply in terms of whether the children are expected to enjoy the activities ... but also what the children will learn or gain from their participation.

One common consideration is physical activity, health and healthy lifestyles ... Mothers' roles as they see it, is to encourage their children to be active and to enjoy and value physical activity ... One important way to accomplish this is seen to be for the whole family – parents and children – to participate together in outdoor and active pursuits on a regular basis.

Another consideration is the importance of children learning to get along with others ... It is through family activities, and doing things together that parents try to help children get along well with their siblings and to solve conflicts without resorting to arguments and 'fights' ...

Many parents ... also place emphasis on the role that family leisure plays in teaching children about 'values'. The idea of values is sometimes articulated by parents in terms of children learning about honesty and ethical behaviour through their participation in family activities. But a more common usage of the term relates to children learning about 'the family' as a value and the importance of family togetherness. In this sense, the purpose of family leisure is not simply something that is done for the sake of the children and/or to enhance child development, but also for the sake of the family as a whole and for shared family ideals and family cohesion. ... Family leisure is seen as a way to 'cement' relationships and ensure the stability of the family unit.

...

The purposive nature of family leisure and the high valuations and expectations associated with positive family experiences raise, of course, the possibility of disappointment. ... When family activities and vacation experiences are deemed by parents to be a 'success' ... a strong sense of satisfaction and accomplishment is experienced. However, positive experiences and outcomes are not always achievable ...

... Parents can easily provide examples of difficult, distressing or even disastrous family events. For example, parents often talk about events being 'ruined' or 'horrible'. These negative experiences sometimes result from bad weather or long travel, but more often the problems mentioned are associated with children's behaviours, such as bickering or fighting with siblings, or being demanding and difficult. ...Significantly, though, a common response from parents to 'negative' experiences is not to give up, but rather a determination to try harder in the future. ...

In many ways family leisure reflects the dominant discourse of parenthood, with its focus on the needs of the child and the importance of active parental involvement. ...

...

In addition to family leisure as a refection of parenting discourses, family activities clearly play a role in the reinforcement and reproduction of ideologies associated with parenthood as well. Family leisure, for example, reinforces the ideal of active, involved parenthood. And it adds to this idea by suggesting that parents need to be involved in every aspect of their children's lives, including their children's 'free time'. ... In addition, parental involvement in and control over family leisure and family vacations can be seen as important processes through which ideologies of the family are constructed and reconstructed. These processes of social construction include reinforcement of traditional notions of the two-parent, heterosexual families with children, as well as more recent ideals about involved fatherhood.

Reading source

Shaw, 2008, pp. 1–2, 6–9, 11–13

Comment

In this extract Shaw suggests that family leisure practices both reflect and help construct the dominant discourses of parenthood. These interviews are with parents who are living together, and discourses of parenting and of family overlap. Shaw analyses parenting practices and family values separately but sees them as mutually reinforcing. She discusses how they contribute to the production and reproduction of broader social norms about family. Family leisure activities, she argues, are not pursued primarily for fun, but are almost a duty; they are part and parcel of what 'good' parents are expected to do for their children, to enhance their developmental chances as well as to instil in the children a strong sense of family togetherness and to foster family values. In this sense, organising and managing family leisure time and activities has become one of the responsibilities of parenthood, where notions of parenthood are informed by broader discourses of family, and vice versa.

Figure 5.3

A mother watches her family enjoying a board game

Shaw also reminds us that family leisure activities, like other family practices, are replete with tensions. First, there is the contradiction between the ideal and the reality. The high value attached to positive leisure experiences can make it difficult for parents to make sense of negative experiences. When it is not possible to reframe those experiences and give them new meanings, parents may see themselves as having failed in some way. Secondly, there is a contradiction between leisure as free time and the work involved in setting it up for the family and making it effective.

Normative expectations around parenting mean that this work is rendered invisible. Furthermore, parents are likely to participate in family leisure at the expense of their own 'personal' leisure. Shaw found that mothers in particular are likely to conflate their personal leisure with children's activities.

We might pause for a moment to consider this question of 'the personal', since it is an issue we take up further in Chapter 6. An interesting issue is the extent to which 'the personal' may be considered to be separate from 'family' matters. Any feeling of entitlement to 'personal' space, or time for ourselves that we may have, derives from an individualist perspective; not everyone subscribes to the liberal ideal of the 'autonomous individual' and, for many people, 'personal life' will overlap with, if not wholly incorporate, family life. (You will return to these issues in the next two chapters.)

In the reading we also come back to the ways in which social power is implicated in the patterning of family. Shaw's participants were middle class, and the experiences of families with fewer resources of time and money could well be different. Those who cannot afford to participate in family leisure practices risk being marginalised or excluded. Family leisure thus reflects and constructs different meanings of 'family' in the context of people's different and unequal life experiences.

In Shaw's study, family leisure, like other family practices, was also gendered in significant ways. Elsewhere in her paper Shaw shows us that, although in many two-parent families both parents typically participate in family leisure activities, there is much 'hidden' behind-the-scenes work (such as planning, scheduling, organising, packing, clearing up) that falls primarily on women. There is also evidence that mothers do more of the emotional work associated with family life. Shaw suggests that these inequalities perhaps account for the sense of exhaustion that many mothers express when even thinking about family activities. This reminds us that, when we are thinking through the complexities of family meanings, we must not lose sight of the patterning of meaning that occurs as a result of power relationships and structural inequalities.

Further, as Morgan reminds us, whilst we recognise the significance of practices in constituting families and reproducing 'family', we must also not lose sight of the fact that we also use practices to resist, challenge and undermine the dominant images and forms. For example, Professor of sociology, Jeffrey Weeks and his colleagues have reported on the changing discourses and practices that are permitting gay and lesbian people to construct 'families of choice'. These not only challenge the boundaries of 'family' but also resist the cultural privileging of heterosexuality: 'These non-heterosexual discourses of family and of choice, of care and responsibility, of love and loss, of old needs and new possibilities, of difference and convergence, are prime examples of those everyday experiments which are contributing to the creation of the "new family"' (Weeks et al., 1999, p. 99). Indeed, Weeks and his colleagues refer to '*the* lesbian and gay family' which makes quite a clear statement that they regard the concept of 'family' as being sufficiently fluid as to have some continuing value.

Finally, as social researchers Ochs and Kremer-Sadlik remind us, morality is also embedded in, and is an outcome of, everyday family practices. 'The flow of social interactions involving children,' they argue, 'is imbued with implicit and explicit messages about right and wrong, better and worse, rules, norms, obligations, duties, etiquette, moral reasoning, virtue, character, and other dimensions of how to lead a moral life' (2007, p. 5). Thus, like discourses, parenting and family practices are far from neutral: they have meanings that resonate through layers of social, political and ethical concerns. You will return to these important issues in Chapter 9.

Figure 5.4

Posing for a family photograph: another widespread family practice

Activity 5.8

You might now like to draw on our discussions in this chapter to reflect more broadly on some of your own experiences. How do you see discourses and practices expressing and shaping particular notions of family in your own life? You might, for example, identify various discourses in newspaper articles, or policy statements, or you can find them embedded in films or TV programmes, or magazines or adverts – in short, wherever there is talk, text or image you could look for discourses that help construct particular notions of family. Examples of family practices that you might focus on include breakfast, a birthday party, family snaps, Sunday afternoons, or even just the washing up. Or you might find it interesting to reflect on some childhood memories of past family practices. You could use these to think about how the family discourses and practices you encountered in childhood – your own, and those of other people you knew – have helped to shape the ideas of family that seem the most meaningful to you now.

Do you notice how memories of those discourses and practices invoke particular feelings? It is often when emotions become harnessed to particular ways of thinking and doing family that things acquire the special qualities we associate with 'family'.

You might like to take this one step further and think abut the ways in which feelings impinge, for better or worse, on family meanings. As has been emphasised throughout this book, family meanings are complex and often replete with tensions and contradictions. Some family issues are emotionally poignant or even extremely painful – for example, violence, child abuse, or incest – and consequently can be difficult or even impossible to talk about, or sometimes even to think about. Some issues are impossible to make sense of because of the lack of availability of discursive frameworks – issues prompted by advances in reproductive and genetic technologies might be cases in point. Whilst writing this chapter, I listened to a radio debate about the ethics of creating so-called 'saviour siblings' and it was clear that people on all sides of this emotive debate were thrashing around trying to find ways to make sense of the new possibilities that reproductive and genetic technologies have created. It is as though family discourses and practices have been taken by surprise and are struggling to catch up with technological advances. What I noticed was that raw emotion seemed to be taking the place of rational debate. Can you think of some family practices that are difficult to make sense of, perhaps because they are too emotive, or perhaps because of a lack of suitable discursive frameworks?

Summary

Here are the key points about family discourse that have emerged from our discussion:

■ 'Family' is constructed in discourse and so images and ideas of family carry particular systematised meanings within them.

- At any time, it is always possible to find a range of competing discourses that construct family in different ways, but not all have equal authority.

- Some dominant discourses of family are particularly powerful: legal discourses, and those tied to institutions and professional practices in the welfare sector are examples.

- Despite the way in which dominant discourses can colonise thought, people are not passive recipients of discursive power, but active negotiators of meaning. Even legal discourses can be challenged and subverted.

- Discourses can perpetuate inequalities and result in the marginalisation, exclusion or oppression of some families or some family members.

- Discourses of family carry expectations and values and are underpinned by political and moral agendas.

Here are some key points about family practices that we have covered in this chapter:

- People are breathing, passionate and embodied and it is they who make family through their activities.

- 'Family' is something people do rather than something that they are.

- 'Family practices' are all those practices that are about family, which differs from person to person.

- Family practices *matter* to people; they have an emotional significance.

- Family practices and family discourses are linked; practices both reflect and help construct discourses of family, and vice versa.

- Like discourses, family practices can reflect and perpetuate inequalities.

- Family practices are actively chosen, and can support, challenge or resist dominant images.

- As with family discourses, moralities are also embedded in family practices.

4   Conclusions

In this chapter, we have considered two main theoretical frameworks for approaching the study of family meanings. In the first section, we focused on discourse, and discussed how family, as a meaningful social object, can be said to be constructed in discourse. We saw that a range of discourses impact on family meanings, including those that do not specifically refer to 'family'. Discourses of parenting were the examples that we focused on, but there are others – for example, those around childhood, or ageing, or sexualities, or 'home' – that also influence and are influenced by family meanings.

We considered the complex relationships between discourse and power, and discussed how inequalities shape the patterning of family meanings. Our focus was on gender, but social class, ethnicity, sexuality, disability and age are other dimensions of difference that are constructed in discourses and impact on family meanings.

We considered the ways in which discourses can be highly influential in structuring the social world as well as our experiences of it. But equally we stressed that discourses do not determine social life in any simplistic way. Rather, although some discourses (particularly those that derive from or are backed up by institutional power) may be more dominant, alternative or counter discourses do emerge thus providing the possibility of social change.

In the second section, we considered family practices and their interdependence with discourse. Based on research that focused on family leisure, we explored the complex links among family practices, discourses of parenting, and the patterning of family meanings, and the ambivalent emotions that those meanings depend upon and invoke.

So far in this book, you have discovered that 'family' is a concept that carries rather a lot of what I have called 'baggage'. You have seen that it's impossible to pin down any precise meaning for family. As 'family' lacks a precise definition, it remains necessarily vague. As we have discussed in this chapter 'family' inhabits, and is inhabited by, a diverse range of discourses – sometimes including even those, like discourses of parenthood, that don't make any explicit reference to 'family' at all. It is because of its inherent vagueness that 'family' is able to take on the diverse qualities that it does, as well as invoke its many connotations. You might think of 'family' as having a chameleon-like quality when it comes to discourse.

Discourses of family are many and variable, and they do change (as you will see in Chapter 7). 'Family', for example since the UK Civil Partnership Act 2004, now officially includes same-sex couples. Whether same-sex couples themselves would choose to describe themselves in terms of 'family' is another matter! The Act makes civil partnerships equivalent to marriage, and amends other family legislation so that same-sex partnerships are no longer excluded from its provisions. For example, the law relating to family provision and the administration of estates on death is extended to include gay and lesbian families; the Children Act 1989 is amended to bring children in civil partnerships within the definition of 'children of the family'; and the provisions of the Family Law Act 1996 concerning family homes and domestic violence are amended to include gay and lesbian families. The Civil Partnership Act is a good example of how even dominant discourses of family (in this case, heterosexuality and marriage) can alter to incorporate a greater diversity of family practices.

Over the years, as we have seen in this book, social scientists have been concerned about the ways in which ideas of 'family' served to normalise some domestic arrangements, and to marginalise, or silence, or stigmatise, others. Many looked for more inclusive concepts of family, but others regarded the whole notion of 'family' as possibly too problematic. They looked beyond family for other concepts that could capture significant aspects of relationships and domestic lives without being bogged down by the exclusiveness or the baggage that the concept of 'family' had come to carry. It is in this context that our focus on 'intimacies' and 'personal lives' in the next chapter is situated.

References

Edwards, R., Gillies, V. and Ribbens McCarthy, J. (1999) 'Biological parents and social families: legal discourses and everyday understandings of the position of step-patrents' in Cheal, D (ed.) *Family: Critical Concepts in Sociology*, London, Routledge.

Gillies, V. (2003) *Family and Intimate Relationships: A Review of the Sociological Research* [online], London, Families & Social Capital ESRC Research Group, South Bank University, http://www.lsbu.ac.uk/families/workingpapers/familieswp2.pdf (Accessed 4 June 2008).

Kaganas, F. and Day Sclater, S. (2004) 'Contact disputes: narrative constructions of 'good' parents', *Feminist Legal Studies*, vol. 12, no. 1, pp. 1–27.

Morgan, D.H.J. (1996) *Family Connections*, Cambridge, Polity Press.

Morgan, D.H.J. (1999) 'Risk and family practices: accounting for change and fluidity in family life' in Silva, E.B. and Smart, C. (eds) *The New Family?*, London, Sage.

Morgan, D.H.J. (2011) *Rethinking Family Practices*, Basingstoke, Palgrave Macmillan.

Ochs, E. and Kremer-Sadlik, T. (2007) 'Morality as family practice', *Discourse and Society,* vol. 18, no. 1, pp. 5–10.

Ribbens, J. (1994) *Mothers and their Children: A Feminist Sociology of Childrearing*, London, Sage.

Rose, N. (1987) 'Beyond the public/private division: Law, power and the family', *Journal of Law and Society*, vol. 14, no. 1, pp. 61–76.

Shaw, S.M. (2008) 'Family leisure and changing ideologies of parenthood', *Sociology Compass*, vol. 2, pp. 1–16.

Weeks, J., Donovan, C. and Heaphy, B. (1999) 'Everyday experiments: narratives of non-heterosexual relationships' in Silva, E.B. and Smart, C. (eds) *The New Family?*, London, Sage, pp. 83–99.

Chapter 6

Intimacy and personal life

Shelley Day Sclater

Contents

1   Introduction

In Chapter 5, we discussed two theoretical perspectives that brought new insights into our study of family meanings: family discourses and family practices. We saw that the language of 'family' carried a good deal of moral, political and emotional 'baggage'. This has led some social scientists to search for a new language to validate other ways of living that are meaningful to people but are not captured by the term 'family'. Might there be other more flexible – or less emotive – concepts that capture significant aspects of our lives and relationships without becoming bogged down in the trappings of 'family'?

In this chapter, we introduce two such concepts – 'intimacy' and 'personal life'. We explore how far these concepts shift our focus away from 'family', and ask whether either 'intimacy' or 'personal life' can be used to enrich, or possibly replace, the language of 'family'. In the first part of the chapter, we focus on intimacy, and in the second part, on personal life.

2   From 'family' to 'intimacy' and 'personal life'

So far, you have discovered that the concept of 'family' has a multiplicity of meanings. Social scientists have struggled to make sense of the changes and continuities in 'family' as well as the diversities that seem to characterise families in the early twenty-first century. The powerful concept of 'family' exerts a normative influence, but it fails to capture adequately the wide range of living arrangements and relationships that people count as meaningful. The concept of 'intimacy' represents one attempt to address this limitation.

In her detailed review of sociological work on intimacy, Val Gillies (2003) suggests that 'intimacy' is a field of study of our significant relationships that has 'colonised' (i.e. taken over and dominated) topics previously viewed through the lens of 'family'. Much theorising about intimacy (for example, the work of prominent social theorists Anthony Giddens and Ulrich Beck) is closely linked with broader theories of social change such as 'globalisation' (with a consequent emphasis on diversity) and 'individualism' (with an emphasis on the importance for individuals of self-fulfilment). Individualism, as a social philosophy, favours freedom of action for individuals over collective or state control. In the context of these broad themes, social scientists have theorised about changes in family patterns, relationships and meanings, and have embraced a concept of 'intimacy' that seems to capture diverse contemporary ways of being more effectively. However, Gillies argues that the extent of such change and its impacts on 'family' may have been overstated. This is because theorists have focused on changes to the neglect of continuities, and equated intimacy with sexual relationships, to the neglect of other close relationships, such as those between parents and children, and friendships.

Some social scientists have argued that we need a new language to validate a wider range of significant relationships and living arrangements, whilst others have sought to make the term 'family' more inclusive. Jeffrey Weeks and his co-workers, for example, advocate a continuing engagement with the language of 'family' as a political project.

In the extract you will look at in the following activity, Shelley Budgeon and Sacha Roseneil summarise succinctly the main issue in these debates.

Activity 6.1

In the reading you will see that Beck refers to 'the family' as 'dead and still alive'. What do Budgeon and Roseneil see as the central issue?

Reading 6.1 Shelley Budgeon and Sacha Roseneil, 'What is happening to "the family"?'

In the West, at the start of the 21st century, 'the family' is a sociological concept under severe strain. Processes of individualization are rendering the romantic dyad [i.e. the couple] and the modern family formation it supported increasingly unstable, and the normative grip of the gender and sexual order which has underpinned the modern family is ever weakening. As a result more and more people are spending longer periods of their lives outside the conventional family unit.

Recognizing these tendencies, Ulrich Beck ... has recently, rather provocatively, described the family as a 'zombie category' – 'dead and still alive'. The weight of opinion within the discipline of sociology might well disagree with Beck on this, given the effort which has been expended researching the ways in which the category lives on in changed and diversified forms – lone-parent families, stepfamilies, lesbian and gay 'families of choice' ... , 'brave new families' ... The move by family sociologists to pluralize the concept, to speak of 'families' rather than 'the family', emphasises the 'still alive-ness' of the category, and seeks to maintain attention on family practices ... While we would not wish to deny the ways in which the family remains a central social institution and a key trope in the cultural imaginary, ... we aim here to address the ways in which the category of the family is increasingly failing to contain the multiplicity of practices of intimacy and care which have traditionally been its prerogative and its raison d'être.

Reading source

Budgeon and Roseneil, 2004, p. 127

Comment

Budgeon and Roseneil point to a key dilemma: 'family' remains central to our thinking and the discourse of family is powerful, yet the category 'family' is inadequate to encompass the many and various intimate practices that constitute our lives and relationships.

As this extract suggests, social scientists have increasingly focused on the usefulness – or otherwise – of concepts of 'family'. This issue is particularly significant in the context of debates about broader social change, as well as more specific issues that touch on 'family' (for example, patterns of gender relations, relationship practices and how we organise our personal lives).

Our main concern in this chapter is to see what happens when we 'decentre' the language of family. In order to do this, we will consider how social scientists have challenged the confines of 'family' and have sought to find a language to explore relationships that go beyond it. Whilst you are working through this chapter, it may be useful to keep these guiding questions in mind:

1   How useful are concepts of 'intimacy' and 'personal life' for exploring family meanings?

2   What do we gain and what do we lose when we use concepts of 'intimacy' and 'personal life' in place of 'family?'

3   Should we retain the concept of 'family' or abandon it?

We will return to these questions later on in the chapter.

Figure 6.1
The concept of intimacy often suggests a close physical relationship

3 Intimacies

In her comprehensive review of the sociological work on intimacies, Val Gillies says that 'the phrase "intimate relationship" is a broad and fluid term, in that it can encompass numerous different associations between friends, sexual partners, family and kin' (2003, p. 3). You will notice in this quote that Gillies links 'intimacy' with 'relationships'. Similarly, in her book *Intimacy*, Lynn Jamieson captures some fluidity of meaning when she adopts a pragmatic description: intimacy, she says, constitutes practices of 'close association, familiarity and privileged knowledge' which involve 'strong positive emotional attachments'; 'a very particular form of "closeness"'... associated with high levels of trust' (1998, p. 189). You might have noticed here that Jamieson highlights the importance of 'practices' (which we discussed in Chapter 5) and also emotional attachments.

Neither Gillies nor Jamieson include the possibility of intimacy with strangers in their definitions of the term but, as we discuss later in the chapter, 'intimacy' as a concept can embrace a wide variety of interactions. As you saw in Chapter 5, acknowledging difference and diversity in family patterns and structures – including lone-parent families, stepfamilies, families of choice, and so on – evinces an ongoing reconfiguration of 'family'; at the same time, this reconfiguration testifies to the continuing significance of 'family' as a social unit or network of significant others. On the other hand, there are those within social science who propose that a much wider range of personal relationships (including, for example, non-co-residential intimate partnerships, friendships, or household communities) are important in providing intimacy, care and companionship – practices that have often been associated with 'family'.

In 1992, in his book *The Transformation of Intimacy,* prominent social theorist Anthony Giddens first brought together issues of broader social change and the meanings and patterns of 'family', with a new focus on 'intimacy' His work has been highly influential in sparking off debates and generating research. One of the main issues that has arisen from this research is the extent to which Giddens' model of intimacy corresponds with contemporary experiences. Later in the chapter we discuss some empirical work that addresses that question. But first, it will be helpful to summarise the main points of the model:

- Intimate partnerships are now more a matter of personal choice than of duty or expectation.

- The most important dimension of contemporary partnerships is their relational (interpersonal and emotional) aspect.

- Partners now expect equality, sharing and companionship.

- Partners expect satisfaction and self-fulfilment from their relationships.

- Sexuality is something we all have a right to enjoy.

Figure 6.2
There are
many forms
of intimacy

- Having or not having children is a matter of personal choice.

- We no longer need a long-term partner to become a parent, and the former links among sex, marriage and reproduction have become more permeable.

- Cohabitation, both short and long term, is increasingly common whether as a prelude to, or as a substitute for, marriage.

Giddens argues that the meanings and practices of intimacy are changing, and he sees 'romantic love' as being replaced by the less stable and more contingent 'confluent love'. By referring to 'confluent' love, Giddens is suggesting that contemporary partnerships lack the 'forever' quality of romantic love; instead, a commitment to the relationship will last only as long as the relationship continues to satisfy. Confluent love, he says, approximates an ideal type – what he calls the 'pure' relationship. Giddens sees sex and gender as being at the heart of his 'transformation of intimacy', since the changes he suggests are happening in the meanings and practices of intimacy, both fuel and are fuelled by changing gender relations. Ideals of romantic love – which were always 'skewed' in gender terms – he argues, have fragmented under the pressure of women's demands for autonomy (1992, p. 62). Because of a new ideal of emotional give-and-take, men are increasingly under pressures to become aware of their emotional dependence and to admit vulnerability. Therefore, Giddens sees that older forms of femininity and masculinity are giving way to newer, more open and more equal configurations. He also sees 'confluent love' as more egalitarian in another way: namely, it does not presume a heterosexual partnership.

Giddens' thesis has profound implications for how we understand 'family'. He argues that our closest intimate relationships, once founded on romantic love, are becoming more pragmatic. He sees gender relations as becoming more equal, and sexualities as becoming more open and subject to greater tolerance. Thus the consequences of the 'pure relationship' and the ideas that underpin it challenge several traditional conceptions and beliefs about family:

■ its assumptions about gender roles

■ its assumption of heterosexuality

■ its incorporation of practices based on duty or a sense of obligation. In contrast, the practices of the 'pure' relationship are based on voluntary commitment and personal choice.

A central feature of the 'pure' relationship is that it is based on a new openness to each other, a sharing of emotional closeness, and an acknowledgment of need and vulnerability, and mutual disclosure – in short, what Jamieson calls 'disclosing intimacy'. Taken together, these features of the 'pure' relationship suggest quite a different pattern of intimacy than that which is usually invoked by 'family'.

It is important to recognise, however, that Giddens presents a particular version of 'intimacy' that is focused on intimate relationships between adults. Others would wish to work with a broader concept of intimacy, and would focus on a wider range of intimacy practices. In this broader view, the intimacies of everyday life would include the routine practices of looking after bodies from birth to death; for example, sharing food, cleaning up, caring for the frail and the sick, washing and bathing, and so on. A practice such as brushing someone's hair could count as an intimate act. The significance of caring practices is something we'll return to later in the chapter.

A further point to note is that there is only scant empirical evidence to support Giddens' vision of contemporary intimacy; the 'pure' relationship based on 'disclosing intimacy' remains an ideal that may never be realised fully in practice.

In the extract in the next activity, which is taken from her book *Intimacy*, Lynn Jamieson reflects on how far the concept of 'disclosing intimacy' captures people's personal experiences.

Activity 6.2

Why do you think Jamieson seems unconvinced that 'disclosing intimacy' is a popular practice?

Figure 6.3
Intimate
relationships
are
important
throughout
our lives

Reading 6.2   Lynn Jamieson, 'Disclosing intimacy'

An overarching task ... is to assess the claim that a particular form of intimacy, 'disclosing intimacy' – a process of two or more people mutually sustaining deep knowing and understanding, through talking and listening, sharing thoughts, showing feelings – is increasingly sought in personal life. ... Is there a sense in which the alleged shift to 'disclosing intimacy' is just a story or are actual lives being lived differently? One possible reading ... is that widespread stories about personal life have changed much more dramatically than private practices. In other words, 'disclosing intimacy' is not becoming the crux of personal life as it is lived, despite a much greater emphasis on this type of intimacy in public stories about personal life. ...

...

This book suggests that the story of a shift to 'disclosing intimacy' is too selective a story to be anything other than a very partial view of an emerging future.

One of many reasons why the story of disclosing intimacy is not more fully resonant with private lives is because it is not the only current story of how lives should be lived. ... New public stories have not drowned out previously dominant stories ... despite marked shifts over the duration of the twentieth century. ... In the second half of the century stories of 'the family' speak less of the good of the family itself, as an institution, as a domestic, economic and social unit, and more of good family 'relationships'. By the closing decades of the century, the story of 'a good relationship' holds up one dimension of intimacy above all others, the knowing and understanding of 'disclosing intimacy'. ...

... [But] there are other ways of being intimate and several possible dimensions of intimacy which can be distinguished from 'knowing and understanding'. ... Love, practical caring and sharing remain as or more important in many types of personal relationships. ...

...

The suggested shift to voluntary, equal, relationships of disclosing intimacy is particularly difficult to sustain with respect to parent–child relationships. ...

...

The overwhelming majority of parents do not treat their children as-if-they-were-equal but protect their children from their own thoughts and feelings. Even child experts who advocate attentive, listening, responsive parenting do not advocate a mutual disclosing intimacy between parents and children because children are to be protected from adult worries and burdens. ...

The suggestion that couple relationships have become more like friendship based on 'disclosing intimacy' is only marginally easier to defend. ...

For any particular couple, what makes for a good relationship, what is in and out of balance when generating intimacy through talking, 'knowing and understanding' versus the doing of more practical loving, caring and sharing, is complicated and difficult to untangle. ...

...

Perhaps the main reason for doubting a shift towards disclosing intimacy is the relatively modest change in gender inequalities. This is highlighted particularly in heterosexual behaviour and couple relationships.

Reading source

Jamieson, 1998, pp. 158–66

Comment

There are four main reasons why Jamieson seems unconvinced that a concept of disclosing intimacy adequately captures what people are doing in their personal lives:

1   'Disclosing intimacy' may be more of a popular public story than a private practice across a range of relationships.

2   'Disclosing intimacy' would be inappropriate in some relationships, for example, parent–child relationships where protection of children from adult concerns is more socially acceptable.

3   The possibilities for 'disclosing intimacy' in some relationships is mitigated by inequalities; for example, gender inequalities.

4   Evidence suggests that practical loving, caring and sharing is more important than 'disclosing intimacy'.

3.1   Alternative views of the 'transformation of intimacy'

Giddens puts a positive gloss on the transformations that he proposes have taken hold. He sees the potential for greater equalities (including gender and sexuality), greater 'democratisation' in families, and greater freedoms for us to express and be who we are (1992, p. 184). But other social scientists take a more pessimistic view and have, for example, identified an underlying individualism – a high value given to personal autonomy by the 'me' society – that may not incorporate any consensus on values. Intimate relationships have also been characterised as fragile and impermanent, and as likely to be jeopardised by inherent uncertainties, risks and anxieties. Prominent social theorists, Beck and Beck-Gernsheim talk about the 'normal chaos of love' (1995). They too see a pervasive underlying individualism and argue that it can involve a quest for connection, to address a profound sense of loneliness. Lynn Jamieson argues that intimacies are much more complex than the body of sociological work suggests. She highlights the diverse range of meanings and practices of 'intimacy' and reminds us of the continuance of gender inequalities and social class differences in intimate lives.

Summary

- Debates continue in social science about the meanings of intimacy and changing patterns of intimacy.

- In considering patterns of intimacy, it is important to identify continuities as well as changes.

- The main trend in social science has been to focus on intimacy as a relationship between adults and to emphasise the sexual relationship.

- But the concept of intimacy can be interpreted more broadly to include a wide range of close (in physical or emotional terms) or caring relationships.

3.2 Diverse intimacies

In this section of the chapter, we explore the broad scope of the concept of intimacy by discussing three diverse examples. Whilst reading the extracts and working through the activities in this section, you might find it helpful to hold three general questions in mind:

1   How useful is the concept of 'intimacy' for understanding family meanings?

2   What new insights does it afford in our quest for family meanings?

3   Does it tell us more, or less, about 'family', or something different altogether?

We will return to these questions after we've explored the three examples.

3.2.1   Intimacy in public-care settings

In the first example, we look at intimacy in relation to caring in Julia Twigg's work on 'bathing as care work'. Twigg sees community care as a service that touches some of the most significant and intimate aspects of our lives. The maintenance and care of the body is highly important for all of us, but can assume a centrality in the lives of older people or people with disabilities. This kind of care has often been 'kept in the family', possibly because of its intimate and highly personal nature. In his book

Family Connections, David Morgan discusses practices of care and reminds us that 'family practices are, to a very large extent, bodily practices' (1996, p. 113).

In community care, our bodies are cared for, not by ourselves, or by family members, but by strangers and professionals. Care of the body, wherever it takes place, involves intimate practices such as bathing and washing that challenge the boundaries of *all* our social relationships. Moreover, caring practices affect how we feel about ourselves, and particularly our senses of privacy, autonomy and vulnerability.

In this example, the concept of 'intimacy' takes us well beyond 'family', but it also enables us to reflect on 'family' as though from a distance and to bring into focus the kinds of practices that constitute 'intimacy' and 'family'.

Activity 6.3

Read the extract from Julia Twigg's paper on 'Help with bathing at home for older and disabled people'.

On the basis of Twigg's discussion of nakedness, can you identify any common theme(s) that characterise different forms of intimacy?

Figure 6.4

Caring relationships are captured in the concepts of intimacy and personal life

Reading 6.3   Julia Twigg, 'Nakedness'

Nakedness has many and complex meanings both in terms of how it is experienced socially and in the metaphors that attach to it and to its representation ... I will confine the account to the social experience of nakedness and to two themes in that: intimacy and vulnerability.

Nakedness is closely associated with intimacy, particularly in modern Western culture with sexual intimacy. The link between nakedness and closeness is both a literal one, in that nakedness permits direct physical touch and closeness, and a metaphorical one, in that to be naked is to divest oneself of protection and disguise. Nakedness creates vulnerability, and this takes on a particular character when the experience is asymmetrical. To be without your clothes in the context of those who are clothed is to be at a disadvantage. Denying prisoners or patients their clothes, interrogating people naked, are common techniques for undermining individuals and creating vulnerability. It is in order to mitigate such effects that doctors are taught how to examine patients in ways that limit their exposure.

Bathing in the community inevitably involves such nakedness in front of another who is clothed. For older people it may also involve a second form of asymmetry in the sense of being naked in front of someone who is young. Nearly all the representations of nakedness in modern culture are of youthful bodies. There are very few unclothed depictions of aging.

Reading source

Twigg, 1997, pp. 224–5

Comment

In this extract Julia Twigg discusses nakedness in the context of the meanings of receiving help with personal hygiene at home. Her work explores personal care *as intimacy* and so expands the concept of intimacy beyond its usual confines, most particularly the idea of intimacy with strangers.

Twigg's work highlights some general themes that characterise different forms of intimacy – for example, embodiment, power, trust and vulnerability – and help us interrogate the variable meanings of 'intimacy'. Being in an intimate relationship with another can make us feel powerful, but in some contexts can leave us feeling exposed and vulnerable. Intimacy, then, can involve trust that the other will 'respect the boundaries' and not exploit us.

Twigg's work prompts us to think how meanings and practices of intimacy overlap with those of family, or how they might constitute something different. It suggests that issues of care, trust and vulnerability have to be carefully negotiated within *all* relationships, be they those of professional care or those of family. Thus, there are boundary issues to do with the personal, the body, privacy and autonomy that are invoked by both 'family' and 'intimacy'. But, if you reflect for a moment on these overlapping dimensions, it soon becomes apparent that they are the *same but different* in the two settings.

As with 'family', the *meanings* of intimacy are different according to context (the crucial issue of 'context' is explored in further detail in Chapter 7). Intimacy in a care setting can thus involve many of the *same practices* as are important in family settings, but they *mean different things*, not least because they are practices that take shape in different discourses: a professional discourse of care in the one case, and an everyday discourse of family in the other. For example, in normative ideas of 'family' that incorporate notions of duty, obligation and expectation, practices of care are framed differently than they are in 'intimacy' where they appear more as matters of personal choice and negotiation.

From this example of nakedness in a public-care setting it is possible to tease out some of the ways in which using a language of intimacy casts a different light on 'family'. Conversely, you will have noticed that some dimensions of 'family' disappear from view when we study this instance of intimacy. For example, that all-important sense of 'belonging' (which we discussed in Chapter 3), or a sense of emotional closeness (which may or may not be positive) that so often arise from 'family' is not present in the professional care relationship. When we notice these absences, it suggests that the language of 'family' is capturing something important that is not necessarily implied by a concept of 'intimacy'.

There are other examples of intimacy that turn the kaleidoscope in yet a different way. We will consider one such example now.

3.2.2   *Intimacy in the lives of sex workers*

Activity 6.4

Read the extract from 'Difficult relations: sex work, love and intimacy' by Deborah Warr and Priscilla Pyett. These authors carried out a qualitative study in Australia in which female sex-workers talked about the difficulties in sustaining intimate relationships in their private lives alongside engaging in sex work. One of the main findings was that sex work can disrupt private intimate sexual relationships, requiring intimacies in both settings to be carefully distinguished and negotiated.

As you read the extract, notice how this example illustrates the fluidity of 'intimacy' and the deep significance of context. In this case, the same practice (i.e. condom use) had radically different meanings in the two settings of 'work' and the personal (or 'private') lives of the female sex-workers.

1   How do sex workers negotiate intimacy at work and in their private or personal lives?

2   What general conclusions about intimacy might we draw from this study?

Reading 6.4 Deborah Warr and Priscilla Pyett, 'Public and private intimacies in the lives of female sex-workers'

All the [24] women in this study reported tensions associated with having a private sexual relationship while engaging in sex work. Fewer than half the women reported being in a current relationship and only five were living with their partners. Several women saw their partners very infrequently. ... Only two of the women with private partners said they used condoms in these relationships. One relied on condoms for contraception as a deliberate strategy to protect herself from STDs [sexually transmitted diseases] because she was unsure of her partner's commitment to the relationship. Most of the other women felt, however, that not using condoms enabled them to experience their private relationships as qualitatively different from the sex they engaged in through work. Indeed, many women refused to use condoms with their private partners lest they experience their private sexual relations as 'just like a job'.

...

Sex work consists in the selling of services which are modelled on practices that are central to ideas of heterosexual intimacy. For female sex-workers and their private partners, this represents a substantial challenge to heterosexual expectations of love, commitment and sexual exclusivity in intimate relationships. Indeed, it is clear that sex work practices, in so far as they simulate or even parody the features of love-making, can profoundly disrupt the special characteristics of intimate sexual relationships. For the women in this study, their involvement in sex work provoked resentment, jealousy, disapproval and disrespect, which impacted on their own and their partner's capacity to enjoy intimacy. When the woman was tired after work and did not feel motivated to have sex, her partner's resentment was likely to be aggravated. Women longed for affection but a lack of desire for sexual intercourse could be misunderstood by their partners as resulting from sexual satisfaction at work. Because they associated condoms with a commercial sexual transaction, using condoms in a private sexual relationship substantially reduced the women's capacity to experience love or intimacy through sex. For their partners too, condom use could be interpreted as a lack of trust.

Reading source

Warr and Pyett, 1999, p. 293 and p. 300

Comment

1 The use of condoms was the linchpin in the way the sex workers in this study negotiated intimacy at work and in their 'private' or personal lives. The condom carried great – and different – symbolic significance in the two settings. With clients, the condom worked to put a boundary around intimacy and acted as a

physical as well as a metaphorical barrier. This symbolically excluded the sharing of passion and pleasure and emotional closeness that ordinarily is associated with making love with a private partner. In private sexual relationships, the deliberate shunning of the condom reinforced this separation as well as the different meanings of sexual intimacy in the two settings. It signified trust and commitment, elements of intimacy that were not present in the work relationships. But, even so, private intimacies remained fragile, as the women's partners did not always easily share their meanings, which had to be negotiated anew in the relationship.

2   This specific study suggests several general points about intimacy:

(a) Intimacy, like 'family', is fluid and is constructed through practices. As with 'family' the meanings of these practices depend crucially on context.

(b) Intimacy can be very fragile and requires negotiation.

(c) It is useful to think about 'intimacies' in the plural to highlight a diversity of practices and relationships that could be included in the term.

3.2.3   What is this thing called love? Insights from across the generations

In our final example of diverse intimacies, we focus on an empirical study of love and romance. It is these kinds of emotional, physical and sexual partnerships that perhaps most often are invoked by the term 'intimacy'. Yet, even within this category of relationships, 'intimacy' has fluid meanings. Joanne Brown (2006) compared narratives of love from people in their pre-forties, with those from people in their post-seventies. Interviewees came from a range of backgrounds, though none was from a minority ethnic background.

In the extract, Joanne Brown discusses some of the differences between the accounts of the older and the younger interviewees.

Activity 6.5

1   What does the extract suggest is the main dimension of difference between the accounts of love given by the older and the younger interviewees?

2   Suggest two general points about intimacy that you take away from this extract.

Reading 6.5   Joanne Brown, 'Love and romance across two generations'

'What is this thing called love?' is not a question that the older people ... were preoccupied by. Although marriage and partnership were central to their lives, they did not subject their feelings for their partner, or the concept of love itself, to scrutiny. A preoccupation of what love is ... clearly demarcates the two age groups interviewed.

Without exception, all of the older interviewees prioritised a discussion of marriage, scarcity, war and death of a spouse when asked to talk about experiences of romance. ...

What Mrs Archer and Mrs Frost emphasised (like all of the older interviewees) was the material, structural conditions of their lives (low wages or unemployment, saving up for a marriage, etc.). Marriage itself was part of a material, structural or familial arrangement, rather than a romantic dream. ...

... [T]he younger interviewees have deconstructed romantic love and are struggling with dichotomous [contrasting] views of it as possible/impossible, desirable/ undesirable, a social construction/an emotional reality, a substitute satisfaction/a real fulfilment, and so on. They hold their relationships up to sociological and psychological scrutiny implicitly, if not explicitly, and clearly have expectations from their relationships and from themselves that are significantly different from their older counterparts. Although the older interviewees spoke about how structural conditions of their lives affected their marriage plans and marriages, they did not ask searching questions about their own psyches or their partner's psyche and thus they did not provide psychologically inflected commentary on their lives. Also, although they recounted their love lives in the context of larger societal and world context (war), they did not overtly question the socio-cultural positions that they occupied (e.g. gender expectations). The younger interviewees ... all, to some extent, did speak about their life histories through what we might call a psychosocial lens.

Reading source

Brown, 2006, p. 171 and p. 215

Comment

1   The extract suggests that reflective observation constitutes the main dimension of difference between the accounts of love given by the older and the younger interviewees. The younger interviewees subjected themselves and their relationships to an ongoing interrogation that drew on psychological and sociological ideas as well as therapeutic discourses.

2   Brown's evidence suggests two general points about intimacy:

   (a)   It suggests the fluidity and multiplicity of meanings of intimacy. Like 'family', 'intimacy' is not a unified or stable concept.

   (b)   It presents a challenge to any simplistic idea that intimacy is being 'transformed'. As is true for 'family' (which we discuss further in the next chapter), historical and social transformations are not linear and comprise a complex mixture of continuities and changes.

3.2.4   How useful is 'intimacy'?

Activity 6.6

Having explored the concept of intimacy from several different perspectives, I now want you to return to our original questions about intimacy:

1   How useful is 'intimacy' as a concept for understanding family meanings?

2   What do we gain and what do we lose when we use 'intimacy' in place of 'family?

3   Should we abandon the concept of 'family' in favour of 'intimacy'?

We will consider each question in turn.

Comment

1   How useful is 'intimacy' as a concept for understanding family meanings?

The concept of intimacy both helps illuminate and helps obscure family meanings. It helps illuminate family meanings because it focuses in on the relationships that, for many people, lie at the heart of 'family'. And it permits a focus on the practices of intimacy in family settings (e.g. caring and sharing) enabling us to build a fuller picture and a deeper understanding of the wide range of practices through which 'family' is constituted. On the other hand, 'intimacy' can obscure or eclipse the wider networks in 'family' by encouraging a focus on dyadic relationships although, in principle, there is no reason why 'intimacy' cannot describe group relationships, for example, communal living.

2   What do we gain and what do we lose when we use 'intimacy' in place of 'family'?

When we use the concept of 'intimacy' in place of 'family', there are both losses and gains. On the positive side, a focus on intimacy may enable us to 'escape the orthodoxy of family ideology' (Budgeon and Roseneil, 2004, p. 133), that is, to represent values beyond stultified notions of 'family values'. 'Intimacy' may be a more egalitarian concept, and it may be more inclusive. Also on the positive side, 'intimacy' permits an expansion of the range of relationships beyond the confines of 'family' (such as, for example, friendships, or partners who live 'apart yet together') that may be included as significant, and opens the way for inclusion of a multiplicity of intimate practices (such as personal care). 'Intimacy' need not perpetuate norms that have become embedded within 'family'; for example, norms about gender and heterosexuality and coupledom. It permits us to take more account of the things that matter to us beyond the boundaries of 'family'.

In short, a focus on 'intimacy' can decentre 'family' and even the couple relationship and, in their place, it opens up a space to explore a wider range of people and things that matter to us in our personal lives.

On the other hand, as Budgeon and Roseneil (2004, p. 127) put it, family remains a 'central social institution' and a 'key trope in the cultural imaginary'. In other words, for all its ambiguities and all its limitations, 'family' means something significant. For example, Jeffrey Weeks and his colleagues (Weeks et al., 1999), writing about non-heterosexual relationships, nevertheless retain 'family' in their concept of 'families of choice'. 'Family,' they say, 'is a resonant word, embracing a variety of social, cultural, economic and symbolic meanings' (p. 86). For them, 'family' captures the rich amalgam of 'care, responsibility and commitment' (p. 94) that lies at the heart of our personal lives. 'Family' resonates with much that is meaningful to us, and exerts an emotional pull that is as difficult to explain as it is to resist.

3   Should we abandon the concept of 'family' in favour of 'intimacy'?

We have continually stressed throughout this book that 'family' is a fluid concept with multiple meanings. This point is crucial when it comes to asking whether or not we should abandon the concept of 'family' altogether. Family meanings are not fixed, and they are not stable. As we discussed in Chapter 5, they take shape within discourses and practices that themselves are subject to a continual process of revision and change. We have seen how social scientists could be tempted to abandon 'family', if only in order to escape its attendant unwanted connotations. But to abandon 'family' may be to throw out the baby with the bathwater. Weeks et al. (1999, p. 99) echo the views of many social scientists when they say:

> Many of the new stories of lesbian and gay lives are very close to those that might be told about rapidly changing patterns of heterosexual lives. That does not lessen the importance of the new narratives about non-heterosexual relationships. On the contrary, they underscore the significance of what is happening to our notions of 'family'. These non-heterosexual narratives of family and of choice, of care and responsibility, of love and loss, of old needs and new possibilities, of difference and convergence, are prime examples of those everyday experiments which are contributing to the creation of the 'new family'.

It is in this context that Carol Smart takes the debate forward in a somewhat different direction. She proposes to move on from 'family' and from 'intimacy' and suggests instead a new concept of 'personal life'. This is the topic you will explore in the next section of this chapter.

4   Personal life

Smart's starting point is a recognition of a paradox: for many years, sociologists have been critical of the term 'family' (for all the reasons we have noted hitherto in this book), and yet that term continues to exert an emotional hold over us. However hard we intellectualise it, however skilfully we analyse it, however much we try to get away from it, 'family' continues to *mean* something to us that we cannot easily put to one side.

Smart begins by telling us a personal story; it's a simple one, and one that many people will recognise. She tells us that she is looking through an old bag in which her mother kept family photographs. The act of sorting through them launches her on an emotional journey that is at once real and imaginary. Through the photographs she is transported into other worlds, other times, other lives and, at the time, she feels herself transformed. 'Dealing with family photos,' she says, 'is not simply a hobby, but part of an active and culturally specific production of self' (2007, p. 3). Thus, her encounter with the family photographs leads Smart to reflect on her own identity as a family member, rooted in time and place by family ties. This epiphany led to a change of intellectual project for Smart: 'In other words,' she says, 'I wanted to write sociologically about relationships and connectedness while remaining grounded in, and even working with, the kinds of real feelings generated by relating to others' (p. 3).

In the following extract, Smart explains the sociological developments in family studies and – more recently, intimacy – that have led to her new focus on 'personal life.'

Activity 6.7

Read the first extract from Smart's *Personal Life* (2007). You might like to make some brief notes on the 'reconfigurations' in family sociology that Smart argues are shifting the field conceptually towards a deeper engagement with personal lives.

Reading 6.6   Carol Smart, 'Why "Personal Life"?'

Ever since the interventions of feminist scholarship into the area of families, the private sphere, domestic life and gender relationships, the term 'family' has been rendered problematic. Michèle Barrett and Mary McIntosh ... mounted one of the most sustained critiques of the term, identifying it as a form of ideology rather than a descriptive concept, and one which sustained women's subordination while deflecting discontent through appeals to the naturalness of the biological unit of the heterosexual couple and their children. Following this, feminist work not only tried to avoid using the term family, but to strip away the ideological veil that shrouded discussions of families by deploying more neutral terms such as 'household' or 'private sphere'. There was also a body of empirical research which focused on abuses, violence and economic inequality in nuclear families. Following on from such approaches, other criticisms were developed, in particular from the viewpoint of same-sex households; in the UK this included reaction to a notorious legal provision which prevented schools from teaching children about 'pretended families' (same-sex relationships) ... The grossness of depicting gay and lesbian households as 'pretended' families led to an absolute aversion to the term. However, the concept of families (as opposed to 'the' family) seemed incredibly tenacious and not only refused to be banished from the lexicon, but seemed instead to expand quite happily to include a range of relationships and households which would never have fitted the original sociological definition of a nuclear family. Thus concepts developed of families of choice ... or of friends as family ... and, although a core notion of family has undoubtedly remained (especially in relation to close biological kin), the term seems to have become more inclusive and more generous in its embrace. David Morgan ... has also helped to shift the field conceptually through his development of the idea of family practices, which captures the idea that families are what families do, no longer being defined exclusively by co-residence or even ultimately by kinship and marriage.

The field is therefore going through a very interesting phase as the sociological imagination stretches and reconfigures in order better to grasp and reflect the complexities of contemporary personal life.

Reading source

Smart, 2007, pp. 26–7

Comment

Smart suggests that 'family' or even 'families' does not capture the complex realities of personal lives and that social scientists must embrace a conceptual shift. She builds on Morgan's idea of 'family practices' (which we discussed in Chapter 5). In the second part of this extract, Smart sets out the main components of the new field of 'personal life'.

Activity 6.8

Now read the second extract from *Personal Life*.

In what ways does Smart's idea of 'personal life' differ from the concept of intimacy we discussed earlier in this chapter?

Figure 6.5

The concept of personal life highlights a wide range of personal relationships

Reading 6.7   Carol Smart, 'The scope of "personal life"'

And this brings me precisely to the concept of 'personal life', a term now increasingly applied to include not only families as conventionally conceived, but also newer family forms and relationships, reconfigured kinship networks, and friendships. But ... 'personal life' is intended to be more than a terminological holdall. The terminology of personal life seeks to embrace conceptual shifts as well as empirical changes to social realities and, for the sake of clarity, I shall enumerate the main components of this field before turning to some of its limitations.

1   First, it is vital to specify what is meant by 'personal'. ... 'The personal' designates an area of life which impacts closely on people and means much to them ... To live a personal life is to have agency and to make choices, but the personhood implicit in the concept requires the presence of others to respond to and to contextualise those actions and choices. Personal life ... is lived out in relation to one's class position, ethnicity, gender and so on.

...

3   The concept of personal life allows for ideas of the life project – particularly significant in the work of Giddens and Beck – in which people have scope for decisions and plans ...

4   The term is also appropriately neutral in that it does not prioritize relationships with biological kin or marital bonds. Such a landscape of personal life does not have hierarchical boundaries between friends and kin. This means that there is more open conceptual space for families of choice, same-sex intimacies, reconfigured kinship formations and so on.

5   Of particular significance is the way in which the concept contains within it a sense of motion. Personal life is never still or stationary in the way that the old idea of 'the family' appeared to be. While the concept of the life course has injected movement into studies of family life, this adds only a social dimension of generational and cohort ageing, whereas it is equally important to capture other kinds of motion. For example, unemployment or divorce can transform personal life, often affecting income, housing and well-being and shifting people into completely different places and spaces ...

6   There is also the potential to overcome the older distinctions made between private and public spheres which have conceptualized family life as a distinct place or institution separate from other social spaces and structures. Personal life is lived in many different places and spaces, it is cumulative (through memory, history and the passage of time) and it forms a range of connections, thus making it flexible ... So personal life is not so concerned with boundary marking and provides the possibility of tracing its flows through systems of education, or work, or elsewhere.

7   The concept also gives recognition to those areas of life which used to be slightly below the sociological radar. Thus personal life includes issues of sexuality, bodies, intimacy and can bring them together, creating a whole that is greater than its parts, rather than treating them as separate subfields of the sociological discipline.

8   Finally, personal life as a concept does not invoke the white, middle-class, heterosexual family in the way that, historically at least, the concept of 'the family' has. This means that important dimensions of class, ethnicity, religion, sexuality, gender, and disability can be written through the narrative and given significance ...

These points are suggestive of the value of reconfiguring the field. But this does not mean that terms such as 'family' or 'family life' should be banned or that notions of kinship and friendship should be collapsed into a formless sludge. These ideas about personal life are intended to provide a conceptual orientation and potential toolbox rather than a rigid, rule-bound manifesto.

Reading source

Smart, 2007, pp. 27–30

Comment

Smart's concept of 'personal life' is intended to embrace all those aspects of our personal lives (including 'family' matters, and including 'intimacy' issues) that are meaningful to us. It is not intended to replace concepts of 'family' or 'intimacy', but to employ a new inclusive language that recognises that 'family' and 'intimacy' reflect only a limited range of personal relationships and issues that are significant to us.

Smart mentions that the main limitation of the concept of 'personal life' is that it may be seen to be too wide in scope. But this openness may be a virtue and Smart goes on to suggest other areas (including work, cultural life and political life) where the concept may be useful. Other limitations of the concept might include its capacity to deal with issues such as emotion, embodiment and social class. But these, as Smart recognises, are challenges for the future.

Whilst the concept of 'personal life' is a recent one in social science (and thus it has not yet been well explored in empirical studies), there are existing studies that have sought to decentre both 'family' and 'intimacy' and so have opened up a space to focus on 'personal' life in more detail.

We consider one such study in the next activity – Sacha Roseneil and Shelley Budgeon's work on intimacy and care in the context of social change. Whilst you are working through this example, you might like to refer back to the earlier discussion of 'intimacy and care' in Julia Twigg's work. You will remember that we read Twigg's work through a concept of 'intimacy', whereas we are now approaching Roseneil and Budgeon's work through the lens of 'personal life'.

In their study, Roseneil and Budgeon explored the broad question of how some people organise their personal lives, loving and caring for each other in the context of social changes that increasingly demand individualised lifestyles. Roseneil and Budgeon see much that matters to people as taking place beyond 'family' – for example, between partners who are not living together, or within networks of friends. They suggest that in order better to understand contemporary patterns, it is necessary to decentre both 'family' as well as (hetero)sexual couple relationships. Thus they develop a more inclusive concept of 'intimacy' which takes its meanings within a broader frame of 'personal life'.

Within this framework, Roseneil and Budgeon carried out an empirical study of how intimacy and care are practised beyond the confines of 'family'. They conducted in-depth interviews with a diverse sample of 53 people whom they describe as living at the 'cutting edge of social change', in that they did not live with a partner, were aged between 25 and 60, and were living in three contrasting localities in Yorkshire, UK. They investigated how, and to what extent people lived in 'non-conventional cultures of intimacy', and studied their practices of intimacy and care. The researchers found, across a diverse range of lifestyles, that *friendships* occupied a central place in people's personal lives, and there was a high reliance among their interviewees on friends (as opposed to biological kin and sexual partners) for care and support. In the extract, we hear about Karen and Polly who are heterosexual, white, 'single' parents and close friends who have bought a home together.

Activity 6.9

1   Read the extract and make a list of what you might count as practices of intimacy that you find within it.

2   Thinking about the list you have made, what dimensions of intimacy can you identify?

3   In what ways, if any, do these practices and dimensions that you have identified expand your concept of 'intimacy' and reflect a broader concept of 'personal life'?

4   Look back at the dimensions of personal life discussed by Smart in Reading 6.7. Can you identify any of these in Roseneil and Budgeon's study? What do you conclude about the potentials of 'personal life' as an organising concept in family studies?

Reading 6.8   Sasha Roseneil and Shelley Budgeon, 'Intimacy, care and personal life'

Karen and Polly each have a wide network of geographically dispersed friends who figure centrally in their narratives, but they are also embedded locally in a network of friendships held together by a conscious mutual commitment to provide support and care. Many of these friends have chosen to live in the same area ... in order to be close to one another. Karen and Polly's three daughters are close to these friends, and Karen says these friends provide another 'anchor' for her children. Prior to the break-up of Karen's relationship, she had been living several hours away from Polly and this circle, but after the break-up she returned to this city because of her friendships there.

Seeing Karen in a bad emotional state, this group of friends gathered together and physically moved her and her children back to the city, actively putting in place the things she would need upon her return. Contacts in the film industry found her a job, a house was rented and decorated for her and a school was found for the children. Similarly, Jenny, a good friend of Polly's who was living a considerable distance away, had also been having a difficult time recently, and so Polly took it upon herself to oversee the purchase and renovation of a house on the street where she and Karen live for Jenny to move into with her children. It is Polly's 'project' to bring the people in her network closer to her when she sees them struggling in their lives. ....

One of the strongest motivations behind Polly and Karen's decision to buy the house together was to provide a safe and stable environment for the children, in which, as two single parents, they could help each other with childcare. As close friends they felt they could give each other a commitment and provide support to each other and their children in a way that would be significantly more secure than if they attempted to pursue this in the context of a love relationship with a man. In effect, they co-parent the children, and share the management of the household. ... They are reworking the notion of 'stability' often associated with conventional family forms by refusing to invest in a sexual relationship as the basis for security, and replacing this with a reliance upon friendships.

Reading source

Roseneil and Budgeon, 2004, pp. 146–7

Comment

1   Practices that fall under a broad heading of 'giving and receiving care and support' are characterised by the authors as intimate practices. They suggest an important mutuality and include emotional support (being there for a friend, being an 'anchor' for a friend's children, helping to provide 'stability') and material/physical help (help with moving and setting up home, bringing friends into close proximity, help with getting a job, help with childcare). These in turn imply other intimate practices, such as the giving of one's time, and affective communication. These intimate practices are important aspects of personal lives.

2   The *dimensions* of intimacy that emerge from these practices include caring, sharing, reciprocity (i.e. exchange for mutual benefit), trust, and commitment. A significant feature of these dimensions is that they are freely chosen rather than automatically arising out of any sense of preordained duty or obligation.

3   These practices and dimensions that we have identified from the empirical study decentre the dyadic concept of 'intimacy' as well as its association with a sexual relationship. Later in the paper, Roseneil and Budgeon discuss the blurring of the boundaries between categories of 'lover' and 'friend'; friends may also be lovers, or they might become lovers, or lovers might become friends. Karen and Polly made a conscious decision to decentre sexual relationships in their lives in the interests of providing stability for the children. This study puts caring practices as the main identifying feature of intimacy, to which other important dimensions are linked. 'Family' is also traditionally associated with caring, but in decentring the sexual relationship in the ways they choose to organise their personal lives, Karen and Polly have shunted 'family' to one side and in its place have created an alternative system of personal life that adequately fulfils their needs for care and support but that does not carry with it the conventional trappings of 'family'.

4   If we consider Roseneil and Budgeon's study using a concept of 'personal life' we see the dimensions of fluidity, movement and openness, as well as social personhood that Smart identifies with her concept of 'personal life'. We capture an expansive network of friendships that decentre both 'family' and 'intimacy'. These relationships are chosen, they are built on foundations of trust and commitment, and maintained by practices of caring and sharing. These practices of personal life include devoting one's time, as well as material and emotional resources to build and sustain relationships that are of mutual benefit (for example, in terms of providing 'stability' for children). A 'personal life' perspective blurs the boundaries between 'family', 'lover' and 'friend' as it turns the kaleidoscope to focus on what Gabb (2008) refers to as 'significant others'.

Activity 6.10

In our final brief reading, Jacqui Gabb sums up her research on intimacy in a way that highlights not 'family' and not 'intimacy', but a whole range of relationships with 'significant others' that, for Smart, would constitute an important dimension of 'personal life'.

Reading 6.8   Jacqui Gabb, 'Significant others'

It is evident that there are many different networks of support and intimate relationships both within and beyond 'the family' and these are experienced in ways that resist uniform interpretation. Some look inwards to family members and beyond to extended kin. Others turn to different relational connections which take a variety of affective forms, including friendship networks, faith-based communities and (in some cases) pets. All of these were identified by participants, to a lesser or greater extent, as repositories for and sources of intimacy. These multifarious affective strategies not only demonstrate the need for a pluralistic approach, they problematise what constitutes intimacy and an intimate relationship.

...

Responses from participants ... illustrate the need to rethink how boundaries are drawn around intimacy and intimates, to include *all* the relationships that are important in people's lives.

Reading source

Gabb, 2008, pp. 168–70

Comment

You will notice from this extract that neither 'family' nor 'intimacy' can fully capture the range of relationships with our significant others. A concept of 'personal life', by contrast, is sufficiently flexible to embrace such a range. But perhaps that brings with it a new set of problems. For example, is 'personal life' so broad a concept as to be able to incorporate anything, and therefore in danger of becoming meaningless?

Summary

- Concepts of 'family' and 'intimacy' fail adequately to capture the complexities and significant dimensions of our lives and relationships, perhaps indicating the need for a conceptual shift towards 'personal life'.

- 'Personal life' is lived out in relation to dimensions of difference, including gender, ethnicity, class, sexuality and disability.

- The concept of 'personal life' incorporates important dimensions of social personhood, a sense of motion, fluidity and openness.

- The broadness of the concept of 'personal life' may be seen as a limitation on its usefuless. But it may also be a virtue, enabling links to be made between personal lives and other areas such as work, politics and cultural life.

- The concept of 'personal life' provides us with an important tool for examining practices that are important to us but which take shape outside of conventional notions of 'family' and 'intimacy'.

5   Conclusions

I want us to return now to the three broad questions that prompted our discussion:

1   How useful are concepts of 'intimacy' and 'personal life' for exploring family meanings?

2   What do we gain and what do we lose when we use concepts of 'intimacy' and 'personal life' in place of 'family?'

3   Should we retain the concept of 'family' or abandon it?

Throughout this book we have emphasised how difficult family meanings are to pin down. Yet 'family' remains a powerful concept, often exerting a normative influence so that certain relationship patterns and practices are elevated as desirable and proper, whilst others are marginalised and excluded. Social scientists have looked beyond 'family' for concepts that better capture the diversity of living arrangements and relationships that people count as significant in their lives in the contemporary world. In this context we have asked whether 'family' may have outlived its usefulness as a concept in social science. Some have argued that we need a new language to talk about and to validate a wider range of significant relationships and living arrangements. Others have sought to make the term 'family' more inclusive.

The complexity of the debate is compounded because of its location in broader debates about global social change and contemporary social conditions. Several prominent social theorists have sought to link these ideas to changing images of family and patterns of intimacy. Our central concern about what happens when we decentre the concept of 'family' arises in this context.

The work of Giddens and others suggested a number of dimensions said to characterise contemporary partnerships that increasingly approximate the 'pure' relationship and reflect 'disclosing intimacy'. These include choice, self-fulfillment, emotion, reflexivity, equality, sharing, mutual disclosure, companionship and sexuality. Theorising in this vein highlights how contemporary intimacies appear to challenge several basic tenets of traditional conceptions of 'family', including assumptions about segregated and unequal gender 'roles', and assumptions about heterosexuality.

But we also noted that critics have pointed to continuities in intimacies alongside the changes – especially the continuance of inequalities such as gender and social class. Jamieson also suggests that 'disclosing intimacy' need not incorporate only sexual relationships, but can also encompass friendships.

By way of examining the diverse range of practices that might be included in the term 'intimacy', we explored intimacy as caring in public settings, intimacies in the lives of sex workers, and narratives of love and romance across two generations. In each case we considered the implications for concepts of 'intimacy' and 'family'.

Exploring the diversities of intimacy in this way not only enabled us to decentre both 'family' and the sexual relationship, but also enabled us to identify some important dimensions of intimacy, such as caring and the multiple meanings of 'closeness' and the significance of 'trust' which take on profoundly different meanings according to context (e.g. when the intimacy is with strangers). We saw that some of these important dimensions of intimacy overlap with some family meanings, but crucially similar practices can have rather different meanings depending on context, and depending on which discourse they are being read through. Focusing on 'family', or 'intimacy' or 'personal life' is like looking through a kaleidoscope; with one small turn, old patterns twist away as new ones come into focus, and then reconfigure again in different colours and different forms.

For example, as we saw in Chapter 2, a significant sense of 'belonging' is a common theme in 'family'. But this dimension does not feature at all strongly when we focus on 'intimacy'. 'Family' suggests a group, with boundaries that keep members 'in' and non-members 'out', although there may be some permeability. Intimacy focuses on relationships – most often dyadic ones – rather than a group or a bounded unit. In this sense, it is more flexible and more able to incorporate diversities. 'Personal life' brings into focus neither a bounded group nor a dyadic relationship, but rather it brings the needing, desiring and interacting individual – a social individual – into sharpest focus.

In common with 'family', 'intimacy', as a concept, is both robust and fragile. Like 'family' its meanings are fluid rather than fixed, and highly dependent on context. Like 'family' it comes into being and is sustained or transformed through human practices that can have powerful symbolic significance (as we saw in the research on sex workers' use of condoms in two different 'intimate' settings). Likewise our examination of the example of love and romance suggested the fluidity and multiplicity of meanings of intimacy, in this case across generations. Like 'family', 'intimacy' is subject to a complex mixture of change and continuity.

Jamieson reminded us that inequalities must not be erased from the picture. Neither a focus on 'family', nor 'intimacy', nor 'personal life' automatically brings structural inequalities into focus. (In referring to 'structural inequalities' we mean those inequalities that are rooted in the way society is structured; for example, differential life chances according to social class). Each concept is as likely as the next to obscure these from view, an observation that suggests that perhaps it matters less what concept we use than what perspective we take with any concept. This highlights the importance of how we use concepts, and the theoretical frameworks (such as those of 'discourses' and 'practices' we discussed in Chapter 5) in which we embed them.

By way of a final observation, we might ask whether 'family' is or is not a useful concept for social science. Should we abandon it altogether? The debate continues in social science and the jury is still out. On the 'no' side we have people like Jeffrey Weeks and his colleagues (although they are by no means alone) who have deliberately hung on to a notion of 'family' but have sought to open up the concept and have it encompass a number of forms of 'non-standard' intimacies. Or we might retain the concept but use it with irony, for example by appropriating it for our own ends but being aware of its limitations. In Chapter 5, we saw parents who appropriated a dominant welfare discourse to further their own aims. In a similar way, we might draw on the power of 'family' without having to subscribe to it fully as, for example, in the quip 'friends are the new family'.

On the opposite side we have those such as Roseneil and Budgeon who are actively seeking to dismantle the dominance of familial discourses with all that they imply for a range of inequalities, oppressions and exclusions. They see 'family' as dangerously perpetuating heterosexual and exclusionary norms, and are critical of researchers such as Weeks for using such terms as 'families of choice' which they see as diverting attention from more radical extra-familial alternative living arrangements.

There is, of course, always a possibility that concepts such as 'intimacy' and even 'personal life' may become as stuck in dominant discourses as 'family' became. If we jettison 'family' we may throw the baby out with the bathwater. Jamieson, amongst others, draws attention to friendship as intimacy and sees friendships as more likely than other kinds of relationships to approximate the 'pure' relationship that Giddens talks about. But she also talks about 'intimacy', and she also talks about 'family', which suggests that it is in our *use* of these various concepts that the interesting consequences lie. In other words, what is perhaps more important than the concepts themselves, is the way that we use them. We might, for example, use concepts such as 'family' that we regard as limited, precisely because we want to focus on the limitations, or exploit its power.

Further, as we have suggested, there is no guarantee that the new concepts we generate will not, themselves, become rigidified or stuck in dominant discourses that circumscribe their meanings. If we use any concept, be it 'family', 'intimacy' or 'personal life', then it is incumbent upon us to interrogate that concept, to examine its connotations, to uncover its assumptions, and not to take anything for granted. In each new context, we can explore the advantages and disadvantages of each concept that we use, and in this way enrich our study of family meanings.

References

Beck, U. and Beck-Gernsheim, E. (1995) *The Normal Chaos of Love* (trans. M. Ritter and J. Wiebel), Cambridge, Polity.

Brown, J. (2006) *A Psychosocial Exploration of Love and Intimacy*, Basingstoke, Palgrave Macmillan.

Budgeon, S. and Roseneil, S. (2004) 'Editors' Introduction: Beyond the conventional family,' *Current Sociology,* vol. 52, no. 2, pp. 127–34.

Gabb, G. (2008) *Researching Intimacy in Families*, Basingstoke, Palgrave Macmillan.

Giddens, A. (1992) *The Transformation of Intimacy: Sexuality, Love and Eroticism in Modern Societies*, Cambridge, Polity.

Gillies, V. (2003) 'Families and intimate relationships: a review of the sociological literature' [online], Families & Social Capital ESRC Research Group Working Paper No. 2, http://www.lsbu.ac.uk/families/workingpapers/familieswp2.pdf (Accessed 9 June 2008).

Jamieson, L. (1998) *Intimacy: Personal Relationships in Modern Societies*, Cambridge, Polity.

Morgan, D.H.J. (1996) *Family Connections: An Introduction to Family Studies*, Cambridge, Polity.

Roseneil, S. and Budgeon, S. (2004) 'Cultures of intimacy and care beyond "the family": personal life and social change in the early 21st century', *Current Sociology,* vol. 52, pp. 135–59.

Smart, C. (2007) *Personal Life: New Directions in Sociological Thinking*, Cambridge, Polity Press.

Twigg, J. (1997) 'Deconstructing the "social bath": Help with bathing at home for older and disabled people', *Journal of Social Policy,* vol. 26, no. 2, pp. 211–32.

Warr, D.J. and Pyett, P.M. (1999) 'Difficult relations: sex work, love and intimacy', *Sociology of Health and Illness,* vol. 21, no. 3, pp. 290–309.

Weeks, J., Donovan, C. and Heaphy, B. (1999) 'Everyday experiments: narratives of non-heterosexual relationships' in Silva, E.B. and Smart, C. (eds) *The New Family?*, London, Sage.

Weeks, J., Heaphy, B. and Donovan, C. (2004) 'The lesbian and gay family' in Scott, J. Treas, J. and Richards, M. (eds) *The Blackwell Companion to the Sociology of Families*, Oxford, Blackwell.

Part 3
Contexts

Introduction to Part 3

Jane Ribbens McCarthy

In this text, we have concentrated throughout on the meanings of family. In Part 1 we did this through a focus primarily on research evidence, while in Part 2 we explored different conceptual and theoretical frameworks to either modify the tricky concept of 'family', or find another language to talk about relationships.

In this part of the book, we will shift our emphasis slightly again, to focus on how meanings are embedded in, and shaped by, the contexts and circumstances of people's lives. At various points so far, we have stressed the idea that meanings as sense-making occur in particular contexts. Indeed, one of the ways in which they may be said to 'work' or 'not work' for people concerns whether or not, or how far, they help people to make sense of the circumstances in which they find themselves. So Part 3 focuses on the idea of 'meanings-in-context', and here we introduce you to two key notions – contexts and cultures – which underpin the next two chapters.

Contexts and cultures

In Chapter 2 we considered what we mean by 'meaning'; here we also need to think about what we might mean by 'context', and how we might think about the relationship between such meanings and contexts.

In the following chapters we take context to refer to dimensions of historical time, as well as space and place. So we will consider family meanings in diverse contexts, both historically and across the world, in relation to where and in what times people are living. But we do not take a view of context as something that is 'external' to people's lives. It is also about the ways that people place themselves in their social worlds. Whether or not contexts have a 'reality' of their own (itself a major source of philosophical debate), the social and personal significance of contexts is inevitably always mediated through the particular meanings that such contexts hold for people. This relates back to our discussion in Chapter 2, of how meanings 'matter' to family studies because they are a core feature in their own right of the social worlds we want to understand, and thus help to constitute the very substance of the social worlds that are the focus of study. When we talk about 'meanings-in-context', it follows that each of these terms is deeply implicated in the other. It is also important to consider that contexts comprise numerous elements, including material substances such as bodies and the physical environment, as well as personal and interpersonal features such as beliefs, emotions and patterns of interaction. These contexts are all shaped by processes over time and structured by inequalities and differences of power that may be formalised through institutions such as governments, organisations or labour markets. Illness, for example, is experienced physically, in terms of the body itself. Any individual's responses to illness will be embedded in a variety of contexts, such as memories of childhood and family encounters with illness, experiences amongst friends or acquaintances, media representations of illness, medical institutions, access to insurance, and so on. But the body itself may also be inscribed with the effects of inequalities, such as childhood nutrition, or patterns of working life. These contexts, and the physical experience itself, will all be understood and interpreted through a range of possible systems of meaning (including the various medical discourses exemplified in Chapter 5).

Contexts thus become part of human interactions through the meanings they hold, and this is sometimes captured through the term 'culture'. While we sometimes associate the word 'culture' with the idea of 'cultural activities' or 'high culture' (as in opera, or art galleries), in the social sciences it is used much more broadly, to refer to all aspects of our lives that are social – the result of human actions and interactions. 'Social scientists use the term culture to refer to the ways of living of people. Within it are included beliefs, values, customs, institutions, languages, technologies, art and all other products and processes of human agency, individual and collective' (Chaudhary, 2004, p. 34).

'Culture' thus refers to a considerable range of phenomena, including 'meanings', or sets of ideas. Referring to a cultural context rather than a political or economic one tends to draw attention to the sets of meanings through which the everyday lives of people are experienced, rather than to material inequalities or processes of power – even though these are all inevitably intertwined. But, certainly, social scientists sometimes find that economic or political explanations alone are not enough in helping to understand people's patterns of behaviour and ways of living. Instead, it is necessary to include attention to the beliefs and meanings which underlay these.

Furthermore, as we discussed above with regard to 'contexts', it is not possible in the social sciences to see the physical environment as somehow separate from culture, because people are always interpreting and shaping their physical environment. For human beings in interaction with other humans, nothing stands outside of culture. As Nandita Chaudhary expresses it, 'culture belongs between the person and the environment' (2004, p. 36).

The terms 'culture' and 'context' are thus closely related, and indeed quite often linked, most specifically as 'cultural context':

> Linked with the notion of culture is the idea of context ... customary practices are believed to be bound together by ritualistic, affective meanings and behaviours that are publicly shared and individually experienced. In this manner, the physical environment, cultural practices and social beliefs are synthesised in everyday settings.
>
> (Chaudhary, 2004, p. 35)

However, as an abstract term, 'culture' is sometimes in danger of being mistaken for a solid and fixed entity that exists outside of individuals, rather than something that is always fluid, dynamic and constantly in a process of being re-created. As with 'family', then, 'culture' may *be experienced as* quite 'solid' and 'external' to individuals. This experience may occur because culture is not the product of the individual but is created through the interactions between people, and, furthermore, culture pre-exists the experience of any one individual. Sometimes academics, too, have been drawn into writing about culture as if it is something fixed and clearly identifiable. To avoid this mistake, it is important always to bear in mind that cultures are never fixed, but always in flux.

But this then leaves us with the opposite question. If cultures are so fluid, how do we pin any particular patterns down to the point where we can describe them as constituting 'a culture'? Such issues cannot be answered in any absolute way, but only by reference to our particular purpose at that point in time. For different purposes then, we may want to draw boundaries around particular cultural contexts, and make particular comparisons, in order to answer the specific questions we have in mind at that moment.

We can thus identify cultures sometimes by reference to large sectors of population across the world, but also at other times by reference to much smaller groups. The key factor is that they must be sets of people who interact over a period of time to the point that they develop their own particular sets of meanings and ways of doing things together. So it's possible to talk about particular professional cultures, family cultures, neighbourhood cultures, urban/rural cultures, school cultures, and so on. In each case, what we are doing is focusing on what is shared between people within that particular setting, or context, and how this perhaps distinguishes them from people who are not part of that context, even if this occurs in quite subtle ways. Quite often this will be linked to some notion of physical space, whether this is cyberspace or geographic space. Thus, in studying family lives across the globe, Therborn (2004) draws on the idea of 'geoculture' to indicate how cultural variations in families may be linked to a 'geographic anchorage' that includes both physical territories and patterns of political power.

This brings us full circle back to the question of contexts again. When we speak of 'contexts', then, we might be referring to:

- the family context or household structures

- social characteristics that shape people's experiences and life chances (such as social class or ethnicity or gender)

- specific neighbourhoods

- broad historical trends

- regional differences

- wider social institutions

- different nation states

- different regions of the world that may share something in common around their economic, political or cultural situations.

And so on!

In Chapter 7 we explore meanings-in-contexts primarily in terms of the contexts of time and place (or geocultures). To do this, we will draw primarily on qualitative evidence of family meanings in earlier periods of history, and in various cultures across the world. We also consider, more briefly, how quantitative evidence may also be used to compare families and family meanings across varying societal contexts. Then, in Chapter 8, we turn to the policy and professional contexts of the contemporary UK, to consider examples of how particular family meanings may be embedded here too.

References

Chaudhary, N. (2004) *Listening to Culture: Constructing Reality from Everyday Talk*, New Delhi, Sage.

Therborn, G. (2004) *Between Sex and Power: Family in the World, 1900–2000*, London, Routledge.

Chapter 7

Family meanings across time and place

Jane Ribbens McCarthy and Megan Doolittle

Contents

1   Introduction

So far in this book, our discussions have centred on family meanings primarily in relation to contexts and communities found in European and New World countries. We have explored how family is understood in diverse ways in everyday lives in such contexts, how it is shaped within research, and how different theoretical and conceptual approaches may help to illuminate or obscure aspects of families and relationships. In this chapter, we extend this discussion to consider family meanings across a much greater range of contexts, historically and globally. In the process, we will:

■ introduce some of the basic conceptual and methodological considerations that are encountered when studying family meanings across a range of contexts

■ offer some insights into how family meanings may vary across time and place, and the tensions between paying attention to broad generalities and localised particularities

■ consider what a focus on context can add to our discussion of the ways in which theories and concepts may highlight some meanings of 'family', while rendering others less visible

■ explore how, and in what ways, an attention to meanings-in-contexts may enable us to see how our own assumptions about family meanings are embedded in the contexts in which we live, and which are familiar to us.

Overall, then, in this chapter we hope to give you a flavour of the ways in which studies of meanings-in-contexts can be both academically and personally challenging, potentially unsettling taken-for-granted assumptions and theoretical frameworks. We may thus learn much about ourselves by trying to understand the lives of others, and then reversing the gaze onto ourselves. We hope that this process will build on the pursuit we began in Chapter 1: to make our own familiar ways 'strange' in order to gain a clearer picture of the family meanings of others. But, as you will see, this is no easy undertaking.

Before we proceed further, however, we have to note that there is a particular difficulty in the language we use here, in that references to 'us' and 'our own', can assume that 'we' all know who is included. However, this is something that needs to be closely interrogated.

Activity 7.1

Take a few minutes to consider who you might be including when you refer to 'my own', or 'our own', in relation to your life, and perhaps make some notes for future reference.

1   If you think about families you know (including perhaps your own), how do you identify people 'like me', or perhaps 'not like me'? Who might not be included?

2   If you think about people across the world, whose 'family' and personal lives would you expect to be most different from those you know closely?

3   How do you think you could gain some insight into, or information about, such different lives?

Comment

1   There are many and varied ways in which families may be experienced as 'like' each other, or 'different'. We saw some of the ways in which researchers might interpret and represent such commonalities and differences in Chapters 2 and 3, for example, with regard to the different localities discussed by Becker and Charles in their study of family lives in Swansea. Class and ethnicity are two of the most obvious bases for such identifications, but there may be all sorts of subtle ways in which distinctions may be made within such categorisations. An individual might, for example, trace their origins differently through different family members, or identify themselves differently according to the situation they are in at the time (even if this is not a consciously thought-out strategy). Nationality, citizenship status, region and neighbourhood might be other bases for identifying 'families like mine'. Household structure is another potential source for seeing some families as 'like the ones that I know', and with whom we may feel we have something to share about 'our' experiences. I am sure you may well be able to think of other such bases for finding commonalities and differences with others.

2   Conversely, families that you might see as different from those you know well might be situated on the other side of the world, or living in the next street, or even next door! You might understand the basis of such differences in many ways, including all those identifications listed above.

3   Finding out about lives and family meanings that are 'different' in these terms may be a difficult process, depending on all sorts of constraints and opportunities that may or may not be present. Personal contacts are probably the main way of getting to know about other people's family lives. But family and friendship networks are often limited in the first place by our sense of whether or not we identify with others, as well as by broader processes that shape where we live and which people we know well. Furthermore, the anxiety about being evaluated

and judged (and found wanting) in terms of our family lives may make all of us reluctant to allow 'others' to get too close to our daily experiences and family meanings. Reading novels and academic studies, or watching films or TV programmes, are alternative routes into extending our knowledge of family meanings in varied contexts, but may need to be consciously sought out. Furthermore, such sources may each present particular 'versions' of family lives, which have been produced for various reasons, e.g. to increase TV audience ratings.

Starting from 'our own' understandings and knowledge always risks privileging certain points of view about who is included in 'we', and marginalising those who might be seen as 'other'. And yet, in themselves, these terms need not imply such marginalisation, since any viewpoint is always a view 'from somewhere' – indeed, how would it be possible to start from anywhere else than our own understandings? The important issue, perhaps, is to ensure that in developing academic knowledge, we try to avoid assumptions about where this 'somewhere' is. This is very difficult to achieve, however, in a world that is shaped by major inequalities of power and resources, which means that some voices and understandings 'from somewhere' are more powerful than others. Indeed, the development of academic knowledge is one such resource, which tends to be strongly based in anglophone (i.e. English-speaking) and continental-European points of view and institutions, often shaping the work and understandings of international charities and organisations such as the UN (as you will see further in Chapter 8). Furthermore, colonial histories mean that such westernised perspectives have often been actively dispersed across global contexts. In this respect, we might refer to such European and New World perspectives as dominant discourses (in the terms discussed in Chapter 5), and it can be very hard to think outside them. Even where academics actively work from other cultural perspectives, it is very difficult to avoid entering into a dialogue with established and powerful anglophone knowledge-bases. In this very process of dialogue, however, it may be necessary to translate one set of culturally based understandings and knowledge into another – more powerful – one, which may compromise and reshape the original cultural meanings.

In our quest to understand family meanings in context, there are various (western-based) social science disciplines on which we could draw, including anthropology, history, comparative sociology, and cross-cultural psychology, among others. In this chapter, we pay most attention to qualitative studies based in history and anthropology, as these are particularly appropriate frameworks for our present purposes. We also include some discussion of comparative sociological approaches, concluding with an overview discussion of what is meant by comparative approaches and the issues they raise.

You may like to note, however, that this discussion of meanings-in-context is one that you have already encountered in earlier chapters, where issues of categorisation and comparison were raised, if not given sustained attention. You saw, for example, how Becker and Charles' study of different locations in Swansea (Chapter 2) raised some difficult issues about how to understand and characterise variable family meanings in different contexts. Indeed, the authors drew upon anthropological approaches in their study, and you may remember that they used anthropological kinship terms in their analysis. Anthropology is thus not limited to the study of faraway places, and, indeed, may have much in common with the project of Professor Caswell's friendly cyborg Borg, whom you encountered in Chapter 1. In our focus on methodological themes in this chapter, we are also building on earlier discussions, since qualitative studies of everyday family meanings (which you encountered in Chapters 2 and 3) have some close affinities with anthropological and historical studies of the systems of meanings of other cultures and time periods; more quantitative, structured, approaches to the study of families and households, however (such as the studies in Chapter 4), have much in common with comparative sociological studies of family lives across the globe. We hope that your reading of this chapter will also raise questions of how far, and in what ways, the theoretical and conceptual frameworks of family discourses and family practices, and intimacy and personal lives (which you focused on in Chapters 5 and 6) may be limited to, or can work beyond, the contemporary western cultural contexts within which they have been formulated.

The contribution that can be made from historical perspectives has also been apparent in earlier discussions, when we considered how census categories developed as a basis for quantitative data in Chapter 4. In the next section, you will encounter examples of insights that may be gained from using qualitative approaches to the analysis of historical evidence.

2   Family meanings in historical contexts

2.1 Imagining traditional and modern families?

You saw in Chapter 1 how the idea of the family has often been closely linked with the natural and biological world, and it is only in the past fifty years or so that historians have thought of 'the family' as a suitable field for serious study as a social and cultural phenomenon. Another very common set of ideas about families in the past is that there has been a shift from something called the 'traditional' family to a 'modern' family. The 'traditional' family is usually imagined to be a large group of kin living together, including children, parents and grandparents. Such families were thought to live as stable groups with few breaks in marriage and inheritance patterns. They were also imagined to live in the same communities across many generations, with very little geographical or social mobility. This is contrasted with a notion of the 'modern' family, which consists of a married couple with their children – the classic nuclear family form – although some sociologists refer to the nuclear family itself as 'traditional'.

Family historians have attempted to trace a specific shift from so-called traditional to modern families, linking wider social and economic processes of modernisation to family forms, structures and patterns. One of the most startling and significant findings in this process was made by Peter Laslett and his colleagues, in the 1960s and 70s, who used a methodology called 'family reconstitution'. Their study was based mainly on parish records of births, deaths and marriages, to establish that in Britain, and probably Northern Europe more generally, there had never been a common pattern of families and households containing more than two generations of parents and children (Laslett, 1965). The nuclear family form appeared to be a very long-established 'tradition' going back to the end of the medieval period and perhaps even longer. Other research followed which examined the evidence for various family forms and structures, mainly drawing on quantitative data. However, tracing family forms through the study and categorisation of records of births, deaths and other demographic data did not reveal much about what 'family' meant to those living in the past. Indeed, such research assumed that there was a distinct entity called 'the family' that could be identified and categorised.

We would now like you to read two extracts which draw on qualitative sources to put forward an argument that 'family', as a term, had rather different meanings before the industrial revolution and other modernising processes occurred. At the same time, there are also some continuities in the ways families are understood, which span many centuries. The first excerpt by Naomi Tadmor analyses the use of the language of 'family' in eighteenth-century England.

2.2   Meanings of 'family' in eighteenth-century England

Naomi Tadmor drew on a selection of five English texts from the 1700s, including diaries and novels, to examine closely what the writers meant by 'family' in these texts.

Activity 7.2

As you read the following extract, consider three aspects of Tadmor's analysis:

1   What are the significant meanings of family which Tadmor outlines?

2   Why have historians tended to ignore the meanings which she has identified?

3   What are the continuities with family meanings in Britain today?

Reading 7.1   Naomi Tadmor, 'The concept of the household-family in eighteenth-century England'

In seventeenth- and eighteenth-century England, we are told, the English family was characteristically nuclear. [...] But what concepts of the family did people have in seventeenth and eighteenth-century England? Did they focus exclusively on the nuclear unit as the prototype of household and family relationships, or were other concepts of the family significant in their world-view? If we attend to the language people used, it seems that the latter was the case. Very often, when English people spoke or wrote about 'families', it was not the nuclear unit that they had in mind. 'Family' in their language could mean a household, including its diverse dependants, such as servants, apprentices and co-resident relatives. Accordingly, Samuel Johnson [in his Dictionary of the English Language, 1755] defined 'family' as 'those who live in the same house'.

This meaning of the term has been noticed by many scholars: indeed, it is mentioned in the opening pages of several studies of the history of the family. But though they have noted this contemporary usage, historians rarely focus upon it when establishing their own guidelines for analysis. Some historians simply mention the archaic usage while clarifying the terms of their discussion, but then proceed to attend to what they regard as family relationships; and most importantly, these have been the nuclear family relationships. Others have devised and developed their own detailed categories for defining household and family types measuring exact degrees of complexity and extension. These categories [...] have become extremely influential in family history. Their main purpose has been to facilitate quantitative research and to enable comparative studies of household and family types across different cultures and historical periods. Nevertheless, one may ask, how illuminating are these categories if they do not engage in dialogue with the terms used by historical actors? [...]

In contrast with much recent work, this essay does adopt the archaic concept of the family – the household, including its diverse possible dependants – as its central concept for analysis. This concept, it is argued, should be seen as fundamental in two senses. First, it was fundamental in contemporaries' own understanding of what families and households were. Secondly, and following from this, this concept also illuminates a wide canvas of social action; for example, when people left households or joined them, as servants, apprentices, wards or even as long-term guests, their actions were very often understood as familial actions. To be sure, there was a concept of 'family' in seventeenth- and eighteenth-century England emanating from relationships of blood and marriage. But, as this article aims to show, there was also a related yet different, and highly significant, concept of the family emanating from relationships of co-residence and authority.

The archive in which I trace this concept is linguistic. My premise is that a systematic study of words and expressions – that is, active usages employed in the eighteenth century when referring to families – can yield important information about the ways in which family ties were understood; and the keyword on which this article focuses is 'family' itself. [...]

[...]

The concept of the household-family is widely current throughout these [...] texts. [...] The following quotations present a set of ordinary but well-defined examples that demonstrate some of its main features:

> I dined on the remains of What *my Family* had for dinner ...

> I would be little justified to *my family*, that you have no reason to complain of hardships from me ...

[...]

In each of these examples a 'family' is referred to, but who are these families? [...]

When Thomas Turner wrote the first example [in his diary] he was a childless widower. Both his parents were also dead, and his relatives were living elsewhere. In other words, it is impossible that on this occasion he was referring to anyone from either his nuclear family or his extended family. Who, then, were the persons whom he designated as 'my family'? The people who on that day remained and dined at home were Thomas Turner's maidservant and the assistant in his shop. Both were members of Turner's household, but neither was related to him by blood or marriage.

[...]

The speaker in the [second] example is a literary character, Mr B. in Samuel Richardson's novel *Pamela* [1740]. Like Thomas Turner, [...] Mr B. is a single man. He is also an orphan. However, he is not a widower but a bachelor. The persons he refers to as 'my family' consist of his numerous household servants, and in these lines he rebukes one of them while justifying himself towards the rest.

[...]

[...] All these families [including some further examples not given in this extract] have some characteristics in common. They are household units: they consist of persons living under the same roof and under the authority of a householder. The heads of these families are single persons, in each case single men. Finally, there are no kinship relations between the heads of these families and their family members. [...] and probably none of these units would be referred to today as a 'family' except perhaps in a metaphorical sense. Nevertheless, they bear witness to a significant form of social and familial organization. They present an extreme, though by no means a rare formation of the household-family, and therefore provide us with a key for understanding some of the basic principles of this historical family concept.

[...]

The main difference between Thomas Turner's concept of the household-family and the standard categories of classification is that the latter rest on the concept of the nuclear family, and particularly the conjugal unit [i.e. a married couple]. Thus, for example, households that include relatives beyond the nuclear core are defined as 'extended', whereas households that include no nuclear core are defined as 'solitaries'. [...] In contrast to these definitions [...] in the eighteenth century families could exist quite apart from notions of conjugality. [...]

[...] however, it should be stressed [...] that there were other concepts of the family that existed alongside, or in conjunction with, the concept of the household-family. Most notably, there was a concept of the family as a lineage, and a concept of the family as a circle of kin; [...] Thomas Turner, for example, used the concept of the lineage in his diary mainly in relation to the crown, the nobility and historical events. He used it regularly when referring to his aristocratic neighbours, the Pelhams. There was also a concept of the family as a circle of kin – from which, significantly, the servants were excluded. For example, when Turner described a festive dinner which he and his wife had in company with '*Mr Fuller's own family*' and others, no servants are mentioned as present. This was probably the nearest he came in his diary to expressing an idea of the family as a co-resident nuclear unit. And, of course, many usages could also have overlapping connotations. When Mr B. refers to himself as being 'the last in my family' he is invoking concepts of both lineage and kinship. [...]

I have tried to show that the concept of the household-family was a central and widely used one in the eighteenth century. [...] I have argued that it is through a rigorous examination of the language of texts that we can develop a better understanding of the eighteenth century household: one which takes greater account of the notions and practices of the historical actors themselves.

Reading source

Tadmor, 1996, pp. 111–40

Comment

This article makes several key points in thinking about the family historically:

1 Tadmor focuses mainly on the meanings of family which other historians have not taken seriously. The main point she makes is that 'family' was closely connected to the household and those living together, whether or not they were related. The other key feature of this kind of 'family' was that all its members were under the authority of the head of the household, as husband and father, if there was a wife or children living there, but also as master of apprentices and servants. She also points to the importance of lineage in the meanings of family, of the linking of previous generations to the present one through inheritance of

Figure 7.1
Mr B.
attempts to
seduce his
maidservant
Pamela. An
illustration
from the
novel by
Samuel
Richardson

name, land or other property. Finally she includes the importance of kinship, of ties of blood and marriage. Thus she argues that familial connections based on both kinship and contract coexisted in households and families in the past.

2   Tadmor argues that historians bring their own ideas about 'family' with them when they look at the past. Thus, they have examined evidence with particular concepts and understandings of what they are looking for, and in this process they may not be able to see meanings which are radically different from the present day. This is not to say that even the most highly skilled historian will be able to find the ultimate truth about what family meant in the past – and Tadmor would not claim to have done this. But an attention to language is likely to be a rewarding and revealing approach. She also points to the emphasis which many historians have placed on quantitative research about families that relies on categories which can then be compared with other places and times. This is a rather inflexible way of representing the fluidity and complexity of family life, as we saw in Chapter 4, and as we will consider further later in this chapter.

3   If we think about what Tadmor says, we can see that families in the past may have had very different sets of meanings to those of today. But there is some continuity with these older discourses, including the idea of co-residence as carrying important connections with family. This is something you saw in Chapter 4 with your focus on the census, which is still shaped around the household and used to formulate data about 'families'. In addition, kinship and

lineage are both widely understood to be connected with what 'family' means today. In many respects, too, these examples resonate with the discussions concerning the slipperiness of the term 'family' in earlier chapters, and the layers of family meanings noted in Becker and Charles' study based in Swansea.

2.3 Family naming practices in nineteenth-century Western Europe

These changes and continuities can be traced in the excerpt in the next activity, in which John Gillis discusses families and naming practices in the nineteenth century in the wider context of Western Europe and its white colonial societies (including the United States). He writes about how names and naming practices help to establish boundaries relating to inclusion and exclusion in families. Family names are often taken for granted today, and surnames are the main tool for researching individual family histories. You may have looked into your own family tree, and if not, you probably know someone who has done, as it has become a major leisure activity in recent years. Gillis locates this practice of tracing a lineage through names as a modern one, part of a major transition in nineteenth-century Western-European families, when families became distinguished from households as a particular set of relationships. He is most interested in family practices, rituals and symbols which relate to this transition, and how these can be seen to define families in historically specific ways.

Activity 7.3

As you read the extract, we'd like you to consider the following:

1 What three aspects of naming practices does Gillis identify?

2 In what ways does his portrayal of the changes to the idea of family in the nineteenth century differ from the meanings of family Tadmor found in the eighteenth century? And in what ways are they similar?

Reading 7.2   John Gillis, 'Names and naming'

Families not only saw but spoke of themselves in an entirely new manner. By the mid-nineteenth century, the definition of the word *family* distinguished it from *household* or any other residential unit. The idiom of parenthood and siblingship was reserved to flesh and blood alone, and children ceased to address their parents as 'Sir' and 'Madame'; the terms they had once used in speaking to all adults now seemed inappropriate for those special persons they were calling 'Daddy' and 'Mommy' for the first time. Such terms of endearment, together with the pet names Victorians became so fond of using, swathed each family with a language of its own making, as transparent to them as it was opaque to those who spoke

Figure 7.2
A British
middle-class
christening
c. 1900

another family tongue. Language defined the boundaries of particular families just as it defined the borders of nations. Caught up in their own rhetorics, in the stories they told themselves and nobody else, imagined families took on a life no less real than the imagined communities that had come to underlie the national consciousness.

Names too were endowed with a magic they had not had previously. In the eighteenth century, naming had ordinarily not taken place until there was assurance that the newborn would survive, and the names given were symbolic of ties other than those of family. Catholics chose from a limited stock of saints' names, while Protestants preferred names that were emblematic of virtue – Patience, Preserved, Chastity – rather than family connections. Frequently, the same name was used more than once, transferred from a dead to a living sibling. But from the mid–nineteenth century onward, names took on unprecedented significance, and the christening ceremony, previous a relatively minor part of Christian baptism, became its most meaningful moment, an important family occasion, a rite of passage not into an extended spiritual community but into the family world itself. ...

Only the nobility had been able to lay sure claim to a family name in earlier centuries. As late as the eighteenth century, the connection between the individuals and surnames was tenuous ... Names were more likely to be attached to land than to family ... Many ... among the poor were called solely by their first name or nickname for their entire lives. However, by the end of the nineteenth century, the possession of a surname divided people by gender rather than by class. It would be some time before women would gain (or regain) the right to retain their own name in marriage, but already the family name was the first thing a child learned, the first sign of its intelligence, and its initiation into its own special family world.

Names became the family's symbolic link with its past and the promise of its future. They were carefully recorded in family Bibles and entered in the family trees that in the Victorian era became a sure sign of membership in the middle class. While the aristocracy had always invested itself in its pedigrees, the middle–class passion for genealogy was entirely new. In the second half of the century, dozens of genealogical societies were founded on both sides of the Atlantic. ... What had been considered a vanity and an affectation earlier became an indispensable emblem of connection for family members who found themselves increasingly isolated from one another.

Reading source

Gillis, 1997, pp. 74–5

Comment

1 Gillis looks at three aspects of naming practices in thinking about the changes to the meanings of family in the mid-nineteenth century.

   (a) First, he shows how the language used between family members became more intimate and emotionally explicit, and how these practices had the effect of drawing boundaries between families, and of making each family group more distinct from other sets of relationships of its members, and from each other. He compares this to the sense of national identity forged through a shared language which was emerging at this time in places like Italy and Germany.

   (b) Secondly, he points to the changes in the rituals of naming children, and the more personal and individual kinds of names they were given. These emphasised the uniqueness of each child as it joined its particular family, rather than the entry of a child into a wider spiritual and social community.

How far western societies, in the last two centuries or so, have seen the emergence of a particular notion of the individual is an issue that will be taken up later in this chapter.

(c)   Thirdly, he draws our attention to the changing meanings of surnames, which were previously connected to land. By the end of the nineteenth century they were universally used as a marker of membership to a family for all classes. He then goes on to link the spread of surnames to a growing concern to trace lineages and to connect present-day families with the past, as they found themselves more physically isolated in distinct, separate and private family groups. This he links to the growing privacy of the home during this period as production became separated from domestic life, a point Gillis develops elsewhere in his book. Very gradually more and more people worked in factories, workshops and other settings, rather than in places where they slept and ate together.

2   Gillis sees family meanings as undergoing important changes between the eighteenth-century world that Tadmor sets out, and the late nineteenth century. The household is less significant than the emotional and ritual bonds between parents and children, and thus servants, apprentices, lodgers and friends lose their central place in meanings of family. However, the idea of lineage continues across both periods, extending from the wealthy down to the humble as families took up naming practices of the wealthy for their own families. You may also have noticed resonances with some of the contemporary themes of family meanings discussed in Chapter 3.

Summary

1   By looking at different historical moments, we can begin to see that family meanings are never fixed, but constantly shift within changing social contexts. Just as today, people in the past took up, used and altered meanings of family as they made sense of their everyday relationships.

2   Tadmor's attention to language – of listening in order to look – shows us that it is important to step back from our assumptions about what we are looking for. By doing so, we can explore meanings of family even when they appear strange and unfamiliar to us, in this case in the distant world of eighteenth-century England.

3   Gillis' use of family practices relating to names is also very revealing in uncovering the shaping of meanings, and how these can change over time but also include continuities with the past.

In the next section, we turn from considering such qualitative evidence of family meanings in previous historical periods to focus on evidence of the meanings of family from across the world.

3   Family meanings in global contexts

Some social scientists have argued that 'the (nuclear) family' is found across all societies:

> A widespread view in family studies has been that 'the family' is universal, performing similar functions in societies all over the world. Murdock's (1960/2003) thesis on the universality of the nuclear family was largely unquestioned for decades. Critics suggest, however, that notions of a universal family can only be sustained by imposing a particular understanding of one family form (the Western nuclear family) on a great variety of social arrangements across societies and cultures.
>
> (Ribbens McCarthy and Edwards, 2011, p 31)

Murdock saw sexual coupling, and the raising of children, as biological imperatives, such that societies could not continue without the existence of 'the family' – hence its universality. A challenge to this view argues that, while the presence of a younger generation of workers and carers may indeed be necessary for social life to continue, sexual coupling and the care of children may occur in all sorts of social networks, while migration may provide a labour force even when birth rates fall below the level needed for each generation to be reproduced in a particular society. So, by insisting on the universality of 'the family', a form of cultural imperialism may occur, potentially blinding researchers to the ways in which various aspects of social reproduction are embedded within, and take their meaning from, particular and variable cultural contexts.

Whether or not it is either accurate or helpful to assert the universality of 'the family', such an approach points to a key tension for social scientists: on the one hand, there may be reasons for wanting to generalise about the meaning of 'family' globally, across societies and cultures, in order to explore what is shared about human experience at a very broad level, or to provide a basis for policy developments; on the other hand, there may also be strong arguments concerning the need to pay attention to variability and difference, with due regard to the significance of understanding meanings in local contexts. From this point of view, social scientists want to explore differences between people's views of the world, seeking to understand these by reference to cultural contexts. This is a major focus for anthropologists:

> What social and cultural anthropologists generally share ... is an interest in different ways people have of looking at the world they live in. These different ways are not individual idiosyncrasies, but different views of the world learned as people grow up in different societies, or within one of the different groups that make up one larger society.
>
> (Hendry, 2008, p. 2)

3.1 Concepts of family and kinship in anthropology

In order to be sensitive to such differences in world views, anthropologists developed a methodology known as 'ethnography', which involved living in the community they were studying for long periods of time, and seeking to understand all aspects of the social lives of people living there. This could be experienced as very challenging at a personal level, sometimes characterised by a disorientation known as 'culture shock' after spending a period of time immersed in another way of life:

> All kinds of things that had once been totally familiar suddenly seem odd, as if one were seeing them for the first time. Consequently, everything becomes questionable: why have I always done this or assumed that? This questioning attitude is perhaps the most basic feature of anthropology. Most people most of the time simply get on with their lives. It could hardly be otherwise, given all that there is to do. It is only under special circumstances that we stop to reflect, and the experience of another culture is a common stimulus.
>
> (Metcalf, 2005, pp. 2–3)

The first challenge an ethnographic study of another culture entails is to learn the language of the people being studied, as well as paying close attention over time to the minutiae of everyday practices of living. Anthropologists have thus been wary of applying the concept of 'family' in studying other cultures, where we have to consider how far ideas and concepts have simple equivalents in different languages:

> The words used for 'family' among the Dhoria Thakors [in Gujarat in India] are *katam (kutumb)* and *parivar*. These are interchangeably used to signify the family reality, though the more commonly used word is *katam*. This word encompasses more than a household and, in some contexts, a lineage segment. The dispersed households of a joint family generally occupy houses adjacent to each other, have a common courtyard and a common entry-exit gate, own fields adjacent to each other, share a common well, possess a common shrine, constitute a primary group for rites of passages, and have a regular flow of inter-household ritual gifts.
>
> (Lobo, 2005, p. 281)

In this description of the Dhoria Thakors, then, we can see that an array of relevant features of social life are implicated in 'family' life, including: household, lineage, proximity of residence and agricultural production, shared space and boundaries, a shared water source, a common shrine, shared rites and ritual-gift exchanges. In order to understand family meanings here, we need to explore the range of interconnected meanings and practices around each of these features of social and economic life. In this regard, it may only be through seeing how a word is used in context that its meanings can become clear – as we saw with Tadmor's careful analysis (discussed above) of what 'family' meant to the individuals whose words and lives she studied in historical context, and as we saw in the qualitative research discussed in Part 1 of this book.

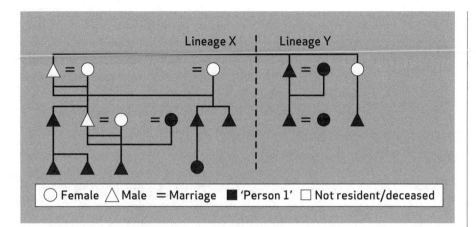

Figure 7.3
Anthro-
pological
diagram of
kinship
patterns
(Source:
Morphy,
2006, p. 24)

'Person 1' = head of household

Instead of the language of 'family' then, earlier periods of anthropology focused very strongly on kinship patterns, often developing complex technical language and graphic diagrams to provide a way of making comparative descriptions across cultures.

Understanding varied societies and cultures is no easy matter, however, and simply avoiding the term 'family' may only go a small way towards opening up our minds to other ways of seeing the world. Thus, the term 'kinship', once so central to anthropology, has also come to be highly disputed as inevitably and inappropriately imposing western ideas of kinship structures on other peoples. This is discussed in some detail by Morphy (2006), for example, with regard to the contemporary census classification of households and relationships of indigenous Australians which used Anglo-Celtic kinship terms that are completely inappropriate, resulting in census returns that were 'not only wrong, but incomprehensible' (p. 29). In recent years, then, anthropologists have suggested other terms that might be used in place of kinship – such as 'reproduction' (Robertson, 1991) or 'relatedness' (Carsten, 2004) – to study those areas of social life and relationships that might, in European and New World industrialised societies, be assumed to come within the remit of 'family'. And this is all part of a broader discussion within anthropology about how researchers can ever fully understand cultures other than their own, and then re-present them to (often western) academic readers – sometimes described as a 'crisis of representation' within anthropology.

In the following example, anthropologists John Monaghan and Peter Just discuss varieties of social formations in different societies, and consider how easy it might be for a western visitor to assume the nuclear family system as a universal basis of family meanings and practices, when in fact this would be highly misleading, failing to understand other people's experiences and lives.

> Anthropologists have learned that societies get along quite well with family units that are both more extensive and less extensive than the nuclear family. A family

can be as minimal as a mother and her children or as elaborate as an Indian joint fraternal family in which parents live with their unmarried children, their married sons, and the wives and children of those sons ... And in yet another model for domestic arrangements, there are societies in both the Amazon basin and highland New Guinea where men and adolescent boys live together collectively in a men's house while women, their daughters, and their young sons live in separate households. Their husbands and fathers visit them from time to time, but rarely spend the night.

A single society may easily accommodate a variety of family types. Similarly, we must not regard these domestic units as static, but rather as being subject to a complex developmental cycle. Among the Dou Donggo [who live on the island of Sumbawa in Indonesia] ... the newly weds ... move into their own house immediately on marriage. Their house is usually built near to that of the bride's family (so she will be near her mother when she bears her first child), so ultimately a village compound is created consisting of a group of sisters and their households. If you were to look at many Dou Donggo households you would see what looks like a 'nuclear family' resembling our own Western model. But it would be quite misleading to see it that way, since the 'nuclear family' is but a part of a wider picture. Similarly, child-rearing, which is one of the central undertakings of the family, is virtually never surrendered to a child's parents alone, but is shared by grandparents, aunts and uncles, and others who happen to be nearby. Children move about from house to house, eating where they are hungry and sleeping where they happen to be when darkness falls. Indeed, in practical terms the nuclear family is a very inefficient child-rearing unit, poorly suited to the task.

(Monaghan and Just, 2000, pp. 83–4)

For people from the Dou Donggo, then, it is the nuclear family pattern as it is understood in western societies that might be difficult to comprehend. Such variable contexts around the world thus raise major issues about what language to use, including appropriate terms and concepts for understanding 'family' meanings, indicating the care needed in listening in order to know how to look. Furthermore, there may be deep political and ethical issues concerning who is doing the looking, under what circumstances and for what purposes. These issues in turn have significant theoretical and methodological implications, and we will consider some of these now through the example of one particular ethnographic study.

3.2 Localised and globalised meanings – an example from India

Susan Seymour undertook a thirty-year ethnographic study of a particular village in Orissa in India, living there with her own family for various periods of time. We encourage you to read the following extracts from her study both critically (thinking about the issues involved in this sort of ethnographic study), and reflexively (thinking about any responses you have yourself to the family practices and values that are described). Bear in mind that, in writing up her study, Seymour explicitly states that she wanted to introduce her readers to 'difference', to expand their ideas of what is 'normal', and encourage empathy towards practices they might otherwise find hard to understand. We should note, then, that we are presented with an account of these families that has been written by an 'outsider' to the community, who comes from a much more affluent, powerful and privileged society, and is writing specifically with an American audience in mind.

Early in her book, Seymour provides an overall description of family structure and ideology in India which she characterises as patrifocal, i.e. male oriented in terms of both the practices involved and the underlying beliefs. She contrasts this with the autonomous nuclear family unit of the 'American cultural system':

> India's culturally idealized family system ... traces descent and inheritance through males (patrilineality); encourages sets of related men to reside together and bring wives in from the outside (patrilocal residence); gives males authority over women; and bases family honor, in part, on the sexual purity of women, using such institutions as early arranged marriage and purdah [i.e. religious beliefs involving the seclusion of women] to control female sexuality. This extended family unit, commonly referred to as the 'joint family,' is male oriented in both its structure and associated beliefs and values; hence, my use of the term 'patrifocal family structure and ideology'.
>
> (Seymour, 1999, p. 8)

This description of 'the family' in varying cultural systems thus resonates with Bernardes' discussion of 'general' concepts of 'the family' (as discussed in Chapter 1), which are abstracted and generalised notions that may or may not resemble the intricacies of everyday lives and family meanings. However, elsewhere in the book, Seymour provides a very different, specific and nuanced discussion of how the women she interviewed discussed their changing family lives in the context of their particular communities.

Activity 7.5

As you read the following extract from Seymour's ethnography, which includes interviews with a mother and her two adult daughters, we'd like you to bear the following questions in mind:

1 What meanings of 'family' can you identify in the quotes taken from these interviews?

2 How are these seen to be changing?

Reading 7.3.1   Susan Seymour, 'Women, family, and childcare in India'

At the conclusion of my interviews with mothers, daughters, and grandmothers, I always inquired if there were something I should have asked about that I had not. This question usually resulted in women asking me questions about women's and men's roles in the United States and in our then making comparisons between Indian and American systems of family and gender. One of the most poignant responses to this question, however, came from the New Capital Misra family.

MOTHER: *You have not asked about family obligations, what we should do, that which is there in family life, like my husband's older sister who was widowed just before we were married. She had to come, together with her sons, to stay with us. They had to come here to get a good education and all, to get their family settled. This was for seven or eight years. Other family members had to be given money, too.*

When she paused, I ask, 'So you had to help out?'

MRS MISRA: *[correcting me]: [It's] not that we had to. Not true, because my brother-in-law is also there, and he also has a lot of money, but he doesn't spend it. … Indian families – you must look at their difference. I never thought of [not taking on my husband's family responsibilities]. I never asked anything to my husband [in the early years of marriage]. I always asked to my parents, my mother.*

MENAKA: *Out auntie (Mother's sister), since she was earning, she always gave us the best of dresses …*

MOTHER: *I never asked Mr Misra for anything. How could I do it?*

MENAKA: *That's where self-sacrifice comes in.*

MOTHER: *Because I know that he's in difficulty.*

NAKIMA: *But I'm sure the same would not be true for a girl, even if she's not working, a girl of today. She would certainly put her foot down. I mean that things have changed to a certain extent.*

MOTHER: *That was one of the reasons why we wanted you to work, to stand on your own feet.*

NAKIMA: *Even if a girl's not earning, even if she's just a housewife, she would certainly rebel.*

'You mean there would be less acceptance of the husband's earnings going to other relatives?' I ask.

MOTHER: *That's why my in-laws …*

NAKIMA: *[cuts her off]: Especially nowadays, the mentality is you give money as a type of investment. You give somebody some money, and you expect a return back.*

'Rather than an expectation that it's just a responsibility to help out with relatives?' I ask.

NAKIMA: *Yes.*

Reading source

Seymour, 1999, pp. 265–6

Comment

1   Mrs Misra's understanding of 'family' distinguishes between her husband's family and her own, and both of these 'family' relationships involve exchanges of resources and support during adult lives. In responding to Seymour's enquiry about what might have been left out of their earlier conversations, then, Mrs Misra makes it clear that 'family' for her means access to resources and obligations to support relatives. Thus, Mrs Misra's widowed sister-in-law and nephews received financial and practical help from her husband, and also shared accommodation – even to the extent that Mr Misra struggled to provide for his own wife and children. As a result, Mrs Misra then looked to her own parents for additional support. But this was not seen as an inevitable obligation, since her husband's brother did not provide such support to their sister.

2   According to one of the daughters, Nakima, this pattern of support has changed, to become a relationship of exchange rather than a gift.

In discussing these quotes, Seymour relates the women's comments to the broader patrifocal context. As you read the next extract from Seymour's discussion, can you identify how she traces the ways in which the women draw on, and reinforce, ideas of patrifocal family lives, but also modify them and reframe them in the light of changing circumstances?

Reading 7.3.2   Susan Seymour 'Women, family, and childcare in India'

It is significant that Mrs Misra's immediate response to the question 'What had I failed to ask?' was to begin talking about 'family obligations.' She put our discussion of changing women's roles and marriage practices back into the patrifocal family context in which the well-being of the extended family unit is supposed to take precedence over the needs of the nuclear unit of husband, wife, and children. She spoke of the heavy financial commitment that her husband assumed when they were first married. It was sufficiently heavy that she was reluctant to make any special requests of him. ... As Menaka appropriately expressed it, her mother had exhibited 'self-sacrifice,' an essential ingredient of being a good wife. Traditional patrifocal family values stipulate that as a wife a woman should put the needs of her husband's extended family above her own and those of her own children.

...

[But] ... this mother-daughter dialogue addresses a potentially significant change in attitude toward family and gender roles. Nakima, Mrs Misra's youngest daughter, asserts that 'a girl' (a woman of her generation) would no longer silently accept the financial sacrifice as her mother had done. She would 'put her foot down,' meaning she would not be willing to sacrifice her own well-being or that of her children in favor of the well-being of the extended family. ... Both [Nakima and another interviewee]... identify a locus of change: that is, educated wives who are capable of asserting themselves and opposing the collective interests of the traditional patrifocal family. It is fear of such threats to the unity and coherence of the joint family that makes some men reluctant to educate their daughters and other men hesitant to have highly educated daughters-in-law.

Reading source

Seymour, 1999, pp. 266–7

Comment

In her discussion, Seymour links this specific conversation to wider accounts of expectations and obligations around different sets of family relations. She also links the language of 'self-sacrifice' to broader ideals of the 'good wife', and finally connects these two different elements of the analysis together, i.e. how a good wife should behave in terms of family obligations.

But there is also a suggestion that these beliefs and expectations about gender roles are changing and modifying, and that this may be linked to the education of women.

Later in the book, Seymour moves her focus again, to a very broad and generalised discussion of family meanings in relation to differing understandings of the individual and selfhood across global contexts.

Activity 7.6

1   How does Seymour characterise western and non–western individuals?

2   What do you think she means by 'cultural models' and why does she use this term?

Reading 7.3.3 Susan Seymour, 'Women, family, and childcare in India'

Placing value upon interdependence, rather than upon independence and personal autonomy, is widespread in India and integral to the successful functioning of the traditional patrifocal family. Studies ... in several regions of India all agree on this fundamental principle. Children are socialized ... to identify with the family as a whole and to put the interests of that collective unit ahead of their individual interests. ... [There is a] complex web of interactions that discourage the development of an autonomous self in favor of what Alan Roland (1988) has called a 'we-self' – a person whose sense of identity is based upon a deep-seated emotional connectedness with others.

...

Although it is important to recognize that societies may construct quite different conceptions of the individual and of selfhood from one another and may, therefore, select from the range of human potential different qualities for emphasis, it is also important not to overdraw the distinctions. Western 'egocentric' individuals must also be capable of becoming social beings; they can never be totally autonomous and independent of others. Reciprocally, non-Western 'sociocentric' individuals cannot be totally interdependent and other-oriented. They must be capable of at least some autonomous thought and action. Interdependence –independence might best be conceptualized as a continuum along which cultures fall according to the particular mixture of collectivist and individualist elements that they exhibit at any one time. One must, however, always remember that the effort to characterize such societal orientations requires building cultural models with which to examine the actual behavior that different members of a society exhibit.

In these two models it is, in fact, the tension between the two different constructions of self that often becomes culturally salient.

Reading source

Seymour, 1996, pp. 268–9

Comment

1 Seymour characterises western individuals as 'egocentric' and 'independent', which is associated with an 'autonomous' sense of selfhood. Non-western individuals are characterised as 'sociocentric' and 'interdependent', with a 'collective' sense of selfhood. Each of these has different implications for meanings of family, such that the more autonomous sense of selfhood might mean that people experience themselves as individuals most clearly *apart* from 'family'– resulting in a tension between 'being yourself' and 'being family' – whereas a more collective sense of selfhood might mean that individuals

experience themselves precisely *through* being part of 'family'. Such differences of experience are likely to be associated with quite different approaches to child-rearing. One concrete example can be seen in the historical changes of naming practices discussed earlier in this chapter: in the contemporary UK it has become common to give children highly unusual names, signifying the uniqueness of the individual. From present UK perspectives then, it would seem unthinkable to follow historical practices of giving a younger sibling the same name as an older sibling who had died, and there is much less likelihood of calling a child after another relative.

2   These characterisations are said to represent 'cultural models' which express different values and priorities. Seymour is concerned to explain that individuals living in all cultures have to find ways to accommodate both interdependence and independence, which she suggests should be seen as a continuum rather than alternatives. You may recall in the UK research discussed in Chapter 3, for example, how some interviewees identified themselves much more than others by reference to their family identities. The cultural models are, then, abstractions against which to understand lived experiences of the tensions between autonomy and connection, personal and collective interests.

A difference of orientation towards individuality and connectedness is a common feature of discussions concerning cultural variations, with anglophone societies particularly characterised as emphasising independent and self-directing autonomous individuality (as discussed in earlier chapters). Such an understanding of the individual may also be seen to underpin such diverse cultural features as liberal democratic political systems, and the knowledge base of psychology. Nevertheless, it is crucial not to overstate such themes, or there is a danger of overlooking the tensions and variations within and between western developed societies, while characterising the majority of the world by the dichotomised and simplistic term, 'non-western'. In Chapter 3, for example, we saw some of the variability within the UK around whether families are understood as collections of 'individuals' or as units of people who together experience a shared identity.

Summary

■ Understanding family meanings in varied global contexts is a difficult enterprise, whether we are trying to explore the cultural meanings of localised small groups or to develop cultural models that might provide insights into diversities across whole regions of the world.

■ Different cultural systems may encompass much larger and more varied groupings, relationships and patterns of residence than are encompassed by the term 'family', as it is often used by social scientists in Europe and the New World.

■ In exploring such issues, people may start to see what is taken-for-granted about their own cultural contexts, whatever those may be. Nevertheless, anthropologists warn that this may often be an uncomfortable process, exposing us to a sense of vulnerability and uncertainty in the context of unknown and unfamiliar customs and practices.

4 Comparative approaches

4.1 Quantitative comparisons of families and family meanings across Europe

While anthropologists struggle to describe the nuances and complexities of family meanings in diverse contexts through in-depth qualitative studies, some sociologists and historians may use more quantitative methodologies to develop comparative descriptions. Such comparisons may refer to different time periods (as in the work of Laslett we mentioned earlier), or to different groups or regions within any one society (as in the changing UK statistical patterns discussed in Chapter 4). Such data sets are generally collected by governments or international governing bodies, and are thus defined by reference to the nation state. They are also likely to be collected in more systematic and extensive ways by affluent societies that have the resources to collate such information, as well as a greater need for such information in order to plan and provide services. Such data sets can then be used by social scientists to compare patterns of family lives and meanings across societies, and sometimes across entire regions of the world. Nevertheless, cultural differences – both within and

Figure 7.4
Flags of Europe

between different nation states – concerning the underlying meanings of the terms used, and the practices of everyday lives, may create considerable problems for such quantitative comparative studies. There is thus always the danger of comparing things that can't really be compared.

These difficulties are discussed by Linda Hantrais (2004) in her comparative work on family change in Europe. In discussing some of the methodological difficulties in such work, Hantrais points to the importance of language, and whether the same term is exactly equivalent in different European languages. Other difficulties arise from all the myriad ways in which data is collected for rather different purposes, or using rather different terms, with significant consequences for the statistical information that results. Among the many examples that Hantrais discusses are issues about definitions of households, homelessness and main residence, questions about how to understand intergenerational relationships and the age limits of 'dependent children', and identifications of 'reconstituted families' and 'lone parents'.

Despite such methodological difficulties, such data sets are used to develop comparative descriptions of family lives across Europe, based, for example, on statistics of demographic trends such as marriage and divorce rates.

Table 7.1 Marriage and divorce rates across Europe (1960–2000)

	1960	1970	1980	1990	1999/2000
Marriages per 1,000 population	7.7	7.7	6.3	6.0	5.1
Age at first marriage for men	26.7[e]	25.9[e]	26.0[e]	27.7	30.3
Age at first marriage for women	24.1[e]	23.2[e]	23.3[e]	25.3	28.1
Divorces per 1,000 population	0.5	0.8	1.4	1.7	1.9[e]
% of marriages dissolved by divorce by marriage cohort	15.0	22.0	28.0	n.a	n.a

[e] Eurostat estimates

(Source: Eurostat (2002a, tables F-3, F-8, F-9, F-15, F-18), quoted in Hantrais, 2004, p. 51)

Such comparative work raises the thorny issue of how we draw the lines for comparison, with consequences for where we see difference and where we see commonalities. As you will see from the quotation below, Hantrais offers descriptions of broad trends of family patterns across the whole of Europe, whilst distinguishing varying patterns between different groupings of countries.

> In sum, non-institutionalised family forms have become more widespread. Marriage rates have been falling, age at marriage and childbearing is being postponed, and family and household size has been declining ... Lone parenthood, most often as a result of divorce or separation, has become a more common experience. The proportion of one-person households has increased, but the

number of multigenerational households has decreased, despite the fact that young people are remaining longer in the parental home.

Although the direction of change in family structure across Europe during the latter part of the 20th century is similar, distinct clusters of countries can be identified that share characteristics with regard to the pace, timing and extent of change in patterns of family formation, family structure and the development of alternative living arrangements ... Denmark and Sweden, followed by France, stand out as the member states where postponement of family formation and the development of alternative family forms seem to have been taken furthest. By contrast, Poland and Slovakia combine the most traditional family forms with the most conventional patterns for the timing of family formation.

(Hantrais, 2004, p. 63)

Once such family patterns have been discerned through statistical analysis, questions may then be posed about how to explain such patterns and the resulting implications for policy-makers. A further feature of a comparative study, then, may be the study of people's values, which may be thought to relate to such differences in family lives, perhaps shedding more light on the underlying family meanings. Hantrais also discusses how these generalisations may be used as a basis for large-scale models of overall value orientations, characterised as traditional versus non-traditional, and materialist versus post-materialist. While the specifics of these models need not divert us here, you may notice how these quantitative studies can thus lead to large-scale characterisations of whole regions of the world, in rather similar ways to the outcomes of the studies of anthropologists. This is something we encountered with Seymour's comparative discussion of different understandings of the individual and selfhood.

4.2 The pitfalls and benefits of comparative approaches

In spite of the methological difficulties involved in such studies, however, both quantitative and qualitative researchers persist with comparative work. Jane Ribbens McCarthy and Rosalind Edwards discuss the reasons for this in their general overview of what is meant by 'comparative approaches':

Despite [many] methodological and conceptual difficulties, cross-cultural comparative studies can be a key source of insight into aspects of family and personal lives, and social reproduction more generally. This is particularly relevant to aspects of family lives that may otherwise be completely take-for-granted because they are so deeply embedded in the particular cultures in which researchers live their own lives. ... Such differences of understanding and of values raise questions of how far it is possible to establish common standards across different societies e.g. around such issues as 'good parenting' (Barlow et al., 2004).

(Ribbens McCarthy and Edwards, 2011, p. 32)

Without such work across cultures, then, ethnocentrism may abound, disguised as science, with the result that the understandings of family lives of other cultures are rendered invisible at best, or defined as pathological or deviant at worst. Exploring taken-for-granted cultural assumptions about families may thus be important, not only for understanding other societies or historical periods, but also for variations in family lives across social classes, ethnic, migrant and refugee groups within any particular society. At the same time, such cultural sensitivity raises difficult questions about how to evaluate differences in family lives, especially where there may appear to be significant inequalities and abuse of power. This need not necessarily lead to a perspective of total cultural relativism, but may suggest a need for scholars of family studies to be more explicit and reflexive about the value stances they take.

'Cultural relativism' is explained by Mary Ann Hollinger as a process in which:

> ... we are more open to viewing the world through the lens of 'the other'. In the process we recognize the limitations of judging other cultures by the standards of our own ... Inherent in the notion of cultural relavitism is the willingness to study and learn from other cultures ... [through] deep engagement ... and meaningful dialogue ... In ... cultural relativism, the family scientist temporarily suspends ethical and moral judgements ... If one ceases to operate from the assumption that one's own culture is normative for all others, family practices that originally seemed absurd or irrational can begin to make sense when situated in their larger ... context.
>
> (Hollinger, 2007, pp. 251–2)

Despite all the difficulties of studying families across time and place, Ribbens McCarthy and Edwards suggest important reasons for undertaking comparative studies, in terms of uncovering implicit values and taken-for-granted assumptions that might otherwise be imposed (by governments and social scientists) on peoples whose own family meanings might be quite different. Whether or not this leaves us in a position in which we are advised to avoid making any evaluative judgements about family lives and practices from other cultures is a question to which you will return in Chapter 9.

Summary

- Comparative approaches that draw on quantitative data sets – most often collated by governments – encounter many difficult methodological issues about how the data is collected and whether it is really comparable.

- Nevertheless, comparative studies may seek to develop broad generalisations about trends in family lives across large regions of the world, which may or may not also attend to differences between countries, or between regions or groups within countries.

■ Comparative studies of family values may also be used to develop broad generalisations based on models of value orientations.

■ Despite the difficulties of comparative approaches, whether based on quantitative or qualitative data, such endeavours may be important for the development of policies. They may also be important in drawing attention to taken-for-granted assumptions and implicit values, a process that may enable us to gain a better understanding of diversities *within* societies as well as *across* cultures around the globe.

5   Conclusions

In Chapter 1 we stressed the need to see how peoples' family meanings help them to make sense of their lives *in context*. By bringing varied contexts and circumstances into focus, we may gain new insights into cultural diversities. Different family meanings, and meanings of family, may thus be understood to reflect the ways in which people make sense of their lives within the contexts and circumstances they experience.

> In part, culturally diverse families can be better understood by focusing on the contextual aspects of their lives. Instead of targeting their supposedly typical characteristics, it is the circumstances of their lives that will assist us in developing frameworks for understanding cultural pluralism ... By focusing on the matrix of choices families have, on the meanings they draw on and create from the world around them, and on how they cope with societal hierarchies and power differentiation, we will gain great insight into the interrelationships between families and their lived experiences.
>
> (Sherif Trask and Marotz-Baden, 2007, p. 55)

In this chapter, we have taken a brief journey through time and place, using a variety of disciplinary and theoretical perspectives and different methodological approaches, to consider how we can understand family meanings in a wide range of contexts. A continuing tension throughout has centred on how to make generalisations, in terms of:

1 how we can group people together to make a basis for comparison

2 how far we risk overlooking differences between groups or regions within any one society or historical period

3 how far we can generalise about different orientations to families and relationships at a really broad cultural level.

In studying cultural variations, then, there is a key dilemma between, on the one hand, wanting to develop generalisations as a basis for comparisons, and, on the other, wanting to understand the uniqueness of each point of view – whether it is an individual, a community, or a society under discussion. For example, can we usefully categorise families along lines of ethnicity, when doing so may group together people with very diverse family lives, ignoring differences of class, education, locality, gender and so on?

> This ... is the very space of anthropology, **a paradoxical space between the practice of and the suspicion of generalisation.** At one and the same moment, one pursues contradictory impulses and aims to do justice to both equally. On the one hand is the individuality of detail ... On the other hand lies the aspiration of the comparative anthropologist towards ... generality and moral clarity: **this** is the human condition.
>
> (Rapport and Overing, 2007, p. xi, original emphasis)

Such paradoxes notwithstanding, we hope that this exploration of family meanings across time and space has enabled you to develop a greater understanding of how family meanings may vary, how far we may risk imposing our own taken-for-granted assumptions on the lives of others, and the difficulties of understanding the life experiences of people living in diverse circumstances.

Activity 7.8

You may now like to turn back to the notes you may have made at various points in reading this book, about your own understandings and experiences of family and relationships – which we have particularly suggested for activities in Chapter 1 and in this chapter. In what ways has your study of this chapter shed a different light on your own experiences? Are there aspects of your own understandings that you might previously have 'taken-for-granted' or seen as 'natural', but now view as more contingent, shaped by your cultural and historical situation? Have you encountered any different ways of seeing the world that you have found interesting or challenging? Some fairly practical examples might include:

- how children's names are decided

- how far we might extend our meaning of 'family', perhaps to include friends, or household members such as lodgers

- how many, and which, people may be involved in caring for children

- how far obligations towards relatives may extend, and whose needs should take priority in this.

There are also some very broad and pervasive issues raised by looking at 'families' across contexts of time and place, which prompt questions such as:

- What is the position of men in relation to women and children?

- Do we need to be separate from our 'family' in order to 'be ourselves'?

But you may have many other thoughts to add to these questions.

Comment

We hope you have found this to be an interesting and insightful exercise in self-reflection, which may be potentially useful in your interactions with others whose family meanings you may understand as similar and different to your own in myriad ways. Comparative approaches seek to see both into and beyond the specifics of particular lives, and to consider them in broader contexts. In this process, anthropologists consider such contexts in both material and cultural terms, exploring how contexts are shaped by systems of meanings as well as by interpersonal and organised structures of power.

In this chapter, we have primarily focused on how anthropological and some historical work may challenge our most basic thinking and cultural assumptions about meanings of family. But alongside the search for insight and understandings of variable family meanings, policy-makers, governments and international organisations need to know how to develop appropriate policies in the light of what is known about family lives within any one society, as well as across different societies and communities. This is where the large-scale data sets come to the fore, and, indeed, such comparative quantitative research can raise all sorts of additional questions for academics in the study of family lives.

In Chapter 8 we explore family policies and professional practices more directly than we have done so far, primarily by reference to the contemporary UK context. In this next chapter, we hope that what you have learned so far about family meanings will lead you to question taken-for-granted assumptions embedded within policies and practices. In the final chapter, we will then consider how we can start to respond to such complexities and subtleties of family lives and meanings across diverse social contexts. We will also explore how family meanings are underpinned by particular values and moral understandings.

References

Carsten, J. (2004) *After Kinship: New Departures in Anthropology*, Cambridge, Cambridge University Press.

Gillis, J.R. (1997), *A World of Their Own Making: A History of Myth and Ritual in Family Life*, Oxford, Oxford University Press.

Hantrais, L. (2004) *Family Policy Matters: Responding to Family Change in Europe*, Bristol, Policy Press.

Hendry, J. (2008) *An Introduction to Social Anthropology: Sharing Our Worlds* (2nd edn), Basingstoke, Palgrave Macmillan.

Hollinger, M.A. (2007) 'Ethical reflections for a globalized family curriculum: a developmental paradigm' in Sherif Trask, B. and Hamon, R.R. (eds) *Cultural Diversity and Families: Expanding Perspectives*, Thousand Oaks, CA, Sage, pp. 244–78.

Laslett, P. (1965) *The World We Have Lost*, London, Methuen.

Lobo, L. (2005) 'Household and family among Thakors in a North Gujarat village' in Patel, T. (ed.) *The Family in India: Structure and Practice*, New Delhi, Sage, pp. 267–86.

Metcalf, P. (2005) *Anthropology: The Basics*, London, Routledge.

Monaghan, J. and Just, P. (2000). *Social and Cultural Anthropology: A Very Short Introduction*, Oxford, Oxford University Press.

Morphy, F. (2006) 'Lost in translation? Remote indigenous households and definitions of the family', *Family Matters*, vol. 73, no. 3, pp. 23–31.

Rapport, N. and Overing, J. (2007) *Social and Cultural Anthropology: The Key Concepts* (2nd edn), Abingdon, Routledge.

Ribbens McCarthy, J. and Edwards, R. (2011) *Key Concepts in Family Studies*, London, Sage.

Robertson, A.F. (1991) *Beyond the Family: The Social Organisation of Human Reproduction*, Cambridge, Polity Press.

Seymour, S.C. (1999) *Women, Family, and Child Care in India*, Cambridge, Cambridge University Press.

Sherif Trask, B. and Hamon, R.R. (eds) (2007) *Cultural Diversity and Families: Expanding Perspectives*, Thousand Oaks, CA, Sage.

Tadmor, N. (1996) 'The concept of the household-family in eighteenth-century England', *Past and Present*, no. 151, pp. 111–40.

Chapter 8

Family meanings in social policies and professional practices

Megan Doolittle

Contents

1   Introduction

In this chapter we continue our focus on family meanings in varying contexts by exploring the ways in which family meanings appear in the contexts of social policies and in the very wide range of measures that relate to everyday family life. Among these are education, health, housing, poverty, security against violence and crime, benefits and care for the most vulnerable. Even though many of these are not explicitly 'family' policies, they can have major implications for families. If we think even more broadly, policies also cover administrative matters and the legal system which reach deeply into family life, such as taxation, inheritance and marriage. In these areas assumptions about what family means are embedded through long-standing sets of rules and practices.

Policies and the practices associated with them can be developed and carried out in different types of contexts, at various levels, with the most prominent in the UK being the different national governments (the UK, Scotland, Wales and Northern Ireland). But also, local levels of policy-making, such as local authorities, and international policy bodies such as the European Union and the United Nations, can be very influential in developing and implementing policies relating to families. Most nations develop policies and practices across all these fields and levels, and we will be using the terms 'government policies' or 'state policies' as a general way of referring to these complex arrangements. Unlike Chapter 7, where we concentrated on family meanings in different times and places, our analysis and examples in this chapter will focus on the contemporary UK.

Activity 8.1

Think about what you have been doing over the past week or so. Try to identify some of the government policies relating to families which you have engaged with over this period.

Comment

Most people think of social policies as being for people with problems, and you may have found it difficult to pick out areas that directly affect you in everyday life. Some areas that occurred to me were:

■ Health. We are constantly exhorted to improve our own health and that of our families. You may have considered issues of healthy eating for example, when doing your shopping. The UK government issues a wide range of health information to individuals, schools, businesses and health professionals that permeate our everyday decisions about whether to serve pizza or broccoli (or both!) for dinner.

■ Education. If you are responsible for school-age children you are probably frequently engaging with schools on issues such as attendance, curriculum, health and safety, and teaching practices. Almost everyone in the UK has been to schools of some kind, or has actively sought alternatives such as home schooling, and education is a core area of government policy that engages with families.

■ Housing. Governments heavily regulate the complex arrangements for building, purchasing and renting homes. Houses and flats are designed and built in line with a myriad of rules and standards that relate, in part, to particular notions of the kinds of people that will live in them. Once built, such structures are difficult to change to suit more flexible patterns of living, and this constrains the choices people make about their living arrangements. Decisions about how to pay for housing frequently involve family participation and even contributions. We tend to take these for granted once they are in place, but they are influenced and shaped by such regulations.

■ Social care. Many of us are responsible for looking after others, including children and young people, people with illnesses or disabilities, and older people. These arrangements are likely to include some element of family involvement, including doing direct physical care; making arrangements for others to do the caring such as relatives, friends, childminders or care workers; making financial contributions for care through current income, savings or insurance. Even those most anxious to avoid any dependency on family may worry about the possible need for care arrangements in the future.

■ There are other kinds of policy engagements which you may have encountered that aim to resolve more acute social problems, such as the youth justice system, children's services which intervene in cases of harm or abuse, or divorce and separation arrangements.

Policies interact with the legal system, and it is through the law that they are ultimately imposed on the unwilling – whether it is parents being fined for the truancy of their children, or the government being forced to amend laws which transgress human-rights legislation. However, families and those who implement policies that affect them are not simply passive receptacles for government ideas (as you saw in the discussion of Nikolas Rose's work on 'governance' in Chapter 5). In day-to-day encounters between welfare workers such as social workers, benefit officers, care workers, teachers, nurses, lawyers and a whole array of those who provide services professionally or voluntarily, people bring their own meanings of family to bear, whether as 'client' or 'practitioner'. In these everyday encounters the meanings of family held by welfare professionals may or may not conform with their clients' assumptions about what family means to them. Ultimately, policies that ignore the family meanings of those who are supposed to benefit from them are likely to be difficult to put into practice effectively or to achieve all of their aims. An example of this might be the Child Support Agency established in 1991, which required separated parents to financially support children they no longer lived with. The Agency repeatedly failed to fulfil its aims in the face of widespread disagreement and resistance to the particular ways it defined such responsibilities, despite a series of enquiries and reorganisations.

Policy-makers must also grapple with the issue raised in the last chapter about how to develop overarching general policies when problems and difficulties are experienced at the individual level. You saw in Chapter 2 how definitions of family have to be flexible in a crisis when emergency services have to deal with individual and unpredictable situations. There are always going to be tensions between a general principle enshrined in a policy which might be designed to ameliorate a social problem – such as the need to support children of separated parents – and the particular situations of those who have to comply with the policy: for example, fathers on low incomes, with step-families to support as well as children from previous relationships, who find that their own circumstances do not match those envisaged by the policy.

Policies relating to families will necessarily have particular meanings of family embedded within them, but policy-makers are also asserting a set of values that may not be shared by those at the receiving end. As we shall see, such values are often unstated assumptions, relying on taken-for-granted understandings of what families are. Such assumptions can have very significant consequences for the ways that policies are developed, and also affect how practitioners and welfare workers implement them on the ground. The implicit meanings of family that policies and practitioners engage with are not neutral or value-free, but contain assumptions about what families should be, and how they should behave.

You might find that you strongly agree or disagree with the policies and practices we discuss in this chapter, an indication that your own values are being evoked. But our aim is to step back from such judgements and opinions in order to examine the meanings and values which policies and practices contain. We will begin with some general issues relating to meanings of family in the contexts of contemporary UK policy, before moving on to examine more specific interactions between welfare professionals and families. In this process, we will be bringing to the surface questions of values as well as meanings in the context of policy.

2   Family policy and family meanings in changing times

2.1 Family meanings and policy-makers

In our first activity, I would like you to look at an extract in which Janet Finch sets out the difficulties that policy-makers face in their attempts to establish the economic and social responsibilities of families, when 'family' itself so difficult to pin down. Her focus is on the fluidity of family networks that extend across generations and over different locations. She shows that this way of thinking about family is necessary in order to shape policies that are flexible enough to achieve their aims.

Activity 8.2

Please read the extract now. You will see that Finch uses the example of the care of older people through kinship networks which cross national boundaries, to show how more rigid definitions of family can prevent the development and implementation of policies which fully engage with family life as it is experienced.

Reading 8.1   Janet Finch, 'Kinship as family in contemporary Britain'

The regulation of individuals' lives, whether through the law or through public policies, inevitably touches on personal, intimate relationships both directly and indirectly. Historically this has been conceptualised principally as 'family' policy and 'family' law, with the concept of family being quite tightly defined. In UK policy and law, 'family' has normally referred to the specific relationships of partnering, parenting and sharing a household. However there is plenty of evidence that wider kinship relations remain important – possibly increasingly important – to the way in which our fellow citizens live their lives. ...

...

All this argues for a much more fluid, and a more individualised, concept of intimate and personal relationships in which both co-resident family and wider kin are regarded as important but not accorded a unique status; rather they are part of a larger picture in which the boundaries are highly permeable. This is very challenging for the law and public policy which, in regulating those aspects of personal relationships where governments deem it necessary to intervene, normally has based interventions on biological ties (between parents and children) and contractual ties (between husband and wife or, more recently, same sex civil partners). Both of these routes identify, with a reasonable degree of clarity, the individuals between whom a degree of obligation is assumed, but increasingly this may not accord with the realities of people's lives. Thus, for example, the law may seek to enforce the obligations of a biological parent who no longer lives with the child or wishes to have contact, but make no interventions to support the more meaningful, living relationship between a child and an active step-parent. Thus there is a sense in which our relationships have to be simplified in order for the law and public agencies to deal with them, but at the same time this courts the danger of a mis-match between public interventions and lived realities.

...

... In considering this issue in more depth I shall use as my main example support for older people, when they are in circumstances where they cannot fully provide for or care for themselves. This is an area in which public policies have not, for some decades, attempted to require relatives to provide either practical or financial support, but there is substantial evidence that the relationships of kinship and friendship continue to provide an important source of support when that is needed. ... [W]here family members have a history of long distance migration .. [this] raise[s], in acute form, the question of whether support for older people depends on proximity, and is disrupted by distance. ... Harriss and Shaw's [research] ... focuses on caregiving to older people where families are stretched across continents, in this case British Pakistanis.

One aspect of this is to bring other different family members together in a complex way through the creation of global care chains ... which include short-term visits of relatives to those who remain in Pakistan and sometimes new migration to the UK, either of a potential caregiver, or of a person who needs care. However migration under these circumstances is often not straightforward. Harriss and Shaw show how it may be thwarted by immigration policies which treat such circumstances with suspicion ... However, these are seldom cases simply of cynical manipulation of the immigration system. In many circumstances the emotional dimension of the relationships, and the sense of responsibility associated with it are much more important driving factors.

This example illustrates neatly the ambiguity of social polices in interfacing with kinship as it is lived in the contemporary world. In this instance it is immigration policy which is at odds with the lived experience of kinship, being more focused on restricting the number of migrants into the UK rather than on facilitating family support. In part this is a dilemma of where to draw the line of who counts as 'legitimate' family. Any requirement to draw such a line for administrative purposes will be at odds with an individual's definition of which particular relationships count as committed relationships. One of the case studies discussed by Harriss and Shaw illustrates this definition dilemma rather poignantly. It concerns a young woman living in the UK who wanted to take responsibility for the care of an aunt who had been much involved in her upbringing in Pakistan, and applied to bring her to the UK in order to provide practical and financial support for her. This incited the suspicion of immigration officials who saw the niece–aunt relationship as insufficiently close to be a legitimate basis for taking on such responsibilities.

...

In such circumstances it is inevitable that the law and public policies will not readily be able to impose definitions of who 'should' (or should not) take responsibility for supporting older people, when that is required.

...

However from a more theoretical standpoint, it is significant that public policy is recognising the potential importance of kin as a personal resource to individuals. The fact that these policies are proving difficult to implement is itself a reflection of the nature of those relationships, which are highly individualised and not amenable to being described in a standardised way. Attempting to standardise the consequences of being an aunt or a cousin is more or less guaranteed to make any policy ineffective, yet there are circumstances where aunts and cousins do potentially have an important role to play as a personal resource for individuals. ... The challenge for public services is to be able to operate in a highly flexible manner which recognises that, in seeking to draw in kin to the support of a young person, the range of relationships which could prove productive will differ in each case.

Reading source

Finch, 2006, pp. 295–302

Comment

Finch emphasises that the flexible and dynamic relationships of family and kinship are difficult for the state to draw upon and define in consistent and effective ways. The use of a fluid definition of 'family' gives her greater scope for including relationships of care and emotional connection which might lie outside narrow definitions of 'the family' set out in some policy areas, in this case immigration law, but which are still relevant both to the lives of those seeking to resolve social problems in their own lives and in terms of making effective social policies.

Figure 8.1
Relationships of care

2.2   Policy and politics of changing families

Finch shows us that in the past social policies have relied on defining family in limited and particular ways, emphasising marriage and parenthood in specific legally recognised and morally sanctioned forms, but these definitions have become difficult to sustain in the face of social changes to family lives in the twenty-first century. In the next extract, Fiona Williams examines the question as to whether or not there is there a new definition of family which policy defines and reinforces. She examines a number of policy areas to answer this question, and here we look at two of these: lone parents and minority - ethnic parents. She concludes with a discussion about values embedded in family policies.

Activity 8.3

As you read this extract, consider the following questions:

1   What does Williams mean by the 'normative' family?

2   Why is the normative family important to policy-makers?

3   What changes does she highlight in the ways policy relates to families?

Reading 8.2   Fiona Williams, 'Policies and changing families'

Policies and laws are important in shaping family and personal relationships both in terms of the assumptions they make about normative family life – the proper way to be or 'do' family – but also in the resources they provide to improve people's well-being. ...

...

Some of the most noticeable changes in family forms have happened over the last 20 years, and in that time it has been possible to see four shifts in the way policies have reshaped an understanding of marriage and family relations.

1   There has been a move in economic and welfare policy away from the 'male breadwinner' family towards an 'adult worker' model where both men and women are earners.

2   Marriage, partnerships, separation and divorce have become more of a private matter to be sorted out between the adults involved and are less subject to a morality 'from above'. Marriage and parenthood are no longer seen as inevitably belonging together.

3   Parenthood and parenting have become less a private matter and much more an issue of public regulation in ensuring parental responsibilities, in which the welfare of the child is the central moral and social concern.

4   There is increased recognition for previously excluded parents or partners: in particular, same-sex partnerships.

Each of these shifts carries with it sets of assumptions about what family lives and personal relationships should be. On the face of it, they appear to reflect what has been happening – women are working more, people may become parents whether they are married, cohabiting, divorced, unmarried and single, gay or lesbian, and parents are more focused on their children. So is the normative family in state policy similar to the family lives and personal relationships that we are part of? It is through this question of the tensions between the prescriptions of family policies and the realities in family lives and personal relationships that we look at the policies and politics of changing families and personal relationships. ...

...

The power of the post-war male breadwinner family was that it marginalised and often pathologised those who fell outside its frame. Male homosexuality was a criminal offence until 1967; along with 'people living in sin' and 'unmarried mothers', same-sex couples were seen as belonging to a different, and lower, moral order. The practices of minority ethnic families were often seen as problematic – mothers from the Caribbean who entered full-time work to support their children were deemed to be neglecting them; South Asian families were not offered services on the assumption that they could rely on their extended family networks. The legacy of eugenics meant that it was assumed that disabled people could not make 'fit' parents. [Eugenics was an international movement in the late nineteenth and early twentieth-centuries that sought to improve the health and fitness of the nation and 'race', as it was then described, by encouraging 'fit' parents to have children and discouraging 'unfit' parents.] How much has all this changed? Is there a new normative family emerging from law and policy where parents are preferably but not necessarily married, where their joint paid work keeps them out of poverty and better enables them to exercise their responsibilities to protect their children and keep them out of trouble? And how far does this new family model embrace formerly excluded groups?

...

Lone parents, whether never-married or divorced, exemplify the separation of marriage from parenting, and as such, have been central targets in New Labour's efforts to get people off welfare and into work, to lift children out of poverty and to reinforce parental responsibilities. So, although the moral disapproval associated with their lack of marital status has dissipated, they have become, through their need for support and the poverty of their children, a target for state intervention. Some interventions, such as Sure Start, aim to give disadvantaged children a better start. They are part of a broader, work-orientated policy objective to get 70% of lone parents into work by 2010. The problems with this objective reveal in starker form some of the tensions ... in the move to the adult worker model. Employment rates for lone parents (mainly mothers) have increased by 8%, from 46% in 1997 to 54% in 2003. ...

If lone parents have been taken out of a 'moralising' frame and replaced in a 'social responsibility' frame, then teenage mothers have similarly had their badge of sexual immorality removed. However, it has been replaced by a different requirement of moral responsibility – to obtain educational qualifications and skills and to be in paid work.

...

There has been much greater acknowledgement of multiculturalism and of the need to counter racism. The Children Act 1989 and the Race Relations Amendment Act 2000 place a duty on all public institutions to take measures to prevent racial discrimination. Many government policy documents carry images of a multicultural Britain ... [but this] does not refer at all to what support for minority ethnic families might mean, or whether their needs and experiences might be different. This omission gives rise to a concern that multiculturalism is seen as having been achieved, rather than as something still to be worked at.

Research reports on minority ethnic families' experiences show how racism, lack of respect for religious or cultural differences and material disadvantages continue to be part of the day to day lives of people of African-Caribbean, Bangladeshi, Indian and Pakistani heritage. This means that issues of protection include concerns about protection from racism. There continue to be inequalities in use of and access to care services in health and social care. For example, black disabled children are more likely to be excluded from school and have less access to services and subsequent employment. ... First-, second- and third-generation minority and migrant groups have significant kinship networks and commitments which operate across continents and often go unrecognised in policies for community care or education.

In addition government position-statements and policies in relation to asylum-seekers and, after 9/11, Muslim fundamentalism, often muddy the waters of multi-culturalism and race relations. For example, ... requirements for a greater commitment of minority groups to subscribe to 'British norms' and a 'British identity' tend to overplay the fixedness of cultural identities and religious beliefs. Pakistani and Bangladeshi family practices for arranged marriages, for example, are often presented as though they are fixed and pre-modern, where women are victims, rather than part of complex patterns of kin commitment and subject to challenge and revision from women within those communities. It is also the case that these experiences do not feature in much of the research on family lives and personal relationships.

...

As with all normative models, there are gaps between the *ought* and the *is*. A recurrent example is the different relationships men and women have to the labour market and to the care of children, which has led to parents negotiating a variety of ways of combining work and care. There also seem to be tensions in the balance between the support the state offers and the responsibilities that parents are required to carry out. This points to the central importance of material support, such as income and childcare funding, but it also involves a set of moral considerations. Is the priority of 'making work pay' which inscribes the new morality for parenting, one which also matters most to parents? Is there true recognition of diversity, or is it only skin-deep? And is the parent-state partnership one of mutual trust? Does the state trust the commitment of parents, do policies reflect the way people's commitment operates, and do parents trust the support which the state and other sectors provide? And where do children's views have a place in this partnership?

At the heart of these questions is a more searching one. In the waning influence of an external moral code, and in the remaking of relations of gender, generation, ethnicity, disability and sexuality, people have had to draw on their own frameworks of what is right and proper to solve their parenting and partnering dilemmas (do I stay at home to look after my child or go out to work, should I get divorced, do I encourage my daughter to have an arranged marriage as I did?) These frameworks may or may not be based in faith or tradition. What, then, should be the aims of government? Should its policies seek to *reflect* the diversity of people's lives and the choices they make, or should it be concerned with *setting* new standards and moral codes? If government does the former, it risks perpetuating the inequalities which exist and influence the decisions people make. For example, if parents are paid to stay at home and look after their children, will this not just reinforce less qualified women's lack of power in the labour market? If it sets a new standard, it risks creating a moral frame which elevates some (those in paid work) and despises others (those not in paid work). And if it does both, as New Labour has done, it will be charged with inconsistency.

...

To some extent a new normative family is emerging which is heavily rooted in work, economic self-sufficiency, education and good behaviour. It revolves around the adult couple, based on a current or past sexual relationship, and is beginning to recognise same-sex couples. Its embrace is ambivalent in relation to lone parents, families with a disabled member, cohabitees and minority ethnic families.

Reading source

Williams, 2005, pp. 26–7, pp. 34–6, pp. 38–40

Comment

1   Williams discusses the normative family as one that fits into what is perceived as the 'right kind' of family, which fulfils the roles that society generally assigns to families. The normative is about what 'ought to be'.

2   Policies allocate resources to families to help them achieve well-being, but they also include constraints about the kinds of families that will be supported. Policies include assumptions about what family means.

3   Williams indicates these changes in policies and families:

(a)   The relationship between families and paid work has shifted in recent policies away from a single breadwinner model to one of 'hardworking families' with two earners.

(b)   While marriage and partnership arrangements are increasingly seen as private matters, parenting and looking after children are seen as more important places for policy interventions. This can be seen as an attempt to shift the meanings of public and private in relation to families.

(c)   Lone parents, especially mothers, feel the tensions between earning and caring acutely and policies in this area have included definitions of family that are contradictory and work against each other.

(d)   Inequalities of class, 'race' and ethnicity are sometimes hidden or unacknowledged when policies relating to families attempt to use meanings of family which are superficially inclusive of multiculture and diversity.

(e)   Recent policies have attempted to emphasise definitions of family which entail taking more responsibility for children's behaviour and development. This 'responsibilisation' of the family means that support for families is conditional on them achieving a particular standard of behaviour; otherwise the sanctions of the law may be used to enforce such behaviour.

Williams is careful to put policies relating to families in the context of wider social changes, particularly in changing patterns of earning and greater cultural diversity. She sees family policies as struggling to bring together the policy aim of supporting 'hardworking families', in the language of New Labour, while also ensuring that families provide what is deemed to be an appropriate upbringing for children, and providing sufficient care for those who cannot work.

Summary

■   Family policies are found across many areas and levels of government, both explicitly and implicitly.

■   Policy-makers struggle to find meanings of family which are flexible enough to encompass the diversity of family relationships and situations in society, while being specific enough to achieve their aims of supporting and regulating families.

■ Notions about what is a normative family lie at the heart of many policies, although these norms are never completely consistent; they change over time and in different social contexts.

3   Family policies in practice

We now turn to look at the ways that family meanings are shaped by and through policy in more depth, because it is in the detailed contexts within which policies are implemented that family meanings are both expressed and contested. We are going to look at two different kinds of policy areas:

1   The use of the ecological model to determine needs for various welfare services.

2   The use of the courts to define the right to family life.

These ways of determining the meanings of family are dramatically different. In the first case, the meanings of family are rarely explicitly defined. Rather, practitioners are given the task of assessing the family situation of the people they are working with as part of a wider examination of their circumstances – with limited explicit guidance about what 'counts' as family. Yet, what practitioners and policy-makers are often aiming to achieve is something referred to as 'family stability'. In the second case, the meanings of family are explicitly addressed through the legal process made available through the European Convention on Human Rights, which includes the right to family life. Those who take a case to court are asserting their definitions and practices of family, and in the process these meanings must be made explicit through the discourses of rights and the language of the legal system.

3.1 The ecological model and family assessment

In this section of the chapter, we consider family meanings and definitions of the family within the context of the work of professionals, such as social workers or health visitors. We will try to understand how public services professionals, who come into contact with families, bring particular kinds of family meanings to their work, which can ultimately and significantly impact on the type of intervention or support such families receive. Therefore, understanding how professionals approach 'the family' is critical in understanding outcomes for at least some families. In other words, how 'the family' is understood by professionals can have a direct bearing on the type of public service response 'a family' receives. Added to this, as we saw above, there is always a tension between a general policy and the particular circumstances of its application, which will involve a specific set of people and their relationships.

Among the ways in which professionals think about and work with families, one particular model, the ecological model, achieved a degree of dominance in social work. Policy-makers used it extensively for guidelines for professionals and practitioners, who often drew upon it in their day-to-day practices. This is important for family meanings because, within the ecological model, household and family relationships were understood as being at a particular social level, which is separate and distinct from the individual and also from broader community and social levels.

Urie Bronfenbrenner, a developmental psychologist, developed the ecological model which he called the Ecological Systems Theory in the 1970s. He outlined four nested social systems, each of which contains roles, norms and rules that can powerfully shape human development. The model offers a way of gaining an all-round picture of what is happening, in relation to the person who is positioned at the centre of the situation, at four levels:

1   At an individual biological and psychological level.

2   In the context of close relationships in the immediate household/family.

3   In the larger community and social systems in which the family is embedded.

4   In the overriding cultural beliefs and norms, which influence the other levels.

In policy terms, this model opened out the previous methods of caseworkers that focused on particular families – and especially mothers – as the source of social problems. This tended to place blame on individual parents or children, inviting

Figure 8.2
The ecological model (Adapted from Paquette and Ryan, 2001)

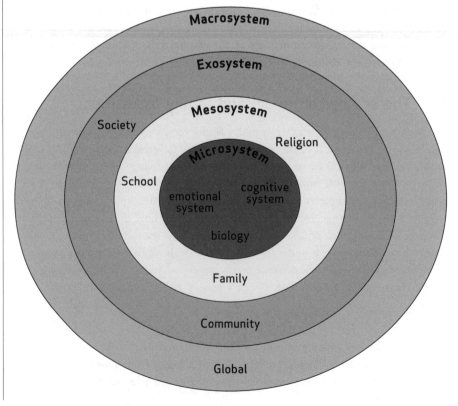

solutions that focused on their perceived needs. The ecological model provided an alternative way to investigate and consider the social contexts that families experiencing difficulties are living within; it thus enabled a wider set of explanations and solutions to be considered.

The key criticism of this model has been that it views society as a system or structure with fixed and distinct levels. The model formulates complex social interactions and social lives into fixed 'levels', rather than thinking in a more fluid way about the various contexts – both direct and mediated – in which family lives occur. For example, the context of neighbourhood is more than just physical proximity; it encompasses networks of relationships that include family members and friends as well as others who are not known personally to the individual. Such relationships cut across three of the levels of the model, rather than being sited at one level only.

A deeper critique can be made about the absence of a theoretical framework to underpin the creation of the model in the first place. It offers no way of explaining how such layers came about and continue to coexist. Like many systems-based theories, it leaves little scope for understanding how change occurs over time through those dynamic interrelationships that cut across and between the different levels. Nor can it help explain those relationships that occur outside its framework altogether; for example, radical alternatives to family life such as communes or religious communities. Indeed it is quite difficult to imagine alternatives within its fixed and bounded terrain.

Within this framework, 'the family' is embedded within larger systems that affect it, and thus the idea of family is there, but its possible meanings remain unexamined. The model suggests that ideas about 'family' are placed in the larger social system so deeply that it is impossible to question or change what 'family' means. Looking at the model from the client's perspective, a particular family is unlikely to understand itself in terms of an ecological system. It is more likely that people understand their experiences of family as a set of fluid relationships which have little to do with interacting in specific ways with different individual, family, community and social levels.

A second and related critique is that the model has little to say about inequalities of power within and between social groups, presuming that people and institutions at the various levels meet and interact across an even playing field. In the model, the historical and social forces which created and sustained the inequalities underpinning social problems are invisible. Stan Houston gives an example of this in terms of inequalities in children's education. According to the ecological model, if children have the same opportunities at the community and/or social levels, there does not appear to be any explanation for their very different experiences:

> A high-achieving school may offer all children, regardless of their social standing, the possibility of gaining a place but we know in reality that the probability of this occurring will differ markedly for children from different classes. This is

because the distribution of social, material and symbolic capital [i.e. resources that they can draw upon if needed] will vary enormously within these classes. ... A more adequate conceptualization of power – than that presented by ecological theory – would demonstrate this reality.

(Houston, 2002, p. 305)

In the context of family meanings, the model allows those who use it to draw on their ideas about normative families without questioning the values and judgements which such ideas include.

It is important to remember that Bronfenbrenner was developing this ecological framework more than thirty years ago, when the concept of family was less problematic in the social sciences. But the ecological model has had a powerful impact on the way professionals work, if only because it provided a convenient checklist for investigating and assessing a wide range of social situations. It has been widely employed across a range of disciplines, and was generally seen as unproblematic despite the growing body of academic and popular work that challenged any fixed notion of family. For example, it has been applied to programmes in the UK, such as Sure Start and On Track, which were community-level programmes aimed at providing a range of services for families. The New Labour government developed these projects with the explicit aim of making an impact on disadvantaged families by working at every level of the model. The United Nations Children's Fund (or UNICEF) and the World Health Organization (WHO) similarly endorsed the model and applied it across a variety of international social issues such as poverty and child maltreatment.

Activity 8.4

The reading in this activity is an excerpt adapted from the WHO's document 'Preventing child maltreatment: a guide to taking action and generating evidence' (2006), which applies the ecological model to develop an understanding of child maltreatment. When you are reading this, keep the following questions in mind:

1   How is 'family' defined?

2   What role does 'the family' play in explaining child maltreatment?

3   What are the effects of using this model?

Reading 8.3   World Health Organization, 'Preventing child maltreatment'

No single factor on its own can explain why some individuals behave violently towards children or why child maltreatment appears to be more prevalent in certain communities than in others. As with other forms of violence, child maltreatment is best understood by analysing the complex interaction of a number of factors at different levels – an understanding that is vital for dealing effectively with the problem of child maltreatment. The following figure presents an ecological model outlining the interplay of these different factors.

The first level of the model, that of the individual, addresses biological variables such as age and sex, together with factors of personal history that can influence an individual's susceptibility to child maltreatment. The relationship level examines an individual's close social relationships – for instance, with family members or friends – that influence the individual's risk of both perpetrating and suffering maltreatment.

Factors at the community level relate to the settings in which social relationships take place – such as neighbourhoods, workplaces and schools – and the particular characteristics of those settings that can contribute to child maltreatment. Societal factors involve the underlying conditions of society that influence maltreatment – such as social norms that encourage the harsh physical punishment of children, economic inequalities and the absence of social welfare safety nets.

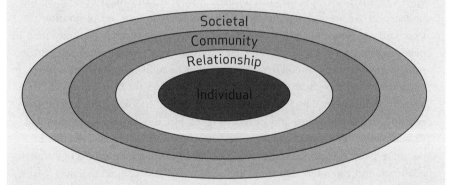

Figure 8.3

Ecological model descibing the risk factors for child maltreat-ment

Factors that increase susceptibility to child maltreatment are known as risk factors, and those decreasing susceptibility are referred to as protective factors. The risk factors listed below are not necessarily by themselves diagnostic of child maltreatment wherever they are detected. However, in places where resources are limited, children and families identified as having several of these factors should have priority for receiving services.

[The document goes on to list various risk factors for maltreatment at these four levels, concluding with the statement:]

Based on the current understanding of early child development, the risk factors for child maltreatment and evidence of the effectiveness of certain prevention strategies, it is clear that stable family units can be a powerful source of protection for children. Good parenting, strong attachment between parents and children, and positive non-physical disciplinary techniques are likely to be protective factors.

Reading source

Adapted from World Health Organization, 2006, pp. 13–16

Comment

1   In these sections of the document, 'family' is not really defined at all. It appears explicitly in the 'relationship level', but it uses the term in a fairly open-ended way, linked with particular kinds of people – 'family members or friends' – rather than a particular form or structure. However, in the conclusion, the kind of family which is necessary for the prevention of harm is described in terms of 'stable family units', 'good parenting', and 'strong attachment between parents and children'. These are statements that identify the way that a family 'ought' to behave. They also assume that 'good' families can be identified as 'units' with parents and children who have positive feelings of love and support for each other.

2   The model is trying to encourage us to understand maltreatment as being the result of a number of different factors, which interact in complex ways. Thinking back to Chapter 5, we could say this document is discursively constructing the ways that the causes and also the solutions to the maltreatment of children are understood. As an international body, the WHO is in a powerful position to impose these views, but it also reflects the policy and practices currently used in many national jurisdictions. It must take into account a wide range of contexts for the maltreatment of children, but, in order to fulfil its particular purposes, it also must avoid the assumption that different practices for bringing up children are all equally acceptable. It acknowledges that some children suffer maltreatment not only at the individual and relational level, but also at the community and social levels – for example, through cultural expectations which condone or prescribe harsh disciplinary practices. Thus it cannot take a position of cultural relativism and can assert that there are some social and cultural practices relating to children that are never acceptable. (You will return to questions of cultural relativism and ethical judgements in Chapter 9.)

3   Figure 8.3 provides a neat visual image of how the individual is 'nested' within larger structures, such as relationships, community and society. In other words, culture shapes societies and communities, which shape relationships, which shape individuals. However, many of the risk factors could be connected to more than one of these layers. For example, individual factors such as physical health are closely related to parenting, i.e. they are relational as well as individual. And parenting can be closely connected to community and society more widely. For example, one risk factor at the relational level is considered to be a 'lack of parent–child attachment and failure to bond' (World Health Organization, 2006, p. 15). However, it was a community norm for mothers to be separated from babies for a period after birth in many UK hospitals in the 1950s and 60s, and thus 'failure to bond' was not necessarily an individual or relational failure, but one which could be seen as being rooted in widespread social practices. Thus risk factors are difficult to place in any one level, and indeed doing so could make it difficult to understand the complexity of factors at work in any child's life. On

the other hand, using the model will show that child maltreatment is more than an individual or family problem. It shifts the way that the problem is perceived as located with the victim and perpetrator to look more widely at their situations.

Summary

■ The underlying reasons for social problems cannot be adequately expressed or explained through a static and fixed model of social relationships.

■ Models like the ecological model can be useful in helping practitioners to organise and structure investigations and solutions that look further than attaching individual blame. However, the model makes it difficult to explain social change or to challenge inequalities, so that these broader issues may come to be dealt with as tick boxes in professional practices, rather than as a basis for supportive interventions.

■ Normative families appear in the ecological model in its assumptions about the place of families at a particular level between the individual and the community. The model does not give any assistance to practitioners in making explicit their normative assumptions about families.

3.2 Human rights and the right to family life

Our second policy example relates to the testing of family meanings through the context of the legal system, in particular the European Convention on Human Rights, and the determination of what family life means in law through the hearing of specific cases. As we saw above, the law is used to enforce policy where other means are unsuccessful, but it is also a set of discourses and practices that shape definitions and meanings. Through hearing a particular case, lawyers argue about meanings of key words and phrases and, in doing so, they show that definitions change through legislation and practices. Thus meanings of family are constantly being challenged and redefined through the hearing of cases where definitions are contested.

The two related cases we will look at in this section concern disputes about whether or not a gay partner can inherit the same tenancy rights from a deceased partner as those to which a heterosexual partner is entitled. The second of these cases drew upon two sections of the European Convention on Human Rights (ECHR):

Article 8 – Right to respect for private and family life

1   Everyone has the right to respect for his private and family life, his home and his correspondence.

2   There shall be no interference by a public authority with the exercise of this right except such as is in accordance with the law and is necessary in a democratic society in the interests of national security, public safety or the economic well-being of the country, for the prevention of disorder or crime, for the protection of health or morals, or for the protection of the rights and freedoms of others.

Article 14   Prohibition of discrimination

The enjoyment of the rights and freedoms set forth in this Convention shall be secured without discrimination on any ground such as sex, race, colour, language, religion, political or other opinion, national or social origin, association with a national minority, property, birth or other status.

(European Convention on Human Rights)

Activity 8.5

The following readings are taken from two law reports from the House of Lords, the highest level of court for civil cases in the UK until 2009, when they were replaced by the Supreme Court of the UK. The judicial functions of the House of Lords were exercised not by the whole House, but by a committee of judges, or law lords, who adjudicated on appeals from a lower court. They determined questions of law that will be applied to all future cases that relate to it. Law reports from such cases are written in a particular way because they are used by lawyers and judges in subsequent cases, and must therefore include quite a lot of very specific information such as the date, the names of judges, and the page references to other case reports. As you read these descriptions and extracts from law reports, see if you can pick out the key issues about family meanings which emerge from the details.

1   What changes in ideas about marriage since 1920 does the first judge set out?

2   How has the European Convention on Human Rights changed the situation for tenants who live with a same-sex partner?

3   What do these cases tell us about family meanings?

Under the Rent Act 1977, when a tenant dies, his or her surviving 'spouse' will not lose their home because they can succeed to the tenancy. He or she will remain protected as a 'statutory' tenant. The parties do not have to be married; the provision applies also to cohabiting couples who had lived as husband and wife. In 1999 the House of Lords considered whether this provision also included same-sex couples. The court considered, at length, the changing meanings and patterns of family, and the judges decided that 'spouse' could not include persons in a same-sex relationship. Note, however, that this point would be different if the case was heard after the introduction of Civil Partnerships in 2005. The judge, Lord Slynn of Hadley, in the 1999 case attempted to set out the definition of family in these ways:

Reading 8.4 '*Fitzpatrick v Sterling Housing Association Ltd*'

It is, however, obvious that the word 'family' is used in a number of different senses, some wider, some narrower. 'Do you have any family?' usually means 'do you have children?' 'We're having a family gathering' may include often distant relatives and even very close friends. The 'family of nations', 'the Christian family' are very wide. This is no new phenomenon. Roman Law, as I understand it, included in the familia all members of the social unit though other rights might be limited to spouses or heirs.

... If in 1920 [when the relevant housing legislation had first been enacted] people had been asked whether one person was a member of another same-sex person's family the answer would have been 'no'. ... An alternative question is whether the word 'family' in the Act of 1920 has to be updated so as to be capable of including persons who today would be regarded as being of each other's family, whatever might have been said in 1920 . ... If 'family' could only mean a legal relationship (of blood or by legal ceremony of marriage or by legal adoption) then the appellant must obviously fail. Over the years, however, the courts have held that this is not so.

...

... [I]t has been accepted that de facto relationships [i.e. those that exist in practice, but are not formally established in law] can be recognised as constituting a family. Thus ... a child adopted in fact who lived with the tenant for many years, but who was not adopted under the Adoption of Children Act 1926, was held to be a member of his family living with him at his death within the meaning of the Act of 1920. ... [T]he judgment of Wright J. in *Price v. Gould* (1930) [another case relating to the Act of 1920] ... in relation to wills and settlements [was] that the legislature had used the word 'family' 'to introduce a flexible and wide term' so that brothers and sisters of the tenant were family for the purposes of the Act. ...

...

The hall marks of the relationship were essentially that there should be a degree of mutual inter-dependence, of the sharing of lives, of caring and love, of commitment and support. In respect of legal relationships these are presumed, though evidently are not always present as the family law and criminal courts know only too well. In de facto relationships these are capable, if proved, of creating membership of the tenant's family. ...

If, as I think, in the light of all the authorities this is the proper interpretation of the Act of 1920 I hold that as a matter of law a same-sex partner of a deceased tenant can establish the necessary familial link. ...

...

... It seems also to be suggested that such a result ... undermines the traditional (whether religious or social) concept of marriage and the family. It does nothing of the sort. It merely recognises that, for the purposes of this Act, two people of the same sex can be regarded as having established membership of a family, one of the most significant of human relationships which both gives benefits and imposes obligations.

Reading source

Fitzpatrick v Sterling Housing Association Ltd [1999] UKHL 42

The Court went on to decide that although Mr Fitzpatrick could be considered a member of his partner's family, he was not considered a 'spouse'. The judges permitted Mr Fitzpatrick to succeed to the tenancy as a 'member of the original tenant's family' under the Rent Act. But, notably, Mr Fitzpatrick succeeded only as an 'assured' tenant, which is less advantageous than the statutory tenant he would have been, had he been deemed to be a 'spouse'.

This anomaly was further considered at the highest level in the House of Lords in the case of *Ghaidan v Godin-Menoza* in 2004. (An extract from the law report relating to this case is in Reading 8.5). In that case, the question was whether the coming into force of the Human Rights Act 1998 (which gave effect in UK law to the rights contained in the ECHR) made any difference to the Fitzpatrick decision. The fact of difference between a 'statutory' tenancy, to which a surviving 'spouse' is entitled to succeed, and an 'assured' tenancy, to which a member of the original tenant's family may succeed, was crucial. In this case, it made a difference to the rent and to the terms of security of tenure. The House of Lords acknowledged that the succession rights granted by statute to the survivor of a same-sex couple were less favourable than the succession rights granted to the survivor of an other-sex couple.

Mr Godin-Mendoza claimed that this difference infringed his human rights. He relied on Article 8 (respect for one's private and family life) and Article 14 (requirement to be non-discriminatory) of the European Convention on Human Rights. He argued that the distinction between a 'spouse' and a same-sex partner in the Rent Act 1977 was drawn on the grounds of sexual orientation and that such difference in treatment was discriminatory. He argued that the court had a duty to take account of his human rights in its interpretation of the Rent Act.

The judge, Lord Nicholls, considered whether there was any justification for treating same-sex couples differently from other-sex couples, and could find none. This is how he set out his reasoning:

Reading 8.5 'Ghaidan v Godin-Menoza'

There is no reason for believing these factual differences between heterosexual and homosexual couples have any bearing on why succession rights have been conferred on heterosexual couples but not homosexual couples. Protection of the traditional family unit may well be an important and legitimate aim in certain contexts. ... The line drawn by Parliament is no longer drawn by reference to the status of marriage. Nor is parenthood, or the presence of children in the home, a precondition of security of tenure for the survivor of the original tenant. Nor is procreative potential a prerequisite. The survivor is protected even if, by reasons of age or otherwise, there was never any prospect of either member of the couple having a natural child.

... The reason underlying this social policy, whereby the survivor of a cohabiting heterosexual couple has particular protection, is equally applicable to the survivor of a homosexual couple. A homosexual couple, as much as a heterosexual couple, share each other's life and make their home together. They have an equivalent relationship. There is no rational or fair ground for distinguishing the one couple from the other in this context. ...

Reading source

Ghaidan v. Godin-Menoza [2004] UKHL 30

Accordingly, the House of Lords decided that it was a matter of human rights that cohabiting same-sex couples be treated in the same way as cohabiting other-sex couples for the purposes of succeeding to a statutory tenancy under the Rent Act. Anything else, it was said, would be discriminatory and contrary to the Human Rights Act.

Comment

1 The first judge sets out a number of changes in ideas about marriage, including an increasing recognition in the courts and more widely of cohabitation and other de facto relationships including, for example, adoption of a child that hasn't been formally legalised and, more recently, an understanding of same-sex partnerships as being 'familial'.

2 The ECHR offered an opportunity to challenge discrimination based on sexual orientation, forcing recognition that same-sex relationships must not only be considered as familial, but as equivalent to marriage, at least in the area of tenancy law. Such decisions thus shape future policy and practice, potentially across many other areas.

3   These cases show us that what 'counts' as family changes over time and according to contexts. What people do in shaping their own meanings of families, whether recognised in law or not, can have very profound implications in the long term. The legislation designed to protect human rights has been successfully used to challenge previous assumptions about family meanings.

4   Practitioner and family interactions

We have seen from the two examples above that policy-makers might want to determine what 'family' means, both in practical and legal senses. As Finch outlined, practitioners and welfare professionals across many fields might sometimes wish to emphasise the complexity and fluidity of family, and at other times to draw its boundaries more clearly. Williams pointed out that people who are the object of welfare policies do not always passively accept the normative assumptions in policy and practice guidelines but determine their own meanings of family. Thus those who implement policies have found that they must listen and pay heed to the ways that the people they are working with understand 'family' in their lives, and how such relationships can be drawn upon at times of trouble or crisis. In the contexts of these encounters between ordinary families and those who implement policy, there is an element of agency on both sides. There are times when people may attempt to mould the way they present their families to fit the preconceptions of those they are dealing with because they do not have the power to insist on their definitions and practices being accepted as reasonable or normal. But there are many ways that people assert their own meanings and practices, whether they fit neatly into the 'hardworking family' of recent political rhetoric or not.

4.1 Battles over boundaries

Our final example of the dynamic and interactive nature of the relationship between families and those who stipulate policy is about a much more everyday kind of experience. In the following extract we see how parents of school children struggle to reconcile the demands of teachers that children do homework with their own views on the boundaries of family life.

Activity 8.6

As you read the extract, you might want to think about other areas of family life where social policy seems to work its way into everyday practices, and to define what families should be doing.

Reading 8.6   Jane Ribbens McCarthy with Sue Kirkpatrick, 'Homework'

In Kirkpatrick's research (2000), when mothers were asked what they felt was expected of them as parents by the school, homework was one of the first things that many women mentioned and its significance was clear in their daily interactions with their children within the home and family. The rhetoric of good parenting, and the desire by mothers to be seen accordingly by schools, may make it hard for parents to voice, or even think, any resistance to these practices. No parent wants to be seen as anything less than supporting of their children, whatever their circumstances.

Yet, in research interviews or in private conversations, parents may at some point express their resentment at having family boundaries invaded in this way, to the point of outright anger at a feeling that parents are being asked to do the school's job for them.

> ... sometimes, if he's forgotten something and he's in tears at nine o'clock at night and he hasn't done it, I just think, well, what the hell are we doing here? ... I find homework a complete pain actually. We both work full time ... and I've got a three year old as well, so when I get home from work I want to have some time ... and you know, he's at school all day – give him a break! I don't agree with them getting homework in the holidays either, 'cos I think, well ... he'll get there ... there's enough time between now and when he's 16 to get there. ...

Similarly, in a private conversation to which I was myself witness, I have heard several middle class mothers complain particularly vociferously when their primary schools set homework for children during the half term holiday. One of these women was herself a parent governor, but still felt unable to voice her feelings as she assumed that this position meant she should be seen to be supporting the school's decisions. But the mothers saw this as breaching a boundary that should have been respected, for freedom from educational responsibilities for themselves and their children, and to provide a space for family togetherness around leisure time. Mothers may also feel that homework during term time should take its place alongside other activities within their children's lives.

...

How then do parents seek to exert any control or have any effect on what is going on in schools? Approaching teachers and schools even for advice or information may be seen by parents as a delicate line to tread. Parents may feel vulnerable to teachers' comments and judgements, and as lacking in basic knowledge of what is, or should be, occurring during their children's school experiences. Parents may have considerable anxieties about antagonising teachers, or being out of their depth on education issues.

Where parents are unhappy with the outcome of contact with schools, they may seek out other resources to supplement school education or to reinforce their own points of view, such as other professional assessments. Another common approach is to try to become more involved with the school, developing closer relationships with teachers and gaining greater knowledge about school activities. This may involve mothers in converting the formal public relationship between mother and teacher into a less formal private relationship – as friendship. Sally discussed how involvement on the PTA could be useful in this way:

> ... the barriers go down a bit, and you do get to know them more as people rather than as somebody's teacher. Like they get to know us, I suppose, rather than as somebody's mum.

Reading source

Ribbens McCarthy with Kirkpatrick, 2005, pp. 77–9

Comment

As I read this, I thought about other practices that schools impose on families relating to school attendance. One flashpoint for parents is the legal requirement on parents to enforce their children's presence at school, and the tightening of rules about taking children out of school to visit relatives, often far away from the UK. Schools have been given the power to fine parents who do this without permission, which is often refused. This indicates that schools must resort to coercion to impose their views, while families continue to prioritise the consolidation of family ties and the value of experiencing travel to other places over the requirements of attending school. This is, perhaps, an indication that family meanings and their associated practices may be widely divergent from those of schools and education policy.

5   Conclusions

In these small examples, we can see how meanings of family are being tested and challenged, directly or indirectly, in the contexts of social policies and practices. Practitioners and professionals are implementing and interpreting policies, while their clients accept, challenge or resist the norms, values and practices that are embedded within them, whether implicitly or explicitly.

In this chapter, we have seen that meanings of family are necessarily part and parcel of policy relating to families, and that policy-makers will always have particular assumptions about what 'family' is or does. Policy-makers and practitioners struggle between the general aims and the specific contexts for their work with the families they are aiming to reach. Static frameworks for implementing such aims cannot address the underlying inequalities between and within families that practitioners encounter, nor can they explain how these have come about. As we have seen throughout this book, such inequalities are deeply embedded in family meanings and, while those who make and implement policies may wish to address and ameliorate such social divisions, there are many tensions and contradictions between such aims and the means, methods and understandings of family which can be drawn upon. Policies and practices are also loaded with assumptions that include value judgements about what constitutes 'good', 'normal' and 'dysfunctional' families, and therefore the evaluation of families permeates interactions between families and the many ways that governments engage with them.

References

European Convention on Human Rights and Fundamental Freedoms, *Article 8* [online], http://www.echr.coe.int/nr/rdonlyres/d5cc24a7-dc13-4318-b457-5c9014916d7a/0/englishanglais.pdf (Accessed 9 July 2008).

European Convention on Human Rights and Fundamental Freedoms, *Article 14* [online], http://www.echr.coe.int/nr/rdonlyres/d5cc24a7-dc13-4318-b457-5c9014916d7a/0/englishanglais.pdf (Accessed 9 July 2008).

Finch, J. (2006) 'Kinship as "Family" in Contemporary Britain' in Ebtehaj, F., Lindley, B., Richards, M. (eds) *Kinship Matters*, Oxford and Portland Oregon, OR, Hart Publishing, pp. 295–306.

Fitzpatrick v Sterling Housing Association Ltd [1999] UKHL 42, http://www.publications.parliament.uk/pa/ld199899/ldjudgmt/jd991028/fitz01.htm (Accessed 27 May 2008).

Ghaidan v Godin-Menoza [2004] UKHL 30, http://www.publications.parliament.uk/pa/ld200304/ldjudgmt/jd040621/gha-1.htm (Accessed 27 May 2008).

Houston, S. (2002) 'Re-thinking a systemic approach to child welfare: A critical response to the framework for assessment of children in need and their families', *European Journal of Social Work*, vol. 5, no. 3, pp. 301–12.

Paquette and Ryan (2001) 'Bronfenbrenner's Ecological Systems Theory', National-Louis University, http://pt3.nl.edu/paquetteryanwebquest.pdf (Accessed 22 July 2008).

Ribbens McCarthy, J., with Kirkpatrick, S. (2005) 'Negotiating Public and Private: maternal mediations of home-school boundaries' in Crozier, G. and Reay, D. (eds) *Activating Participation: Parents and Teachers Working Towards Partnership*, Stoke on Trent, Trentham Books, pp. 59–82.

Williams, F. (2005) *Rethinking Families*, London, Calouste Gulbenkian Foundation.

World Health Organization (2006) 'Preventing child maltreatment: a guide to taking action and generating evidence', World Health Organization and International Society for Prevention of Child Abuse and Neglect, http://whqlibdoc.who.int/publications/2006/9241594365_eng.pdf (Accessed 27 May 2008).

Conclusions

Chapter 9

Family meanings, family values

Shelley Day Sclater, Megan Doolittle and Jane Ribbens McCarthy

Contents

1   Introduction

If there is one certainty that comes out of this book, it is that a good deal of uncertainty surrounds family meanings! We have found that we cannot easily answer the apparently straightforward question of 'what is family?' with any degree of confidence. We have discovered that family meanings are shifting and elusive, rather than fixed and easily accessed; they're slippery, difficult to grasp, and even harder to keep hold of. They're often in tension with each other, and even a cursory glance at our own lives is sufficient to reveal how different meanings jostle for position as we negotiate our way.

In short, we have seen how family meanings are multiple and various, taking shape in contexts that are, at once, individual and social, political and emotional, historical and cultural. Family meanings, if ever we can pin them down, are fixed only temporarily and with reference to very specific contexts and situations. In the normal course of events, they are continually constructed and reconstructed in discourses and practices across a wide range of domains, through the everyday activities of people just leading their ordinary lives. But they are also part of power structures and processes of governance: some meanings incorporate values that constitute a basis for judging our own lives and those of others.

The aims of this final chapter are twofold. First, we review the arguments, issues and evidence from earlier chapters and consider their implications for our quest for family meanings. In so doing, we will consider another important dimension of family meanings that we have not yet brought into clear focus: the moral dimension. Our second aim is to pursue and explore that moral dimension – the values that are embedded in our concepts and perceptions of family. Among the contexts where 'family' takes shape – for example, in our own lives and imaginations, in government policies or professional practices, in academic research or in legal frameworks – the moral layers of meanings are not always obvious or easy to pin down.

It is widely argued that the contemporary world – at least in European and New World societies – is characterised by risk (and a consequential pervasive anxiety), as well as a cultural plurality, which contribute to a sense of moral uncertainty. The term 'cultural plurality' suggests moving away from any implication that white western middle-class culture is the normative standard, towards a recognition that societies are made up of a range of cultural groups. This involves respecting difference and valuing diversity. Referring to the widespread sense of moral uncertainty, Stuart Waiton, in his book *The Politics of Anti-Social Behaviour: Amoral Panics* (2007), sees a moral hiatus in contemporary British society caused by changes in politics and values as well as radical alternatives. The 'good old days' when everyone 'knew their place' and it was a simple matter to distinguish between right and wrong or good and bad, may be a comfortable myth, but the global social world of the late-modern era, it seems, has finally put paid to any such supposed certainty. We cannot take for granted that our personal convictions about what constitutes 'the good' are shared by even our nearest and dearest, let alone by others across local, national and global communities. In this context, 'family' emerges as a highly contested moral terrain.

Of course, there is a sense in which 'family' has long embodied the struggle between competing moral positions – for example, as in the eugenics debates about using 'selective' breeding to enhance the 'fitness' of the population in the late-Victorian period in the UK. What is new in the contemporary context is the greater visibility of difference in a global, plural world; this both permits and reflects a wider range of moral positions. But recognising – and respecting and valuing – a wide range of moral positions means that it is difficult (and perhaps undesirable) to prioritise any moral position over another. However, such hierarchies can, and do, occur (as we saw in our discussion of dominant discourses in Chapter 5) but, crucially, they are always subject to contestation as a result of the plurality of moral voices that jostle to call the tune.

In the discussion that follows, we trace this thread of moral uncertainty and ambiguity as it interweaves through the main themes of this book. But first, it might be useful to set out briefly here what we mean when we talk about 'morals'. We see 'morality' as referring to accepted standards of rightness or goodness. Such standards are neither fixed nor universal (even if some people like to act as though they are!), but vary according to context, and are liable to change. They may be particular to an individual, or to a social group, or they may be more generalised in a culture or a society. Moral standards imply a standpoint from which qualities of 'good' and 'bad' are judged.

Whilst moral standards imply socially acceptable qualities or conduct, they may make reference to broader, more formalised, ethical codes where principles to live by are

Figure 9.1
This image portrays a moral message about what families should be like

systematically set out. For example, people might derive their moral standards from – or justify them with reference to – a particular religion, or to more secular codes such as 'human rights', or to broader systems of formal ethics such as an ethic of care. We will return to this issue later but, for now, it is sufficient to note that there are many different ways of thinking about morality, and different ethical codes that people may draw upon to guide their conduct, inform their opinions, or to justify their behaviour.

Our main argument in this chapter is that 'family', however conceived, is a contested moral terrain; 'family' is a site where contemporary struggles over morals – over what is right and proper, and over what constitutes 'the good' – are being fought out. With this in mind, we can begin our review of the moral dimensions of the family meanings we've discussed in this text.

2   Family meanings and 'family values'

In Part 1 we explored the notion and importance of 'family meanings', and immediately found ourselves on a moral terrain. When we asked 'what is 'family?' we heard different voices talking about what 'family' meant to them. We found that ideas about family differ from person to person, but there were some interesting common threads – most notably when people tended to describe 'family' in positive, maybe idealised, terms. This perhaps reflects what Barbara Cox Walkover (1992) captured when she referred to the 'family as an overwrought object of desire'. That 'family' is referred to in different ways, and is often idealised in people's talk, indicates that 'family' is not a neutral term, and suggests the emotional investments people make in 'family'. Crucially, these aspects of everyday talk alert us to the moral judgements that are embedded in the apparently neutral language of 'family'.

An example of how such moral judgements can be embedded in language is the way in which families are often seen as 'natural', as an inevitable and taken-for-granted part of 'normal' life. When 'family' is naturalised in this way, broader biological discourses are invoked, bringing with them the apparently unassailable authority of science. 'Family' as a social arrangement (and institution) is pushed to one side in favour of 'family' as a biological – and therefore universal – imperative, linked to reproduction, inevitably heterosexual, and resting on a gendered division of labour that is assumed to prevail in 'nature'. We don't have to look far behind those ideas to see that morality appears wherever 'family' appears.

When we stand back and reflect on the assumptions underlying our thinking and our talk about 'family', we can find, embedded in our common-sense notions, a particular idea of what constitutes this 'natural', apparently universal family. How readily – or even automatically – do we implicitly assume, for example, that *all* families approximate the type with which we ourselves are most familiar, and that this type is 'right and proper'? But when we stand back and reflect on our thinking and expose our own assumptions to critical scrutiny, we see how our ideas fit into those of our broader culture, and how some images – in this case, the family as a 'natural' arrangement – tend to dominate. By scrutinising our own assumptions, we can appreciate that normalising such views of family as 'natural' can easily lead to a moral disapproval of those who, for whatever reason, don't fit the image. These kinds of value judgements are embedded in the languages of political, policy and public debates as well as in everyday conversations. Indeed, as social theorists Ellen Friedman and Corinne Squire (1998) demonstrate in their exploration of *Morality USA*, moral positions on family frequently drive public policy. It is as though the state of 'the family' has become a moral barometer of the state of the nation.

In recent years, the supposed demise of 'family' and the alleged decline of 'family values' in many European and New World societies has fuelled something of a moral panic, and families have been blamed for a whole range of modern social ills, ranging from child murder – as in the Jamie Bulger case in 1993 – through youth gang violence on 'sink' estates, to gun crime among young black men. These are all UK examples, but similar ones may be found in other countries. That these anxieties so readily proliferate around a diverse set of social issues, and fix both the 'problem' and its imagined 'solution' at the level of 'family', serves as a constant reminder that families are primary sites for the instilling of moral values. (The links among families, welfare and crime are discussed further in Ribbens McCarthy, 2008.)

Indeed, it is through the supposed decline of family morality, associated with an alleged loss of moral certainty more generally, that sociologist Stuart Waiton (2007) suggests we have seen the rise of *a*moral panics. By this he refers to a deep anxiety about the loss of moral certainties, which has led ruling groups in western societies to develop policies (with regard to families, parents, children and so on) to impose social order through legislation and the control of personal lives, rather than through moral consensus or any shared sense of family values. Thus, in the UK, the USA and Australia, as well as some European societies, there have been attempts to anchor an uncertain morality through statutes that encode an apparently definitive moral certainty around the supposed needs of children. For example, Ribbens McCarthy (2008) discusses the close connections between particular ideas about children's needs and the maintenance of social order. And Day Sclater and Piper (2000) have shown how legislation that 'puts children first' – and so regulates parental behaviour – is supported by dominant discourses that circumscribe 'family' as a moral space that can legitimately be policed by the state 'in the interests of children'.

Yet, as we saw in Part 1 of this book, families are diverse, and their meanings are fluid and elusive: in this situation, where there are so few common assumptions, so little shared ground, what can constitute 'family values'? The notion of family that informs contemporary moral debates, laws and policies is often an idealised one; it may bear little or no relation to actual family lives, nor to the complexities of meaning that inform everyday family experiences and practices. Yet, it is crucial to register just how strong the emotional pull of this idealised image is. As social scientists, we should seek to make the familiar strange. In other words, we should not only recognise that ideas of family can invoke strong emotion, we must also go one step further and open up that very response for further scrutiny. Not only do we then see that the term 'natural' in relation to family risks obscuring how far 'family' may be analysed as a matter of culture and history, but we can then also interrogate our own and others' emotional responses, and examine them for the 'moral work' done by those apparently 'private' feelings. By 'moral work' we mean to indicate how our personal use of the language of 'family' can both reflect and perpetuate broader social and political imperatives.

The recognition of this significant moral dimension to 'family' raises a number of issues in relation to the family meanings we explored in Part 1. These included:

- the difficulties in talking about families when the term 'family' itself conveys ideals and norms

- how to develop a language to describe people's lives and relationships that can accommodate both what is shared and what is variable – without creating stereotypes or making judgements

- how to study families when researchers are themselves so involved in the social contexts in which families occur and are discussed.

In Part 1 we looked at accounts of families generated by two types of data and linked to different research methodologies – quantitative and qualitative. As you saw in Chapter 4, a quantitative approach is appropriate for large-scale surveys, for generating snapshots of families in time or across time, and for establishing dominant trends within populations. But if we are interested in more individual and localised accounts, or nuances of meaning, then a qualitative approach is more appropriate. Together, these two approaches furnish us with a variety of data about the complexities of family meanings.

In Chapters 2 and 3, we focused on the layers and patterning of family meanings as they emerged through qualitative research. From the studies discussed in these chapters, we saw how people talked about their everyday family lives and meanings. And by teasing apart the tangled threads of family meanings that emerged, we 'deconstructed' what is normally taken-for-granted about families, and saw that meanings could not be thought of as either fixed or as telling the whole story. Rather, the meanings we encountered were fluid, partial and shifting, and often in tension with each other.

From our discussion of the family meanings that emerged from the research we encountered in Part 1 of this book, we might draw out three important – perhaps defining – features of 'family': boundaries, proximity, and quality of relationships. Here, we'd like to discuss each briefly in turn.

First is the issue of boundaries and questions of belonging: who is included and who is excluded from 'family'? On what basis do such processes of inclusion and exclusion occur? Research suggests that many people think of family as a 'unit' with boundaries that distinguish insiders from outsiders. This may be a primary defining feature of family for some, though boundaries are defined in different ways for different reasons and memberships are variable. For others, ideas of 'family' may be much looser and boundaries more permeable.

A second significant theme of family suggested by the research we examined relates to proximity: how far is family identified with a physical space where family members can 'be' and 'do' 'family' together? This physical space need not be 'home' or even household, although academic definitions of 'family' commonly emphasise co-residence. For example, as we discussed in Chapter 3, children might not see living together as a necessary element of 'being family' if parents are separated. For the women in Pen-cwm in Swansea, family ties entailed networks of women and children living 'nearby', with any notion of moving away being seen as a threat to 'family'. For the Bengali families in Swansea, by contrast, 'family' was understood through linguistic and cultural ties to the country of origin, even while this was physically very distant.

A third element that we might identify as among the defining features of family relates to the quality of relationships, and to the family practices through which they are expressed. Some ideas of family refer to the 'biological' aspect, which closes the boundary and defines relationships – not according to quality – but with reference to

Figure 9.2
The living room is an important space for doing family together

'blood', where family ties endure regardless of what happens in the relationships. In some tension with this, there is a 'social' conception of family that disrupts those certainties and introduces elements of fluidity and the idea that it is the quality of relationships that is important, including sharing lives over time.

Such is the power of the idealised version of 'family' that relationships – whether biological or social – are seen to involve shared feelings of love and warmth, which are manifested in practices of 'caring for' or at least 'caring about'. (These issues are discussed further in Fink, 2004.) A key quality that recurs across many studies is the sense of togetherness that is said to characterise family. In this way, relationships that don't display those desired qualities may be disqualified from being considered to be 'family' at all, as in the idea that friends can be more your family than your blood relations.

Against this backdrop of a tendency to idealise 'family', it is important to remind ourselves that not all family relationships are experienced as positive, and not all family practices involve warmth or care, and not all families experience a sense of 'togetherness'. On the contrary, there are many whose family lives have been the source of pain and oppression, or worse. Feminist researchers in the 1960s and 70s changed the face of family studies when they drew attention to issues of power and violence that are so easily obscured by prevailing tendencies to normalise, if not idealise, 'family'. They alerted us to the darker side of 'family' that does not always – or easily – show its face in research studies or, indeed, in life. For most people, though, family life is likely to be a mixed blessing, evoking deep ambivalences, and its meanings and significances change over time. This may be particularly important for those whose family lives may seem, to 'outsiders', to be highly problematic (as seen, for example, in Barnard's study (2007) that showed how children whose parents had serious addictions expressed deeply contradictory feelings about their family lives).

We might speculate that the power of the dominant discourse of family – and particularly the way it signifies a cosy togetherness – may well militate against any easy disclosure of discontent, dysfunction or abusive practice. You will remember from the research studies we examined that family meanings came out as overwhelmingly positive. Yet we all know that there are other stories to be told. We have not pursued in this book what Carol Smart refers to as the 'secrets and lies' that are likely to form the backdrop to many a positive family narrative, though a wide range of research has focused on the more problematic or painful aspects of family lives. That these issues tend not to surface in more general family research is itself an interesting phenomenon (Ribbens McCarthy et al. forthcoming), and testifies to the power of the word 'family'.

In this book, we have focused on the readily accessible meanings of 'family' that populate personal accounts and dominant discourses of family, and we have drawn on the tendency to accentuate the positive into our analysis. This has enabled us to

Figure 9.3

Some representations highlight the darker side of family life

conclude that it is probably impossible to be neutral about 'family'. The most we can do is recognise our own ambivalences, and to identify the ambiguities of 'family' and the many different ways in which the term is used. Our analysis suggests that 'family' might refer to something supposedly neutral and factual, or alternatively it might refer to an ideal, to an object of desire, or of anxiety, fear or longing. Sometimes it's not clear at all how the term is being used! Family meanings can slip continually along these different threads, even within a single piece of text or talk. Small wonder, then, if social policies and professional practices try all ways to restore some moral certainty into the wayward concept!

A host of discourses, policies and professional practices do seek to 'contain' family problems, and so to restore prodigal families to the fold. Such families may be categorised as 'dysfunctional', with the implication that they are capable of being restored to 'functional' with appropriate 'support'. This indicates that sometimes all is not well below the surface of family meanings. But it also points to how the power of 'family' so easily can eclipse the negative. It is as though there is no room for negative experience within a dominant conception of family, and that those negative experiences belong in a different realm of discourse altogether. Thus, the family meanings we teased apart in the research studies in Part 1 of this book are not only multiple, fluid, uncertain, and situated, but perhaps also represent strategies for the active management of complicated ambivalences and feelings of anxiety and longing. They are perhaps the outcomes of struggles to present the brave – or even just the acceptable – face of the family and, as such, constitute moral performances.

To frame family meanings in positive terms, is to claim a sense of identity and belonging that can survive through 'thick and thin'; it is also to avoid the shame that a less-than-perfect family inevitably attracts. To frame family in positive terms is also to occupy a moral high ground that relies on invoking just a touch of nostalgia. You might have noticed that images of family that populate a wide range of individual, policy and professional narratives tend to hark back to an imagined and idealised past – usually the 1950s – as though, by comparison, something significant is missing in families today. On closer inspection, such ideals can be identified as fantasies that bear only scant relation to reality; as Stephanie Coontz (1992) put it, this is nostalgia for 'the way we never were'. Clearly, we may take refuge in this kind of nostalgia when we find moral uncertainty difficult to bear. Yet, if such idealisation remains unexamined – along with our own emotional investments in seeing things through an idealised and nostalgic lens – it can paralyse our analyses. A critical examination of these images, and some speculation as to why they persist and hold our imaginations in the present day, can considerably enrich our understanding, as much critical feminist work has shown.

If 'family' necessarily implies such emotional and moral investments, this raises the issue of how professionals and social scientists can use the concept without inevitably setting in train these emotional and moral evaluations. Some researchers have evaded the issue by continuing to talk about 'family' as if it was a neutral category, or its meanings were obvious. But other family researchers have tackled the issue through a continuing commitment to 'reflexivity'. 'Reflexivity' means attending closely to the research process, and to the ways in which the researcher's own assumptions, values and emotions enter into the way she or he does the research, from the development of concepts and initial study design, to data collection, transcription, analysis, writing up and dissemination of findings.

In Chapter 4, we examined some quantitative data that gave us quite a different perspective on family meanings from that generated by qualitative research. We saw how large-scale surveys and data on populations routinely collected by governments necessarily depend on categories that limit what we can see, and which expressly include and exclude. Thus, historically, instruments such as the census, and other statistical data, do not just neutrally represent some pre-existing reality, but have themselves shaped the meanings of families and households. It is perhaps in relation to this quantitative research that we find the clearest picture of what society wants us to count as 'normal' in relation to family. Thus large-scale data, collected over time (longitudinally), can tell us about changes in what is seen as 'normal' as well as helping us understand how such categories can persist over long periods of time.

3   Moral discourse, moral practice

In Chapter 5, we discussed two theoretical approaches: family discourses and family practices. Still concerned with the question 'what is family?' we focused on how 'family' may be analysed as an object of discourse, and how it may be seen as constituted in concrete family practices. We saw how 'family' may be constructed, for example in the UK, with the discourses of everyday interactions, political debates and policy definitions, and the formal codes of law. We also saw how families interact with such discourses for a range of purposes. Sometimes those discourses where 'family' is most effectively constructed do not refer explicitly to 'family' at all; discourses of parenting, or childhood, are examples. 'Family' is of course different from 'parenting' or 'childhood', and sometimes other discourses can provide ways to sidestep notions of 'family' – as, for example, in some contemporary policy debates about children's needs and rights. But, crucially, the discourses that define or prescribe family statuses and relationships have particular notions of 'family' embedded in them, and so contribute to the broader picture of family meanings.

It is through these various discursive constructions of family that the complications of moral uncertainties are played out. For example, in the narratives of legal conflict between parents we saw competing discourses jostling for priority. The dominant discourses of 'parental responsibility' and 'the welfare of the child' are formally encoded in family law, and can, thus, mask other discourses that speak instead of parents' claimed rights. Such discourses are less visible and considered to be less legitimate in the legal arena. We saw that the moral claims that parents made about what they felt to be their entitlements were grounded in their everyday practices of caring for and caring about their children. However, to be heard at all, these claims had to be framed in the language of the law, i.e. through the dominant discourses of welfare and parental responsibility. By appropriating the legal discourse, parents managed to subvert its dominance with their own moral claims of rights and entitlements, which were based on their experiences as parents.

In particular, both mothers and fathers reintroduced 'gender' back into the frame, seeing it as central not only to their dispute, but to all they had done – and in the future would do – as parents. Family law in the UK has been at great pains to erase gender from discourses of parenting and child welfare, and has encoded parenting as a gender-neutral activity. But this is clearly an area where law is out of kilter with parents' everyday experiences, and legal disputes over children become an arena for the playing out of competing moral claims, between mothers and fathers, and between parents and the state. In a broader sense, this example also illustrates how attention to discourse throws a new light on the moral uncertainties, the ambiguities and the skirmishes associated with competing family meanings. If, as we have suggested, a 'putting children first' agenda represents an attempt to provide a firm anchor in the storm of moral uncertainty, its effectiveness is mitigated when parents bring in their own needs and desires, as it were, through the back door.

In the second part of Chapter 5, a further answer to the question 'what is family?' was provided by our focus on family practices: families are what families do. A focus on family practices can also provide insights into how moral uncertainties around families are lived out in everyday lives. In the example of family leisure that we examined in Chapter 5, there is also a layer of morality at play. The moral threads manifest themselves as tensions between, for example, mothers wanting and not wanting to play board games. To participate is regarded as good, because it means you are doing the best for your children, and it signifies the togetherness of a desired family life. To feel ambivalent about participation is to risk allowing your personal needs and desires to nudge aside both the ideal of selfless motherhood and the moral imperative that children must come first. In short, it is to risk positioning yourself as a less-than-good mother. When theorists such as Nikolas Rose argue that we police ourselves, it is this kind of personal positioning in moral discourse that they are thinking about; our desires to be good parents are the motive force behind our (ambivalent) adherence to social norms in everyday family practices.

In the extract we considered from Susan Shaw's work in the US, a further moral dimension appeared in the tension between 'family' leisure and 'personal' leisure. Some parents may not expect to have 'personal' leisure time, or may regard their own leisure as being one of a piece with that of their children, whilst for other parents there would be a greater separation between the two. In both cases, 'family' shapes the boundaries of the personal. The example of family leisure shows that family practices are moral practices – not only when they are about doing 'the right thing', but even when they are about their ordinary business of creating or maintaining 'family'. For example, Shaw found that family leisure presents an opportunity for teaching the children about 'family values'.

4   Beyond 'family' to intimacies and personal lives

In Chapter 6, we pursued two key concepts – 'intimacy' and 'personal life' – as further tools to open out meanings around families and relationships. We found that the concept 'intimacy' foregrounded our intimate relationships, whereas 'personal life' embraced a wider set of personal relationships. We explored how using a different language to alter our focus (moving 'family' from centre stage) brought new dimensions of families and relationships into relief.

So, what do we conclude a focus on intimacies does for our study of family meanings? And what new moral issues does a focus on intimacy raise?

In Chapter 6 we noted that the concept of intimacy both illuminated and obscured family meanings. 'Intimacy' has the potential to encompass a broader range of relationships than are captured by 'family'. For example, Giddens's notion of the 'pure' relationship (1992) was widely welcomed for the way in which it decentred the heterosexual imperative of 'family' and thus created space for same-sex partnerships to be more visible and valued. Beyond that, 'intimacy' – though it often has connotations of the sexual – can apply also to non-sexual relationships, such as relationships of care, as well as intimacies with strangers. In these ways, 'intimacy' appears as a more flexible concept than 'family', and perhaps is able to capture a wider range of contemporary relationship practices.

On the other hand, if 'intimacy' is taken – as it often is – to refer primarily to dyadic relationships, or those between adults, it can push out of focus the wider networks of belonging that are implied by 'family'. Thus, when we focus on intimacy, the family unit or family group, with its boundaries and sense of belonging, may fade from view to be replaced by a focus on particular relationships, both within and beyond the confines of 'family'. Relationships between adults and children, or among children themselves, don't have a straightforward route into 'intimacy', and neither do relationships across generations more generally. This is largely because 'intimacy' has tended to be associated with the sexual, and because intergenerational caring practices are not automatically seen as intimate ones – though there is no reason, in principle, why that should continue to be the case. Indeed, the concept should be sufficiently flexible to apply to a wide range of relationship practices, including the sexual and the non-sexual, the close and the not so close, as well as even intimacy with strangers.

'Intimacy' may have the potential to be a more inclusive and egalitarian concept than 'family', and it may avoid the emotional and ideological baggage that has come to be associated with 'family'. It need not perpetuate – and may even challenge – the norms that have become embedded in 'family'. But, on the other hand, like 'family', the concept of 'intimacy' tends to be sanitised in both academic work and the popular imagination, in the sense that its dark side – those practices such as incest, and physical and emotional abuse – remains obscured from view by the dominant discourses that accentuate the positive. Feminist researchers have long been at pains to expose the potentials for oppressions and violence that lurk behind the cosy facades of familial and intimate relationships, but such knowledge continues to jar against the more dominant idealisations. We might venture to suggest that such idealisations will be apt to predominate as long as issues of power, and the systematic abuses of power – between genders and between generations, for example – are relegated to the margins of either 'family' or 'intimacy', as though 'power' represents an unusual dimension rather than an inherent structural component of all relationships.

In the second part of Chapter 6 we noted that Carol Smart's concept of 'personal life' was inaugurated by her emotional response to some old family photographs. This led her to want to write about issues around 'family' and 'intimacy' that captured all those dimensions of our lives that have significance for us. Her concept of 'personal life' acknowledges our emotional investments in family but also derives from and develops Morgan's important notion of family practices. Importantly, though, Smart does not want to throw out the baby with the bathwater; she still wants to retain some notion of family and of kinship, because she recognises – ultimately, on the basis of her own personal experience – that 'family' *means* something very significant to us. Social scientists can't fully explain it, but neither can they explain it away.

What does Smart's focus on personal lives add to our quest for family meanings? And does it suggest anything about the moral work accomplished by 'family'?

Through her idea of 'personal life', Smart shifts the moral terrain occupied first by 'the family' and later by 'intimacy'. The value of the concept is threefold. First, it lies in emphasising individual takes on family meanings, thus giving legitimacy to personal experiences and visibility to individual voices. A focus on 'personal life' makes clear that family meanings are very much matters of individual biographies, which themselves are rooted in social and cultural time and place. Second, in this approach it is no longer possible to lose sight of diversity; the individualism implied by the concept of 'personal life' implies an equal respect due to each person. Third, the concept may be well equipped to resist the kind of codification and 'getting stuck' in the kinds of prescriptive discourses that bedevilled 'family', and which threaten to fix the meanings of 'intimacy'.

On the other hand, that Smart's concept makes such an appeal to 'the individual' may be considered to be a weakness, particularly as the concept of an autonomous individual is not one that is shared across all cultures, but is very particular to the philosophies of liberal democracies in Europe and the New World. However, Smart's work is critical of the kind of individualism that is implicit in Giddens's and others' work on intimacy. Instead, Smart employs a more social concept of personhood, and emphasises the interdependence rather than the separateness of people. In the midst of moral uncertainty, Smart anchors her concept of 'personal life' in an ethic of care. This has at its heart a recognition of our interdependence, our emotional connections and the centrality of the relational to the personal. (Issues of personal life in the context of social policy are explored in detail in Fink, 2004.)

'Personal life' opens the door to new explorations of family meanings and family values, and the study of the discourses and practices where they take shape. Smart's concept accommodates ideas about both families and intimacies, but also encompasses other aspects of individuals-in-relationships. But, on the down side, like 'intimacy', it loses sight of 'family' as a social unit to which people 'belong' and to which they feel committed, and which provides an important dimension of their identities, rooting them in culture, time and place (Ribbens McCarthy, 2012). On the other hand, might the rubric of 'personal life' offer opportunities to discuss our ambivalences about both 'family' and 'intimacy' more openly, and to explore the moral dilemmas they pose for us?

What is most instructive when we focus on concepts such as 'intimacy' or 'personal life' is that they provide conceptual frameworks which can avoid the kinds of idealisations that 'family' often invokes – although, as noted above, such new concepts can themselves slip in this direction. Nevertheless, moving away from the concept of 'family' might make it easier to look at the broader picture, including what lies in the shadows. Then, we might ask ourselves, how systematic is this obscuring from view of the more problematic aspects of family lives and relationships? What is driving it?

One answer, we suggest, lies in the emotional investments we habitually make in 'family'. Several times in this book we have found it useful to invoke Walkover's notion of 'family as an overwrought object of desire', and at this point in our discussion this idea very well captures the sense of the moral power of family that we mean to convey. 'Family' is a complex amalgam of needs, desires and longings. Its meanings contain and manage our deepest – and often conflicting – needs for belonging, for safety and security, for identity, for recognition, support and validation. Through its practices we manage our hopes and our anxieties, and work through our vulnerabilities. For all these reasons, 'family' *means* something to us, something that is not captured either by 'intimacy' or by 'personal life'. For all sorts of reasons, 'family' has come to connote a whole range of feelings, and it is those feelings that lie behind the moral power of the word. 'Family' remains a resonant concept that, in principle, can embrace a wide variety of meanings, and invoke powerful emotional and moral responses. It is the language that many people continue to use in their everyday lives as shorthand for 'a set of relationships that really matter to me'.

5 Values in diversity

In Chapter 7 we looked at family meanings in diverse contexts, through a focus on global and historical perspectives. We explored how family meanings are situated and contingent in particular contexts of culture, time and place. We noted the need to be cautious about how we make any generalisations about 'cultures', at the same time as we acknowledge and respect difference.

In studying cultural and historical variations, we encounter two key dilemmas. The first of these is the tension between a wish to develop generalisations across social groups, and a desire to do justice to the uniqueness of each point of view – whether it be that of an individual, a community, or a society. When we categorise families along lines of, for example, ethnicity, does this require that we group together people with very diverse family lives, and does this risk obscuring differences of class, education, locality, gender and so on?

The second dilemma is a moral one: an underlying ethical principle we have adopted throughout this book is one of respecting difference. In practical terms, we have presented a discussion of family meanings as inseparable from contexts, and have not sought to make moral judgements about the perspectives of others from the vantage point of our own cultural values. Thus we have considered how meanings, in terms of sense-making, are embedded in the contexts of people's lives. In this sense, family meanings, and their associated values, are not regarded as right or wrong, but are

Figure 9.4 Contemporary families reflect cultural plurality

seen as part of the ways in which people respond to the contexts in which they live, drawing on the cultural and personal resources available to them to make sense of the circumstances in which they find themselves. This approach also draws our attention to the ways in which specific features of a way of life – such as family meanings – are also integrated with broader social and cultural features, such as beliefs about what it means to be a child, or how to relate to the material world.

In exploring this approach in Chapter 7 we asked whether we need to move beyond a position of ethnocentrism which, as Hollinger puts it, is *'the tendency to evaluate and judge other cultures with the standards of one's own'* (2007, p. 246). What are the moral ramifications of cultural relativism, whereby one suspends one's own moral judgements to develop an empathetic appreciation of the other? An example of the moral implications of different cultural practices may be explored, for example, in relation to where children sleep, which varies considerably across time and place. In some cultures children sleep alone in their own bed, or in their own room, and sleeping alone (as opposed to sharing a bed with parents or others) is seen as medically desirable. In other cultures, to leave a child to sleep alone may be regarded as a neglectful or even as an abusive practice, while, historically, sleeping alone in many communities may have been simply unknown. It is thus necessary to appreciate the situated and contingent nature of these sorts of habitual practices in order to avoid a limiting and possibly destructive ethnocentrism.

There are two key difficulties, however, that arise from a position of cultural relativism. First is the difficulty of transcending ethnocentrism when our values and standards tend to be so deeply embedded in our ways of thinking that we may not even realise that there are other ways of seeing things; we may react to others' customs as alien, bizarre or even horrific. Whilst there is no easy solution, we have encouraged you throughout this book to address this problematic issue by using a reflexive awareness to interrogate your own understandings, viewpoint and emotional reactions. In so doing, you have probably become aware of how your own emotional investments in particular family meanings have a social history, as well as a place in your own personal biography. And you will have noticed the pervasive moral or evaluative dimension of emotion. A reflexive awareness will highlight for you the ways that personal meanings are constructed in social contexts and are not just individually formed. Reflexivity, used well, is an excellent tool that makes good analytic use of your own subjective experiences and feelings.

The second difficulty that arises from a position of cultural relativism is that, if we say that we should not judge others' cultural traditions by our own standards, but must respect them on their own terms, does this not lead inevitably to a position of moral relativism where 'anything goes'? Again, there is no straightforward answer but, in attempting to *address* this issue, you can learn a lot from engaging in the debates. Hollinger (2007, p. 253) takes the view that cultural relativism does not have to imply a position of moral relativism. In other words, we do not have to ignore or become 'desensitized' to practices that we disagree with or even find abhorrent (the examples of such practices she cites include infanticide, sex-selective abortions, wife beating and genital mutilation). Rather, we need to extend our reflexive awareness to appreciate the social and cultural implications of particular family practices before we judge or critique them.

Further, if we do take the next step of judging or critiquing others' family practices, it is incumbent upon us as moral citizens to make it clear from which ethical standpoint we make our observations. In other words, we can use principled ways to argue for a particular point of view. Thus we might locate our viewpoint with reference to any one of a number of formal ethical codes, or we may prefer to ground our critique in a particular religion, or a discourse of human rights. For example, someone who adheres to the religious principles of Roman Catholicism would be likely to consider termination of pregnancy, or embryo research, as violating a right to life and so as contrary to the fundamental ethical principles of their religion. Detention without charge or trial is widely considered to be contrary to principles of human rights; while disciplining children by means of physical punishment could be regarded as contrary to principles of children's rights and probably also human rights. As we discussed in Chapter 8, the European Convention on Human Rights and Fundamental Freedoms includes provisions designed to ensure respect for private and family life, as well as freedom from discrimination. These various formal ethical codes, then, have implications for family meanings and practices.

But whatever 'anchor' we use to ground our ethical judgements will provide a different perspective on the issue, which in itself is a valuable practice: it enables us to appreciate certain cultural practices whilst rejecting others, as we use an explicit moral framework to affirm what we value whilst also, as Hollinger puts it (2007, p. 254) 'recognising our own responsibilities in a pluralistic world'. When people reflect on their everyday ethical dilemmas, some will tend to stick with a fixed reference point whilst others will be more pragmatic or eclectic. Either way, such ethical reflection can help to avoid the potential impasses of cultural relativism and a consequent moral relativism. It enables us to move beyond the taken-for-granted nature of implicit cultural values – including those embedded in apparently neutral scientific discourses – to make explicit the ethical basis on which we appreciate some family meanings while rejecting others. In making our values explicit, and in being self-critical, we create the possibility for discussion and respectful dialogue with others whose value positions may be different.

6   Policy predicaments

In Chapter 8, we considered how meanings are *conferred* upon families through professional and policy discourses and practices. We saw how such meanings are very often normative and consequently might be difficult to see, particularly in expert discourses. These meanings feed in to how governments think families *ought* to be, making policies and professional discourses prime purveyors of morals in a society. Indeed, it is fair to say that policies are morality driven – governments want to do the 'right thing' by families, but they also want families to do the right thing for society. Tensions can occur, as we saw in Chapter 8, not least because what is considered to be the right thing is apt to change. Furthermore, governments don't always stop to take time and examine what is meant by 'family', and exactly who or what their policies address. In this way, policies that touch on 'family' (and there are many) are a primary site for the proliferation of unspoken norms and values.

Our discussion of policy in Chapter 8 pointed to the enormous moral burden that 'family' and families carry in contemporary European and New World societies. Families are a convenient place for a wide range of social ills to be located (many contemporary 'social problems' from 'school underachievers' through 'gang culture' to gun crime are often attributed to something having gone profoundly wrong with family life), and thus families seem to be the logical place where those social ills can be put right. Thus, government policies stipulate a broad range of interventions and professional practices designed to instill 'proper' morals and standards of behaviour in families and their members . Tensions arise when elisions and slippages occur, as social problems become family problems that, in turn, morph into 'problem families' – who are then subjected to a range of moral interventions, impinging on family privacy and individual autonomy.

But, as we have noted, such is the climate of moral uncertainty that prevails across many European and New World societies that policies and welfare professionals have had to make repeated attempts to anchor the family in shifting moral sands by, for example, foregrounding children and making their supposed needs and interests a number-one priority.

In Chapter 8 we saw how the moral meanings of family were tested and challenged in the contexts of social policies and practices. Practitioners and professionals implement and interpret policies, while family members accept, challenge or resist the norms, values and practices that are embedded within them. The moral messages carried by policy discourses and professional practices encourage families to present themselves as moral, coherent and ordered, thus adding another layer of complexity to how family meanings are played out in policy contexts. Meanings of family are necessarily part and parcel of policy relating to families, as policy-makers make particular assumptions about what 'family' is or does, and about what is 'good', 'normal' or 'dysfunctional'. Yet the inequalities between and within families are difficult for practitioners to address within existing policy frameworks.

7   Family meanings and family studies

This book has introduced you to various aspects of the study of family meanings, and it provides a sound basis for any further learning you might want to undertake in the area of families and relationships. In this final discussion, then, we will very briefly point up some additional areas and significant questions that you may encounter if you go on to read and study further in relation to this key area of social and personal lives. In doing so, we re-emphasise the framework and concerns that have underpinned this text and set these alongside other aspects of families and relationships that we have *not* centralised in this book.

This text has focused on the question, 'What is family?', which has allowed us to explore what is involved in developing a coherent and consistent approach towards such a significant area of social life, when the central concept is so problematic. Whether you have been reading from the perspective of an interested student of social science, someone wanting to develop their knowledge and understanding of social policies, or a professional working with family members, by this point you have encountered a number of avenues for developing a critical understanding of the concept of 'family'.

In this short journey through the varied meanings of 'family', we have considered how difficult it can be to hear, see and understand the multiple and fluid ways in which people make sense of those areas of their lives which are commonly understood – in European and New World societies at least – to come under the rubric of 'family'. Family meanings are not, however, limited to particular social settings – though they may have particular associations with some, such as household and home – but may be embedded in a wide variety of situations, such as medical encounters, schooling, work lives and so on. In other words, family meanings may be found everywhere! In all these various settings, then, meanings of family may be assumed, negotiated, contested and (re)created. In such processes, the practices and experiences of social and family lives are both shaped by, and constructed afresh, in particular interactions. In this book we have thus stressed a view of 'family' and social worlds as 'mutually constituted', such that the families we know may appear to be the most taken-for-granted and 'natural' way of living, with the consequence that it becomes very hard to see how contingent and variable family meanings may actually be.

We have also suggested that one important route towards teasing open some of these processes is to pay careful attention to *how* research around families and research is undertaken, as well as examining and exploring the *data* it produces. In this way, we can both 'know' more about family meanings, and also about how research itself is embedded within the very processes it seeks to explore, drawing on particular concepts and re-presenting them to wider audiences in ways that impact on social policies, professional practices, and wider images and rhetoric of families as found in the media. As part of this, we have stressed how researchers, policy-makers and professionals cannot achieve some form of detached objectivity from which to consider these issues. Instead, close attention to our own assumptions, values and experiences may be crucial towards any attempt to 'make the familiar strange'.

Given that 'family' is such a fluid and variable concept, we have considered whether a critical approach requires us to interrogate the word, or supplement or replace it with another language instead. As we have reviewed in this chapter, we have pursued this issue through the theoretical frameworks of family discourses and family practices, and the concepts of intimacy and personal life. We have also explored family meanings in diverse contexts – cultural, material and temporal – which inevitably implicate dimensions of difference, power, and inequalities.

Throughout these chapters, the notion of meanings-in-context has been central. This notion draws on an established 'hermeneutic' tradition in social science that focuses on meanings as sense-making, with a view to understanding how social actors themselves understand and frame their worlds. Such meanings both express and shape experiences and actions, and are thus part of the very contexts in which people experience their lives. We have, then, argued that contexts and meanings are inevitably intertwined.

We have also put a strong emphasis on seeking to understand meanings without evaluating them; while this may be an impossible task to achieve in any absolute sense, it does caution against imposing any easy judgements on others' family lives. Instead, we have sought to explore how family meanings result from people seeking to make sense in some way of the circumstances in which they find themselves. While the term 'family' may indeed be suffused with moral evaluations and emotional resonances, if we try to see how family meanings are relevant in our own lives we may step beyond these evaluations to develop some empathetic understanding for the family meanings of others living in varied contexts and circumstances.

However, studying family lives and personal relationships through the lens of 'meanings', is just one approach amongst others that may also be found worthwhile or useful. In this general area of family studies, researchers and writers may draw on a range of different academic disciplines and research methods, with varying views of the nature of research and knowledge, and the purposes which such research might fulfil – from a desire to develop greater understanding of families and relationships, to urgent practical or policy driven concerns about how to intervene in people's everyday lives. For example, a psycho-social approach would be concerned with a sense of 'interior' life and the realm of feeling, while some therapeutic approaches might take a view of family as a 'system'. Sociological approaches stress the structural features of power, inequality and conflict, whether amongst family members themselves, or across families more widely. Other approaches might focus on representations of families in the media explored through, for example, a discourse-analytic approach. Within this broad range, studies might be topic-based; for example, quantitative research into change and continuities around family lives in contemporary societies, or qualitative research into the complexities of family 'breakdown' or transformation. Another interesting area would link discussions of family meanings with theoretical debates in sociology, around such themes as individualisation, democratisation and globalisation.

Additionally, you may be well aware already that much research and policy is explicitly directed towards what is 'good' or 'bad', 'healthy' or 'unhealthy' about family lives, trying to develop a solid evidence base for making decisions about practical interventions. Indeed, these are very difficult areas for action and decision making, such that evidence-led practice may seem a highly desirable way forward. Nevertheless, we have argued that there is always the risk of such evidence being based on implicit cultural assumptions and value judgements. On the other hand, if all evidence is open to doubts, we may risk creating a situation of paralysis. In this concluding chapter, then, we have centralised the question of values, and how to pursue an ethically informed practice that respects cultural diversities while also formulating a basis for action.

These are some issues that you may encounter in other discussions and approaches, if you extend your study of families and personal lives, as we hope you will. While this book has used a particular framework selected from amongst many possible approaches, it provides a strong basis for both social science investigations and policy and professional practices.

8   Conclusions

You might remember that in Chapter 1 of this book, Gubrium and Holstein quoted Lewis Carroll's character Humpty Dumpty. He despaired of ever understanding anything in a world where words could mean whatever the speaker wanted them to. The meanings of family can sometimes seem just as slippery, elusive and yet ever-present both in everyday life and in the academic study of families. And yet, despite this, 'family' continues to be deployed and evoked as a concrete entity, a set of practices, or a set of discourses, which is impossible to ignore. For this reason, as well as many others, investigating the meanings of family is an excellent way to begin the study of families themselves. By acknowledging that they are difficult, if not impossible, to define in any fixed way, we are on the road to understanding the tasks involved in researching, conceptualising and contextualising families.

By taking this path, we are also obliged to reflect on our own families and the meanings of family in our lives; in other words, what we bring from our own experiences and meanings when we investigate families in general. By doing so, we hope to understand the place of family and families in our own lives. But more importantly, perhaps, this kind of deliberate reflection allows us to acknowledge the assumptions and values which we bring to our studies of family. In acknowledging them, we can step back and attempt to see other points of view, other meanings, and other conceptual worlds.

We might conclude, therefore, that the meanings of family, while never fixed and stable, are not completely arbitrary. They are shaped and formed through the social worlds in which people live, including everyday lives and relationships. There can be no question that family meanings continue to matter deeply to people living and working in many different contexts, whether they find family values, practices and relationships life-affirming or oppressive – or even both.

References

Barnard, M. (2007) *Drug Addiction and Families*, London, Jessica Kingsley.

Coontz, S. (1992) *The Way We Never Were: American Families and the Nostalgia Trap*, New York, NY, Basic Books.

Day Sclater, S. and Piper, C. (2000) 'Remoralising the family? Family policy, family law and youth justice', *Child and Family Law Quarterly,* vol. 12, no. 2, pp. 135–51.

Fink, J. (ed.) (2004) *Personal Lives and Social Policy*, Bristol, The Policy Press.

Friedman, E. and Squire, C. (1998) *Morality USA*, Minneapolis, MN, University of Minnesota Press.

Giddens, A. (1992) *The Transformation of Intimacy: Sexuality, Love and Eroticism in Modern Societies*, Cambridge, Polity.

Hollinger, M.A. (2007). 'Ethical reflections for a globalized family curriculum: a developmental paradigm' in Sherif Trask, B. and Hamon, R.R. (eds) *Cultural Diversity and Families: Expanding Perspectives*, Thousand Oaks, CA, Sage, pp. 244–78.

Ribbens McCarthy, J. (2012) "The powerful relational language of 'family': togetherness, belonging, and personhood', *Sociological Review*, vol. 60, no. 1.

Ribbens McCarthy, J., Hooper, C.A., and Gillies, V. (eds) (forthcoming) *Family Troubles? Exploring Changes and Challenges in the Family Lives of Children and Young People*, Bristol, The Policy Press.

Ribbens McCarthy, J. (2008) 'Security, insecurity and family lives' in Cochrane, A. and Talbot, D. (eds) *Security: Welfare, Crime and Society,* Maidenhead, Open University Press/ Milton Keynes, The Open University.

Walkover, B.C. (1992) 'The family as an overwrought object of desire' in Rosenwald, G.C. and Ochberg, R.L. (eds) *Storied Lives: The Cultural Politics of Self Understanding*, New Haven, CT, Yale University Press.

Waiton, S. (2007) *The Politics of Anti-Social Behaviour: Amoral Panics*, London, Routledge.

Acknowledgements

Grateful acknowledgement is made to the following sources:

Cover image

Copyright © iStockphoto.

Chapter 1

Text

Reading 1.1: from 'Introduction' by Morgan D.H.J. in (ed.) Cheal, D. *Family: Critical Concepts in Sociology*. Copyright © 2003 David H.J. Morgan, Routledge. Reproduced by permission of Taylor & Francis Books UK; Reading 1.2: Gubrium, J.F. and Holstein, J.A. (1990) *What is Family?* Mayfield Publishing. By kind permission of Jaber F. Gubrium.

Figures

Figure 1.2: Courtesy of Mary Evans Picture Library; Figure 1.3 top left: Copyright © Rob Howard/Corbis; Figure 1.3 top right: Copyright © Jason Hoskings/zefa/Corbis; Figure 1.3 centre left: Copyright © Emely/zefa/Corbis; Figure 1.3 centre right: Copyright © Roy Botterrell/Corbis; Figure 1.3 bottom: Copyright © Anna Peisl/zefa/Corbis.

Chapter 2

Text

Reading 2.2: Becker, B. and Charles, N. (2006) 'Layered Meanings', *Community, Work and Family*, Vol. 9, No. 2, May 2006, Taylor & Francis Ltd. Reprinted by permission of the publisher Taylor & Francis Ltd, http://www.informaworld.com.

Figures

Figure 2.1 left: Copyright © Reuters/Corbis; Figure 2.1 right: Copyright © Antoine Gyori/Corbis Sygma; Figure 2.2: Copyright © Paul Hillery; Figure 2.3: Copyright © Chinch Gryniewicz; Ecoscene/Corbis.

Chapter 3

Text

From *Family Understandings: Closeness, Authority and Independence in Families with Teenagers* by Wendy Langford, Charlie Lewis, Yvette Solomon and Jo Warin, published in 2001 by the Joseph Rowntree Foundation. Reproduced by permission of the Joseph Rowntree Foundation.

Chapter 7

Text

Reading 7.1: Tadmor, N. (1996) 'The concept of the household-family in eighteenth-century England', *Past and Present*, No. 151. Oxford University Press; Readings 7.3.1, 7.3.2 and 7.3.3: Seymour, S. (1999) *Women, Family and Child Care in India*, Copyright © Cambridge University Press, reproduced with permission.

Figures

Figure 7.1: Fitzwilliam Museum, University of Cambridge/Bridgeman Art Library; Figure 7.2: Mary Evans Picture Library; Figure 7.3: Morphy, F. (2006) 'Lost in translation: Remote indigenous households and definitions of the family', *Family Matters*, No 73, Australian Institute of Family Studies; Figure 7.4: Copyright © DK Limited/Corbis.

Chapter 8

Text

Reading 8.1: Finch, J. (2006) 'Kinship as 'Family' in contemporary Britain' in (eds) Ebtehaj, F., Lindley, B. and Richards, M. *Kinship Matters*, Hart Publishing; Reading 8.2: Williams, F. (2004) *Rethinking Familes*, Calouste Gulbenkian Foundation; Reading 8.4: The United Kingdom Parliament (1999) 'Judgements – Fitzpatrick (A. P.) v. Sterling Housing Association Ltd, Opinions of the Lords of Appeal for Judgement in the Cause on 28 October 1999'. Parliamentary Copyright material is reproduced under Licence Number P2005000031, with the permission of the Controller of HMSO on behalf of Parliament; Reading 8.5: The United Kingdom Parliament (2004) 'Judgements – Ghaidan (Appellant) v. Godin-Mendoza (FC) (Respondent), Opinions of the Lords of Appeal for Judgement in the Cause on 21 June 2004'. Parliamentary Copyright material is reproduced under Licence Number P2005000031, with the permission of the Controller of HMSO on behalf of Parliament.

Figures

Figure 8.1: Copyright © John Birdsall www.johnbirdsall.co.uk.

Chapter 9

Figures

Figure 9.1: Copyright © H Armstrong Roberts/Corbis; Figure 9.2: Copyright © Israel Images/Alamy; Figure 9.3: Courtesy of The Advertising Archive; Figure 9.4: Copyright © John Birdsall www.johnbirdsall.co.uk.

Index